# DISTURBING THE WAR

## The Inside Story of The Movement to Get Stanford University Out of Southeast Asia 1965—1975

By Lenny Siegel

Pacific Studies Center

DISTURBING THE WAR: The Inside Story of the Movement to Get Stanford University out of Southeast Asia—1965-1975

Copyright © 2021, by Leonard Siegel

*Cover photo:* Lenny Siegel leads a march to the Stanford Research Institute's counterinsurgency offices in the Stanford Industrial Park and conducts a guided tour, describing other military contractors in the Industrial Park, April 21, 1969.

For simplified access to the source documents and images linked in *Disturbing the War,* go to a3mreunion.org/DisturbingTheWar.html.

Editing, cover design, and layout by Karen McChrystal

ISBN: 978-0-578-80396-8

Pacific Studies Center
P.O. Box 998
Mountain View, California
94042

Printed in the United States of America

# Acknowledgments

I wish to thank my wife, Jan Rivers, for her decades of support. We started dating during the early 1971 Laos Invasion, and we're one of just a handful of activist couples who connected during our Movement who are still together.

I would also like to thank Stanford History professor Barton Bernstein for encouraging me to write this book, though I doubt that it satisfies his stringent academic standards.

Martin Gorfinkel and Jeff Kane played key roles in the creation of the online A3M Reunion Historical Archive. Without their help, utilizing the hardcopy archives would have been much more difficult. I would also like to thank Jeff for placing all the links in this book on the A3M website. And I greatly appreciate the team that put the *Stanford Daily* archive on line. It provided a reliable check on my memory and produced a few surprises.

At a time when the average person may take dozens, if not hundreds of high-quality photos every week, it's hard to imagine the paucity of reproducible photographic images from 50 years ago. So I'm particularly thankful to the Stanford Historical Society, the Stanford University Archives, and the Stanford News Service for retaining and making available most of the images in this book, as well as the Movement photographers who held on to their pictures.

I would like to thank Karen McChrystal of Hidden Springs Press for turning my manuscript into a book. I'm amazed how much the publishing industry has changed since my last book, published in 1985.

Finally, I would like to thanks the thousands of activists at and around Stanford University, including people I often disagreed with, for enacting the story that I've tried to summarize in these pages. I'm proud of what we did.

## Dedication

*"To all of those on and off campuses throughout the country who worked to stop the brutal and unjust Vietnam war, and to those who continue to work for peace and justice. May this book help and inspire you."*

# Table of Contents

# Preface
## Telling Our Stories

Most of you who are seniors came to Stanford in the last year of what some people refer to as "the Time of Troubles," others as "the days of student activism," and still others simply as "the late 60s." For those of you who were not here in 1971-72, I might add that the late 60s lasted longer at Stanford than at most places.[1]

*~Stanford University President Richard Lyman,*
*June, 1975*

Any use of force or violence, *disturbing the public peace,* or any threat to use force or violence, if accompanied by immediate power of execution, by two or more persons acting together, and without authority of law, is a riot. [emphasis added]

*~California Penal Code Section 404*

For the generation of activist college students who attended Stanford University, in Palo Alto, California, during the late 1960s and early 1970s, our time spent there was much more than a time of troubles. It was a time of awakening and a time of triumph. In the ferment of the period, we were able to educate ourselves to the hypocrisy of political and economic power in American society. The worldviews of leaders, followers, and even bystanders were reshaped dramatically. Though we fell far short of many of our long-term goals, our wave of rebellion helped alter events in the U.S., Southeast Asia, and beyond.

---

1. Richard W. Lyman, "Don't do your own thing; do your own thinking," *Stanford Observer,* June, 1975, p. 3. exhibits.stanford.edu/stanford-pubs/catalog/nm202yv2554 p. 349. This is the printed version of his June 15, 1975 Commencement Address.

Though not all veterans of the Stanford Movement remained committed to social and political transformation, it is difficult to find one who regrets, in general, what we did. In fact, we have held Stanford Movement reunions in 1979, 1989, 1999, 2009, 2014, and 2019. All but the most recent attracted more than 100 Movement veterans from all over the U.S. and even abroad. These were our formative years; they launched many of us on careers or avocations of activism. At our 2014 reunion we had a discussion, "Telling Our Stories." History Professor Barton Bernstein, who had spoken at some of the earliest anti-war teach-ins in the mid-1960s, encouraged me to write a book. Instead, I ran for the Mountain View City Council and served for four years.

Over the years I've regaled or bored my two children, Misha and Abe, with anecdotes about my activist years as a Stanford University student activist and outside agitator. The event they seem to remember most is when in May, 1969 I threw a police tear-gas canister into a war and counterinsurgency research center operated by the Stanford Research Institute (SRI) a little more than a stone's throw from the academic campus. Author Ed McClanahan memorialized my precision throwing arm in a short story, assigning me a pseudonym, in "Another Great Moment in Sports."[2] He called it my "clear moment." I'll get to that in chapter 6.

In 2017, while Vice-Mayor of Mountain View, a city of 80,000 people about five miles from Stanford, I told NBC Bay Area about the incident for a documentary they were producing about the military history of the Bay Area. I explained that this was nothing compared to napalming a peasant village in Vietnam, which is essentially what I was protesting.[3] I did not expect many of my constituents, some of whom are Vietnamese refugee families and others who are veterans of that war, to support or even understand my militant act.

---

2. Ed McClanahan, "Another Great Moment in Sports," in *My VITA, If You Will.* (New York: Counterpoint, 1998).
3. "War, Protest & Prosperity: How the Military Created the Modern Bay Area," NBC Bay Area, September 24, 2017.

However, I remain proud of that demonstration, the sit-ins, and barging into university meetings to which I and dozens or hundreds of comrades were not invited. I, along with many of those people, five decades later, remain proud of what the progressive Movement at Stanford accomplished. I was charged, for my participation in that May, 1969 protest, with violation of Penal Code Section 404, which defines a **riot** to **disturb the public peace**. But we know better: We were **disturbing the war**.

I have always wanted to write a book about my time at Stanford, from 1966 through the end of the Vietnam War in 1975. In fact, I wrote the first paragraph above in the late 1970s. It's not just that I enjoy telling my stories. I believe there are many lessons to be learned from our experiences, and I have always felt that the histories that I've read about the New Left failed to capture the flavor—the uncertainty, the evolving militancy, the focus on research and documentation, and the David vs. Goliath spirit—of the Movement that I knew. Furthermore, I believe that history is enhanced when documentary sources are complemented with inside knowledge of the work that eventually produced headlines.

However, while raising a family I kept on organizing and writing about current issues: against war, for housing justice, exposing the mistreatment of tech production workers, promoting environmental cleanup and justice, etc. So I kept putting off my story. In 2018 I helped set up an oral history project, "The Movement Oral History Project: Antiwar and Other Activism in the Stanford Community, 1963-1973." It's a partnership among my activist cohort, the Stanford Historical Society, and the Stanford Library Archives.[4] I ended up recording about eight hours of video. As I reviewed the transcript, I realized, "I've already written a good portion of my book."

---

4. "The Movement Oral History Project: Antiwar and Other Activism in the Stanford Community, 1963-1973," Stanford Historical Society. https://historicalsociety.stanford.edu/discover-history/oral-history/projects/movement-oral-history-project-antiwar-protest-and-allied

I gave the oral history largely from memory, but I've discovered more than once over the years that my memory is not infallible. I needed to ground-truth my stories. The *Stanford Daily's* searchable online archive has been valuable, particularly in checking dates.[5] It turns out that I developed a knack for getting quoted early on, so the *Daily* has a lot of references to me, too. I also have easy access to both the hard-copy and online Movement Archives.[6] I had learned from my parents, who reached maturity during the Great Depression, the importance of never throwing anything out.

Basically, I kept what I believe to be most of the fliers, newsletters, posters, press releases, and other papers published by the Stanford Movement beginning 1966. I organized them by topic and year, and I stored them in file cabinets at the Pacific Studies Center, the non-profit started by the Stanford Movement in 1969. In 2009, with the help of Jeff Kane and my father-in-law, Martin Gorfinkel, we started placing those documents, with brief descriptions, on the web. These documents have proven invaluable in supplementing and correcting my memory. I have included links with my references, so historians and other readers have easy access to original sources. Within those documents are a number of my contemporary reports. I quote from them liberally.

Obviously, this book is not a complete history of the Stanford Movement. At times I mention events in which I did not take part, but I don't pretend to be writing anything much more than a history from my personal perspective. So I often focus on my own role, knowing that thousands of others took

---

5. *"Stanford Daily* Archives." https://archives.stanforddaily.com I am referencing many of these articles, complete with web links, to make it easier for readers to access the originals.

6. "April Third Movement Historical Archive." http://a3mreunion. org/archive/archive.html I am referencing many of these documents, complete with web links, so readers can access the originals. For simplified access, go to http://a3mreunion.org/DisturbingTheWar.html There are many other documents located within this on-line library.

part. We had many articulate, dedicated activists, and there were leaders who showed the charisma that I never had. And it's not even a complete description of what I did at Stanford. Browsing through news reports from those days, I was even busier and more visible than I remember.

I don't say much about the nascent women's movement, the organizations of students of color, or gay rights.[7] Those were indeed important, and I supported them. But my role was tangential. Furthermore, I don't have much to say about sex, drugs, and rock-n-roll. Finally, while I was at Stanford there were numerous fires started by unknown people and even guns fired. Some of the perpetrators likely took part in the Movement I knew, but I only knew about them from news reports. I didn't consider those adventurous actions as part of the mass movement I felt I was helping to build, so I don't say much about them in this book. Rather, I have recalled highlights of my experience, with an eye toward underscoring themes that I believe are important.

It is easy today, five decades later, for participants and others to view the "Time of Troubles" as a climax never to be repeated. Only twice, in Spring of 1969 and the Spring of 1970, did activism electrify the entire campus. The Spring terms of 1968 and 1972 were runners up. Most of the time most of the Stanford community went about its business, perhaps barely noticing, maybe even lending tacit support to our bands of activists.

Sometimes I get the impression that most people think that radical organizers, like Athena, spring to life fully developed. In fact, most of the people I worked with, at least through 1970, adopted their views slowly, carefully, and even painfully.

---

7. To some degree, the Women's Movement emerged in reaction to male chauvinism in the broader movement. See, for example, "Elizabeth Braunstein," Interview with Elizabeth H. Braunstein conducted by Molly Culhane, 2018. The Movement Oral History Project (SC1432). Department of Special Collections & University Archives, Stanford Libraries, Stanford, Calif., pp. 22-23. historicalsociety.stanford.edu/publications/braunstein-elizabeth

I worried that those who arrived on the scene as full-blown revolutionaries were police agents. I trusted activists who had learning curves similar to my own.

The story of the "Movement," therefore, was not simply the individual rallies, sit-ins, street protests, and trials. Rather, it was the melding of research, education, communication, and action to create an evolving community of activists capable of changing the university and, along with similar organizing across the country, influencing national policy.

I am struck, as I look back at the turmoil of the late 1960s and early 1970s, by the *chutzpah* of the Movement. Young people, only a fraction of whom were backed by their parents, took on some of the most powerful institutions in world history, and we made a difference. And it made a lasting difference in our lives.

# Chapter 1: Sputnik

I grew up in Culver City, a suburb on the west side of Los Angeles. It was known as the heart of the movie industry, with large lots containing movie facades. It was also home to Hughes Aircraft and other aircraft companies. We lived on busy tree-lined Braddock Drive in a single-family home that my parents—Henry and Adele—bought nearly new in 1946—so-called Victory Housing—for $10,000. My parents' first son, Aaron—known as "Rusty" for his baby red hair—died long before I was born. My older brother, Sandy, was seven years older than I, and in between were my sisters, Roberta and Irene. My Uncle Nate, a World War II veteran who worked for Douglas Aircraft, lived with us when he was single.

I was born late 1948, the year that Israel declared its independence, just three years after the defeat of Nazi Germany and end of the Holocaust. So I was part of the first generation of Jews who were taught to remember the Holocaust, that it should never happen again. My grandparents had come over around 1890 from Lithuania, fleeing pogroms and the Russian Czar's military draft. So to my knowledge, only distant, unknown relatives were murdered by the Nazis, but the Holocaust was an attack on us all.

The Jewish community was divided between Zionists, who believed that Jews deserved an independent homeland in Arab Palestine, and leftists. In those days, the split was blurred. We would take dimes to temple to help "plant trees in Israel." However, by the 1967 Six-Day War my family had come down on the leftist side. Later I discovered that every Jew had a Communist uncle. My brother spent time with Bolshevik Uncle Hillel, who lived in the nearby poor Jewish enclave of Venice Beach.

My parents became politically active in the late 1940s. They were members of the Southland Jewish Organization. Like many in their generation, they defended Julius and Ethel Rosenberg against atomic spying charges, and they supported the Hollywood Ten, screenwriters, directors, and producers investigated by Congress for their Communist affiliations and jailed for their refusal to cooperate. But my parents were never members of the Communist Party.

In 1947 my father wrote a letter to a Los Angeles County Supervisor:

> I myself am an honorably discharged veteran and demonstrated my loyalty to our country in more than four years service with the U.S. Navy. Now I learn it is proposed that membership in, or support of, the Mobilization for Democracy and other civic groups fighting for the maintenance of civil rights will make one automatically disloyal, or at least highly suspect, and subversive to such a degree as to be unfit to be employed by our County. I am shocked ...

Based on that letter, in 1951 the Federal Bureau of Investigation, implementing President Truman's "Loyalty Order" (Executive Order 9835), opened an investigation of my father because the House Un-American Activities Committee (HUAC) identified the Mobilization for Democracy as an affiliate of the Civil Rights Congress, which was on the Attorney General's list of subversive organizations. As a result, he lost his job as an Aircraft Communicator for the federal Civilian Aeronautics Administration.

Losing his job brought hard times, with four young children at home. But my parents were frugal. They grew up during the Depression. They never threw anything out. We rarely went out to dinner, and that was the Hamburger Hangout. My mom always used to patch the holes in my jeans, and now people buy jeans that have holes in them. My dad even worked as a day laborer for a short while. Eventually, however, he landed a job as a stock clerk at Alvin Metals, a private company owned by a friend who likewise was politically unemployable.[1]

My mother later wrote, "our children grew up in an atmosphere of questioning, challenging, researching, and doing a lot of reading to get the facts as they, too participated in many protest demonstrations."

The first demonstration I clearly remember was supporting Adlai Stevenson at the Democratic Convention in LA in 1960. But there were lots of marches for nuclear disarmament. On one of those marches I heard the pejorative "kike" for the first time. My parents helped form chapters of Help Establish Lasting Peace and the Committee for a Sane Nuclear Policy. Our large "den," which we had added to the house in 1953, hosted many meetings. We just had to take down the ping-pong table.

Back in those days, the threat of nuclear war between the both-over-armed U.S. and Soviet Union was constant. Air raid sirens blared at least once a month, and homeowners built underground bomb shelters.[2] You could see it in movies, from "Dr. Strangelove" to "On the Beach." In October 1962, I was playing basketball or tennis at Culver City's Veterans' Park, several blocks from home, when my mom drove up. She insisted that I come home immediately because the world was going to end. It was the Cuban Missile Crisis, and we found out much later that we were indeed on the brink of nuclear holocaust.

---

1. This period, known as the McCarthy Era for the anti-Communist campaign spearheaded by Wisconsin Senator Joseph McCarthy, went well beyond political grandstanding. It created hardship for many young, progressive families. My wife's father, an African-American civil rights activist, World War II veteran, and Communist, similarly lost his job as a physical therapist working for the Veterans Administration, also in West Los Angeles.

2. The 1961 Twilight Zone episode, "The Shelter," well dramatized the folly of nuclear shelters. In it, a false warning of nuclear attack turned the neighbors against the shelter's owners.

In school they would prepare us for nuclear war with "drop drills." We were supposed to hide under the desk in case a nuclear weapon went off. We were in the middle of the biggest concentration of defense industry in the world, a sure target for Soviet Missiles, and they told us we could be safe if we ducked under our desks. Not only was this absurd, but it was designed to build support for even more military spending.

I think I was in the eighth grade when I decided not to go along. I refused to "drop" in multiple classes. It was my first act of civil disobedience. My French teacher sent me to the principal's office, and they called my parents. My parents supported me, and nothing came of it.[3]

With this family background, it was easy for me to become an organizer, even in junior high school. My friends and I distributed fliers door to door for local candidates. In junior high we set up a forum to discuss capital punishment, the House Un-American Activities Committee, and nuclear disarmament. In the summer of 1964, when I was at UC Berkeley in a math program for high school students, I took part in the demonstrations at the Republican National Convention, including the big march led by Martin Luther King. It was my first large San Francisco demonstration. Back home I joined picketers at Mayfair market in support of the United Farm Workers grape boycott.

By then my mother had returned to school, studying for her teaching degree at UCLA. She connected me with the Student Organizing Committee, and I gathered a group of friends to help register voters in predominantly African-American Watts for the "No on 14" campaign for fair housing. Too young to complete the registration forms ourselves, we "bird-dogged," knocking on doors and chalking the sidewalk if someone inside was willing to register.

---

3. In researching this book, I learned that Joan Baez's first act of civil disobedience was refusing, in French class, to take part in a nuclear war drill. Her action was a few years earlier than mine. See "Joan Baez in Palo Alto: Her First Protest," Palo Alto History. http://www.paloaltohistory.org/joan-baez-in-palo-alto.php

Meanwhile, President Johnson was escalating the War in Vietnam. The draft was on the minds of most high school boys, as more and more young men were being called to serve in the Army. At Culver High, like other high schools, we had a boys-only assembly with speakers from the draft board. There were perhaps two or three people in the audience who had any kind of activist inclination. It was just average, mostly working class, maybe upper middle-class boys. Someone from the draft board said, "Your chance of dying on the freeway is greater than your chance of dying in Vietnam." He was booed. Some of my schoolmates did indeed die in Vietnam.

For me it was hard to separate the fear of dying from the fear of killing. I didn't want to do either. I'm pretty sure my brother applied for conscientious objector status, unsuccessfully, and I was preparing to do the same.

Back in those days, the progressive movement was intertwined with folk music: Woody Guthrie, the Weavers, Pete Seeger, the Freedom Singers, Odetta, etc. We used to listen to the Les Claypool show Saturday nights on KRHM FM. That's how I was introduced to the music of Bob Dylan and maybe Joan Baez. We subscribed to *Sing Out* magazine. We had hootenannies in our den, and I remember a meeting at our house where black civil rights activists sang freedom songs. I even attended a filming, at UCLA, of the sanitized TV show, Hootenanny. Or maybe it was just the rehearsal.

My sister Irene had a high school physics project in which she, with the help of my dad, made a five-string banjo from a kit. Irene already played the guitar, so I claimed the banjo. Like almost every other aspiring banjo player, I bought Peter Seeger's book and record album, "How to Play the Five-String Banjo." I was never very good, and I still struggle to carry a tune, but I still sing folk music and songs of struggle when there is no one around to suffer my voice.

I always did pretty well in school. In the wake of the late 1957 Soviet launch of Sputnik, the first human-made satellite, the U.S. launched academic programs to encourage bright, young students to go into science and mathematics with the goal of winning the "space race." In Junior High school, I was invited, along with other promising students from several schools, to attend computer programming classes at Bendix/Control Data, a military contractor with local offices. We used the Bendix G-15, which was about the size of my refrigerator with the computing power of the watch that I now wear. We used punched paper tape for input, and it used a spinning magnetic drum for memory. When I took my kids to the Smithsonian in the late 1980s, there was the shell of a Bendix G-15, a veritable antique, on display.

In high school I was a nerdy physics lab assistant. We had a Bendix G-15, and then we had a PDP-5, manufactured by Digital Equipment Corporation. I was looking forward to a career in computers and physics. When I was in high school, I read an article in the *Reader's Digest*[4] about how Stanford's Engineering Dean, later Provost, Frederick Emmons Terman, Jr., had created a community of technical scholars that encouraged engineering graduates and professors to establish businesses nearby, primarily at what was then known as the Stanford Industrial Park. This became a global model for university-business cooperation, spawning what is now known as Silicon Valley. But the article mentioned nothing about the central role of the Defense Department. I'll get to that later.

I also learned that the Stanford Linear Accelerator Center did particle physics research, but unlike its counterparts in Berkeley and particularly the Lawrence Livermore Laboratory, it didn't design weapons of mass destruction. SLAC even invited visiting researchers from Iron Curtain (Communist-led) countries. So that got me interested in Stanford.

---

4. I found in my files "He Searches for 'Steeples' of Talent," an article by Frances Rummell and Adelaide Paine, condensed from *Future,* in the December 1962 *Reader's Digest*. Re-reading the article, I realize that some of my understanding about Stanford came from other sources.

In high school I wrote a paper about how revolution is depicted in fiction. The novel that impacted me most was *And Quiet Flows the Don,* officially written by Mikhail Sholokov.[5] Sholokov wrote about the struggles of Don Cossacks during World War I, the Russian Revolution, and the ensuing civil war. My takeaway was that the protagonists were not driven by ideology, but by how institutions and individuals treated their families and villages.

I wanted to stay in California because I did not want to suffer winter. I didn't want to stay too close to home. I wasn't interested in Berkeley because I had two siblings there. And I had seen in the news that Stanford had an anti-war movement, even though some of the activists insisted on wearing ties. So I applied to Stanford. My academic success and tennis letter proved enough for me to overcome Stanford's rumored discrimination against Jews, particularly when compared with Ivy League schools. I was accepted for admittance in the fall of 1966, with a scholarship that covered tuition—at the time $1575 per year.

---

5. A traditional folk song cited in this book was the source of Pete Seeger's anti-war melody, "Where Have All the Flowers Gone?" Lynne Hutchinson, "Happy Birthday, Pete Seeger!" *Performing Songwriter,* May 3, 2013. https://performingsongwriter.com/pete-seeger-flowers-gone/

# Chapter 2: We Accuse—The Community of Technical Scholars

A new counterpart of these medieval "communities of scholars" has in recent years begun to take form in our modern society. These consist of universities which have strong programs in engineering and science, surrounded by companies emphasizing research and development...

*~Frederick Emmons Terman, Jr., 1963[1]*

In the Spring of 1970, amidst militant campus protests against the U.S. invasion of Cambodia, five of us were on trial, in civil court in Palo Alto, for disrupting Stanford University. During one of the breaks, the Court Clerk approached me and asked something like, "My nephew is thinking of attending Stanford. Do you think it's a good college?" Stunned that she would ask someone on trial for threatening the status quo at Stanford, I answered, "It depends upon what he is looking for." And that's been my answer ever since. My years at Stanford were some of the most formative, rewarding, and educational years of my life, but most of what I learned was outside the classroom.

Leland Stanford Junior University was founded by Leland and Jane Stanford in 1885, in memory of their only child, Leland Jr.[2] on their horse farm adjacent to Palo Alto on the San Francisco Peninsula. Leland Sr. was a railroad tycoon who became Governor and U.S. Senator for the state. In addition to the academic campus

---

1. Frederick Emmons Terman, Jr., "The Newly Emerging Community of Technical Scholars," presented, University-Industry-Liason Conference, Colorado Springs, November 5, 1963.
2. It took a while to get used to the "Junior University" appellation on sweatshirts and other expressions of the university logo.

and the two-mile-long Linear Accelerator, the property contains a wildlife refuge, a golf course, a research/industrial park, an upscale shopping center, and Stanford Hospital. Governed by a private, self-selecting Board of Trustees, at the time it enjoyed being called the "Harvard of the West," but unlike Ivy League schools at the time it was a big name in college sports, particularly men's football and basketball. By the time I arrived, academic buildings—classrooms, libraries, and laboratories—had long ago overgrown the sandstone Quad erected by the Stanfords at the terminus of Palm Drive. Today the campus covers 8,180 acres, more than 300 acres larger than the nearby city of Mountain View, where I live.

Stanford, particularly its Engineering School and Electrical Engineering Department, was earning the reputation as the center of a Community of Technical Scholars. In fact, that's what brought me to Stanford in the first place. This was the vision of Frederick Emmons Terman, Jr., who returned to Stanford after World War II to become Dean of Engineering and later Provost.

More than any other person, Terman was responsible for the emergence of Silicon Valley as a global center of high technology. Terman brought in research contracts, encouraged faculty members to form businesses that could utilize the fruits of their research, and created the Stanford Industrial Park, on Stanford land, where those companies could grow, absorbing students as they graduated and sending professionals back to school part-time in Stanford's classrooms and labs. That critical mass expanded into neighboring communities, encouraging more start-ups and attracting tech corporations based elsewhere.

Terman's vision was remarkable, successful, and precedent-setting, but I soon discovered that there was a little-acknowledged partner, the U.S. Department of Defense. The Pentagon funded campus research and procured the products of the spin-off companies. In the 1960s, this meant that Stanford had enlisted in the Vietnam War.

Stanford had about 12,000 students when I entered in the Fall of 1966. About half were graduate students. The student body was predominantly white, Christian, and male. Undergraduate males complained that our incoming class had a predetermined ratio of two men for each woman. The income level of Stanford families was well above average. Most male undergraduates lived in dorms or fraternities. Almost all females lived in dorms or sorority-like "row houses." In fact, it took the spirited ♀FF campaign to force the university to allow undergraduate women to live off campus starting 1967.

While some frosh men lived in all-freshmen Wilbur Hall, I was assigned a shared room in Burbank House, in Stern Hall, where upper-classmen also stayed. Stanford still provided maids to clean our rooms. One of my first meals at Stanford was a ham sandwich on Yom Kippur. During frosh orientation I played touch football on the lawn and billiards in the basement. I listened to my preppy hallmates exaggerate their experiences with women.

The people who organized Orientation were well aware of the growing political ferment among American college students. They asked incoming frosh to read *Beyond Berkeley*, a balanced collection of essays based on the 1964 Free Speech Movement in Berkeley. The authors introduced the collection:

> The issues that arose at Berkeley ought to be faced by educated people everywhere and certainly should be aired in and out of our classrooms on our campuses.... Relationships exist between the unrest at Berkeley and our entire heritage, and students especially would do well to discover these relationships, to think about them, to write about them clearly and alertly, even to argue about them among themselves or with their elders.[3]

---

3. Christopher G. Katope and Paul G. Zolbrod, *Beyond Berkeley*, Cleveland, Ohio: World Publishing Company. 1966. Page xvii.

We didn't have TVs in our rooms, so I had to go to a common room to watch my Los Angeles Dodgers, even with Koufax and Drysdale, lose the World Series in four straight to the Baltimore Orioles. That helped me transfer my sports loyalties to the Bay Area, though I didn't pay much attention to baseball again until the Oakland A's started sporting long hair.

I loaded up on physics and math classes, but I did manage to get into "Popular Ballads and Folksongs," where Professor Claude Simpson introduced us to the British ballads collected by F.J. Child. Many of these songs were performed and popularized by Joan Baez. I enrolled in Western Civilization (known as Western Civ), obligatory at the time for all Stanford freshmen, but I found the "great works" curriculum largely irrelevant. I think I also started my "work study" job at Memorial Auditorium (Mem Aud) my first quarter, as part of my financial aid package.

I didn't have much trouble finding the campus anti-war movement. At the time the leading group was the Stanford Committee for Peace in Vietnam (SCPV), which had led a thousand-strong march into Palo Alto on January 31, 1966 when President Johnson resumed the bombing of North Vietnam. While some activists suggested a protest at Moffett Naval Air Station, several miles away in Mountain View, most participants reportedly preferred a less confrontational substitute: the U.S. Post Office.

SCPV and its allies had joined a national wave of campus sit-ins protesting university complicity with the Selective Service System (SSS), sitting in the University President's office from May 19-21, 1966. University administrators had hosted an SSS examination that SCPV pointed out was designed to "help determine who is sent to kill or be killed in Southeast Asia."[4] To

---

4. "Documentary: Stanford Sit-In, May, 1966." http://a3mreunion.org/archive/1965-1966/65-66/files_1965-1966/66_Sit-InDoc_cover-p17.pdf page 8. The sit-in received national attention in 2012 when a photo was found showing that Republican Presidential candidate Mitt Romney, a Stanford student that year and only that year, had skipped class to take part in a counter-demonstration.

the protesters, the decision to conduct the draft test on campus "symbolized the authoritarian nature of the university's decision-making structure." They wrote:

> We believe that students do not exist for the university, but that the university exists for its students; consequently, it must recognize our right to a major role in making university policy. We demand the right to make the decisions which affect our lives. This protest initiates our campaign to democratize the university.[5]

**Fig. 2.1. October 16, 1965 peace march to Palo Alto. Notice the men wearing ties.**

Over the summer, two Stanford students—Anatole Anton and Stuart MacRae—were hauled before the House Un-American Activities Committee because of their work raising money "to provide medical relief, through the International Red Cross, to victims of U.S. aggression in Viet Nam." Berkeley

5. "Why We Sat-In," May, 1966. http://a3mreunion. org/archive/1965-1966/65-66/files_1965-1966/66_ WhyWeSat-In.pdf

activist, later "Yippie," Jerry Rubin was also subpoenaed. In the spirit of the times, they confronted their interrogators, calling the hearing unconstitutional. Undergraduate McRae testified,

> "I have a responsibility to stand up to this committee and to speak out against its transparent effort to intimidate resistance to the war..."[6]

While McRae, Anton, and the SCPV leadership, some of whom were foreign graduate students, were more radical than the average Stanford student, Stanford students were moving left. Long-haired David Harris, a peace activist who along with other Stanford people had been a civil rights volunteer in Mississippi in 1964's Freedom Summer, was elected student body president in the spring of 1966.

I quickly learned my way around the "bullpen" in the Associated Students office, where activists groups had desks and access to a mimeograph machine. I took part in a peace demonstration underneath the football stadium scoreboard at the Stanford-Air Force game, holding up signs such as "LBJ: The time is running out." Though that day the Air Force mascot, a falcon, was never let out of its cage, we released doves. Some of the activists drove me to the nearby port of Redwood City, where SCPV and others had been protesting napalm shipments to Southeast Asia. I joined Students for a Democratic Society, which early in 1967 joined statewide protests against University of California and State College tuition and to "support increased student representation at Stanford."[7] We wore buttons that demanded, "Tax the rich," which again became a key part of my political platform fifty years later.

---

6. Anatole Anton, "HUAC and the Summer of 1966," http://a3mreunion.org/archive/1966-1967/66-67/1966-1967.html HUAC Hearings on HR 12047," Excerpt, August 16-19, 1966, p. 1165. http://a3mreunion.org/archive/1966-1967/66-67/files_1966-1967/HUAC_Hearings_HR12047_excerpt.pdf

7. "Student Power!! Rally," February, 1967. a3mreunion.org/archive/1966-1967/66-67/files_1966-1967/66-67_rally.pdf

In January 1966, activists and "hippies" started the off-campus Free University of Palo Alto and the on-campus Experiment. The two merged in mid-1967 to form the Midpeninsula Free University. Movement attorney Jim Wolpman later wrote:

> Anyone could teach a class. From Marxism—of every ilk—to Non-violence to Encounter Groups to Crafts to Art to Computers to… It published a handsome, quirky newsletter that printed anything anybody was interested in. It sponsored be-ins, street concerts, a restaurant, a store, a print shop, and more.[8]

The Free U., as it was known, meant different things to different people, but it provided a sense of community at a time when many students and other young people were feeling alienated from the lives they were brought up to live.

Living on campus, initially without a car, I connected with the Experiment. Disappointed in my Western Civ classes, I proposed a class in Alternative Western Civ. Looking back, I don't think I knew what I would have done if anyone had signed up. When my instructor spotted my offering in the Experiment catalog, he suggested that I find another class—that is, he kicked me out. A few years later, when I was leading anti-war demonstrations that he took part in, he told me that he found my ideas much more palatable. I felt the same way about him. Eventually, in one of its spurts of academic reform, Stanford dropped the Western Civ requirement, for better or worse. My alternative class never got off the ground.

Somehow the graduate students who founded the Experiment obtained use of the old Reserve Book Room, centrally located near the Quad's Engineering Corner and White Plaza. The Book Room had moved to spacious new Meyer Undergraduate Library (UGLi), which opened to serve my incoming class. The Experiment hosted counter-classes, published a newspaper, and held dances with major San Francisco

8. Jim Wolpman, "Alive in the 60s: The Mid-Peninsula Free University, 1967. www.midpeninsulafreeu.com

21

rock bands and "psychedelic" liquid light shows. Reportedly, sometimes Ken Kesey, author of *One Flew over the Cuckoo's Nest,* and his "Merry Pranksters" would hang out there.[9]

**Fig. 2.2. Stanford's first sit-in, May 19-21, 1966, in President Sterling's office protested university complicity with the Selective Service System (SSS).**

---

9. For more about the Experiment, see Christopher Hargrove, "Experiment Emphasizing More than Seminars," *Stanford Daily,* February 24, 1967, p. 3. https://archives.stanforddaily. com/1967/02/24?page=3&section=MODSMD_ARTICLE15#article

**Fig. 2.3. Stanford students' effort to provide medical aid to Vietnam drew the unfriendly attention of Congress, November 2, 1965.**

### "Over the Hump"

Our protest at the February 20 speaking visit of Vice-President Hubert H. Humphrey, a spokesman for the war effort, drew national attention to Stanford. In the latter days of the Lyndon Johnson Presidency, anti-war activists worked hard to make university campuses unwelcome to high government officials who symbolized the war effort. At that time, in some ways campus radicals were more upset by corporate liberals such as Humphrey, because they were "wolves in sheep's clothing," than out-and-out right-wingers such as Barry Goldwater.

The sequence of events around Humphrey's visit illustrated the uncertainty and division within the campus anti-war movement, but they also showed how events drive themselves. A few days before the scheduled event, a large group of faculty members called for a silent protest, asking demonstrators to passively wear white armbands. To many people on campus, heckling and even a walk-out would be unbecoming of intellectuals: a failure to communicate.

23

Dozens of activists met in the Experiment building—twice, I think. Many participants expressed concerns about doing anything too militant. In the end the Ad Hoc Committee to Greet Humphrey agreed to hold a teach-in the night before. We would show up at Mem Aud (Memorial Auditorium) early to ensure admission, and we would honor the faculty's silent treatment. Then we would walk out.

The Ad Hoc Committee circulated a flier, "Over the Hump with Humphrey," topped with a photo of American GIs dragging Vietnamese prisoners, with a rope tied around their necks, over a hill. It began:

> HUBERT HUMPHREY, a prime example of "cold-war liberalism," comes to Stanford, not for an honest exchange of views between this academic community and the Administration he represents, but rather to continue the barrage of lies and propaganda that are an integral part of this government's war in Vietnam.[10]

On Monday, February 20, 1967 Memorial Auditorium's 1700 seats quickly filled up. The welcoming applause of non-protestors easily drowned out the silence of the demonstrators. When Humphrey began to speak, a man in the audience—he sounded like Anatole Anton—shouted "What about Vietnam?" Humphrey calmly replied, saying something like, "I'm glad you reminded me to mention that." Humphrey went on to glibly discuss the "Now Generation." He had learned how to play down protest. I remember a later demonstration in San Francisco, where the smiling Vice-President faced an angry crowd, flashing two V-signs as if he was enjoying the adulation of a crowd of campaign supporters.

Hundreds of people walked out, in at least two phases, because we apparently never fully agreed when. We joined hundreds more milling around outside. Demonstrators were

---

10. "Over the Hump with Humphrey," Ad Hoc Committee to Greet Humphrey, February, 1967.
a3mreunion.org/archive/1966-1967/66-67/files_1966-1967/66-67_OverTheHump_p1-2.pdf

frustrated that the protest seemed to have little visible impact. We wanted Humphrey and the press to see us as he left. David Harris gave a speech, from an SDS sound truck, urging activists to "put your bodies on the line," and a few people sat down to block the building's rear exit. When Humphrey, guarded by Highway Patrolmen and the Secret Service, finally left the building hurriedly through a rear corner hustling toward his limousine, the entire crowd—not just protestors—ran to catch up with him. Many shouted "Shame! Shame!..." A few of the speedier demonstrators made it to his car, bouncing on it because they really didn't know what else to do.

There was no serious attempt to prevent Humphrey's retinue from leaving, but it looked like protestors were trying to chase him down, as reported by some of the national press. *Time* magazine even claimed that demonstrators threw a bag of urine at the VP. Activists were incensed by fake reports of our militancy. In early March University President J.E. Wallace Sterling sent a letter to the entire Stanford community calling initial press reports "overdrawn," but warning that "the threatening degree of anger among the crowd ... occurred on a scale which justifies serious concern."[11] A week later, a delegation of four, including me, representing an ad hoc group, sought to meet with Sterling, to ask him to repudiate those reports.[12] His response was dismissive. Despite the overwhelming desire by activists to appear polite and constrained, the departure of Humphrey from campus looked like an escalation of militancy.

---

11. J.E. Wallace Sterling, "Letters from President Sterling," March 3 and 14, 1967. http://a3mreunion.org/archive/1966-1967/66-67/files_1966-1967/66-67_ToStudents.pdf

12. Possibly we met with then-Provost Richard W. Lyman, not Sterling. See "Group to Urge Refutation of Humphrey Statements," *Stanford Daily,* March 9, 1967, p. 1. https://archives.stanforddaily.com/1967/03/09?page=1&section=MODSMD_ARTICLE9#article

## Researching the University

Under the leadership of co-founder Ira Arlook and SCPV leader David Ransom, both graduate students, the Experiment began publishing well-researched articles on Stanford's role in the Vietnam War and the military industrial complex. We built on research, done by the Graduate Coordinating Committee a year earlier, on the business affiliations of the Stanford Board of Trustees.[13] With their help, I learned how to research companies and military contracts. I spent hours in the basement Engineering Library poring through the *Technical Abstract Bulletin* and the plush, well-stocked library at the new Graduate School of Business reading corporate annual reports and business reference books.[14] Today, with the wealth of information available at the touch of a search engine, what took hours and special trips to the libraries back then would take minutes on one's phone or computer. So I guess I learned how to do research the hard way.

As an undergraduate, I wasn't even allowed to use the Biz School library, until I obtained an authorizing letter from a faculty member. But I couldn't complain. Tuition did not pay for the library. According to a plaque on the wall, the library was funded by a donation from the Del Monte Corporation.

Meanwhile, Georgia Kelly, a young harpist active in the Free University, had a proofreading job at the Stanford Research Institute, a wholly owned subsidiary of the University

---

13. Research Staff of the Graduate Coordinating Committee, "Know Your Trustees, February 3, 1966. http://a3mreunion.org/archive/1965-1966/65-66/files_1965-1966/66_KnowYourTrustees.pdf

14. At some point during this period, the Defense Department classified (made secret) the *Technical Abstract Bulletin* and its indices. In 1972 I inquired why, and the Pentagon's response was to show a page from the *Movement* newspaper that described a research project at SRI. See "Correspondence between Leonard Siegel and the House Foreign Operations and Government Information Subcommittee regarding the classification of the *Technical Abstract Bulletin*," July, 1972. http://a3mreunion.org/archive/1971-1972/71-72/files_71-72/71-72_TAB.pdf

headquartered a couple of miles away in Menlo Park. When documentation of SRI's counterinsurgency and chemical warfare research crossed her desk, she passed the information to Dave Ransom.[15] This opened new avenues of research for the activists clustered around the Experiment.

In February, March, and April the Experiment published a series of exposés on Stanford and the War. Frederick Terman's Community of Technical Scholars was part and parcel of the military industrial complex.[16] Santa Clara County was home to some of the country's largest weapons producers, and Stanford and SRI were among the largest non-profit Defense contractors. Several Stanford Trustees served on the boards of military companies. SRI had designed the "Strategic Hamlet" program, a euphemism for the concentration camps in South Vietnam that were emplaced to separate the peasant "sea" from the guerilla "fish." Researchers at both Stanford and SRI were doing studies for the U.S. Army's Chemical and Biological Warfare (CBW) program.

Defense contractors in the Stanford Industrial Park were interconnected. Stanford trained people to work in war industries, gave them experience in military research, and encouraged faculty members to consult for war contractors. In fact, some of the faculty established or sat on boards of directors of local military electronics firms such as Applied Technology, Varian,

---

15. See Georgia Kelly, "The Roots of the Stanford Peace Movement," *Sandstone & Tile,* Winter 2011, pp. 18-20. https://purl.stanford.edu/xd213kr2527

See the video version, "Time of Realization: The Roots of the Stanford Peace Movement in the 1960's and 1970's," April 1, 2010.
http://a3mreunion.org/archive/video/time_of_realization.html

16. Ira Arlook, "Stanford on the March," *Commitment,* February 7, 1969; David Ransom, "Stanford Observed," *Resistance,* March 9, 1967; "Stanford Research Goes to War," *Resistance* special issue, April 4, 1967. http://a3mreunion.org/archive/1966-1967/66-67/files_1966-1967/66-67_Commitment2-7-67.pdf http://a3mreunion.org/archive/1966-1967/66-67/files_1966-1967/66-67_Stanford_Observed.pdf http://a3mreunion.org/archive/1966-1967/66-67/files_1966-1967/66-67_Resistance_4-4-67.pdf

and Watkins-Johnson. Stanford leased out the land and provided services, such as special programs in continuing education, which soon became a special instructional television network.

Consequently, Santa Clara County grew into one of the world's most sophisticated industrial areas. While known more today for the early production of semiconductors—why it's called "Silicon Valley"—and for search engines, social media and smartphones, when I arrived it was dominated by military contractors such as Lockheed, FMC, and Westinghouse, receiving billions of dollars in weapons work each year.[17] Military technology firms plowed money back into Stanford.

On April 13 we held a rally and marched to SRI along with Palo Alto high school students to protest its role in the war. It wasn't a large march, but it set the stage for a multi-year campaign to extract Stanford and SRI from the Southeast Asian War and other military-related activities. This campaign kept the Stanford peace movement in high gear after the reduction in ground combat by U.S. troops weakened organizing on other campuses.

For me, it was personal. The Community of Technical Scholars that had brought me to Stanford was part and parcel of the war machine that I devoted a great deal of my time opposing. I was disillusioned. I didn't drop out, but at the time I didn't see much future pursuing my chosen career in physics and computing.

---

17. My colleagues and I wrote repeatedly about this over the years. See for example, Lenny Siegel, "From Our Own Backyard," Pacific Studies Center, July 1972. http://www.a3mreunion. org/archive/1971-1972/71-72_war_research/files_71-72_war_ research/71-72Research_Backyard.pdf

## The Great Poster War

In early April the Experiment printed four 17 x 22 posters, all headed "We Accuse."[18] Each showed a war scene and the face of one or two Stanford administrators or trustees, including President Sterling, SRI Chair Ernest Arbuckle, and Trustees William Hewlett, David Packard, Charles Ducommun, and Roger Lewis, all of whom served on the boards of major military contractors. The accompanying flier explained, "Those who develop and supply weapons for the war are no less responsible for their actions than the men who order it fought."[19]

In those days, it must not have been easy to print large posters, because the Experiment went up to San Francisco, where the *Oracle* underground newspaper printed psychedelic posters, to get them produced.[20]

Many on campus found the posters objectionable, for we were directly attacking the people who ran the university. The Stanford police at first removed them from the announcement kiosks found in many parts of campus. In a pattern that we repeated many times, we tried to deflect anger over our tactics to a discussion of the issue of university participation in the war effort and the military industrial complex. For example, when I taped them up at the newly created Grove House, Stanford's new experimental co-ed residence, it triggered a hot debate.

In January 1967 I had moved, along with 42 other undergraduates, into a newish, tastefully built, fraternity building on a hill overlooking the campus and beyond. As a result of several serious infractions, the Phi Delta Theta fraternity was

18. See http://a3mreunion.org/archive/posters/posters_1967_we_accuse. html. At some time over the decades I lost my Arbuckle and Hewlett/ Packard posters. If anyone has a copy of either, I would love to see it.
19. "We Accuse," April, 1967. http://www.a3mreunion.org/ archive/1966-1967/66-67/files_1966-1967/66_67_WeAccuse.pdf
20. Interview with Ira Arlook conducted by Natalie Marine-Street, 2019. The Movement Oral History Project (SC1432). Department of Special Collections & University Archives, Stanford Libraries, Stanford, Calif., p. 24. historicalsociety.stanford.edu/publications/ arlook-ira. My psychedelic posters disappeared from my collection over the years, too.

penalized with a two-term expulsion from their house. To replace it, the university accepted a proposal by history professor Marc Mancall to create the Grove House, one of the first co-ed "dormitories" in the country. Technically, its theme was international "development." I wrote a naïve paper on the topic.

But the real theme was residential intellectualism. Students—including many who did not live in the Grove—and faculty engaged routinely in academic discussions, sometimes related to house seminars, sometimes informally around the dinner table. We proved that Stanford students were capable of learning and living in the same building, but some have suggested that was due to the process used to select us from about 300 applicants.[21]

The official retrospective narrative is that undergraduate men and women established brother-sister relationships, as opposed to the competitive dating game found in the single-gender dorms. There was a door separating the men's rooms from the women's rooms. However, the assertion that there was no sex between residents appeared untrue, at least that's what I concluded watching students visit others' rooms. Still, Grovies were able to establish more mature, thoughtful relationships than I saw elsewhere on campus.

I considered the Grove a warm bed of liberalism. Sure, the vast majority of students were already against the Vietnam War. Though many Grove participants became career progressives, while we were in Grove few residents were sympathetic to the radical groups that I participated in. I remember the difficulty I had trying to convince my suite-mates to sign the anti-draft "We won't go" statement. One of my suite-mates, who eventually

---

21. See Julie Makinen, "Res Ed at a Crucial Crossroads," *Stanford Daily,* March 9, 1994 and Joanna Xu, "A Pioneer House's Reunion," *Stanford Daily,* October 15, 2007. archives. stanforddaily.com/1994/03/09?page=1&section=MODSMD_ ARTICLE6#article and https://archives.stanforddaily. com/2007/10/15?page=3&section=MODSMD_ARTICLE12#article

Fig. 2.4. One of four "We Accuse" posters we plastered around campus in April, 1967. I'm still looking for clean versions of posters featuring Ernest Arbuckle (SRI and Stanford Business School); Trustees Hewlett and Packard; and Trustees Ducommun and Lewis.

31

became an activist immigration attorney, questioned the provenance of the revolutionary lyrics in the Cuban revolutionary song, "Guantanamera," popularized in the U.S. by Pete Seeger.

Anyhow, when the Experiment published the We Accuse posters, I taped a set on the wall near the Grove House entrance. Some residents objected, calling them disrespectful.

> Someone posted copies of them in the front hall of the Grove, and by three in the afternoon nine statements from students, tutors, and Mancall were displayed around the posters, both attacking and defending the University's involvement in the Vietnam War and the suitability of this form of protest.[22]

Grove leaders were proud of the rational dialogue of the "Great Poster War," but I was disappointed that many of my fellow Grovies did not yet take seriously the implications of Stanford's role in the War.

The activist groups on campus had no formal membership, and participation was overlapping. Each recognized student organization was entitled to a desk and access to a mimeograph machine in the student government "bullpen" at Tresidder Union. It was easy to get to know key people in all the groups. SCPV declined and disappeared, so many of us gravitated to the Stanford chapter of Students for a Democratic Society.

SDS was emerging as the pre-eminent New Left student group in the north and west. It had national conferences, a national office, and a national newspaper, but it wasn't that organized. Rather, one chapter would pull off a demonstration, such as a protest of recruiters from Dow Chemical or the CIA, and others would read about it or view it in the news, and organize something similar.

---

22. Gail Anderson and Marian Johnston, "'Toward the Residence University,' The Story of the Grove Project," *Stanford Daily Magazine,* May 11, 1967, p. 4. http://a3mreunion.org/archive/1966-1967/66-67/files_1966-1967/66-67_Grove-Project.pdf

I personally liked SDS because initially it rejected the authoritarianism of nominally Communist governments and parties, but it refused to red-bait.[23] Some SDSers traced their ideology to the anarcho-syndicalist Industrial Workers of the World, America's "one big union" at the beginning of the 20th Century, and many considered the American Communist Party stodgy and conservative. The SDS 1962 foundational Port Huron Statement was the "bible" of participatory democracy,[24] a concept that I have promoted throughout my professional and political life. We believed that people, including students, have a right to make the decisions that affect their lives.

Summer 1967 in the Bay Area is best known as the "Summer of Love," when thousands of young "hippies" converged on the Bay Area, particularly San Francisco's Haight-Ashbury neighborhood. But many of us, not only at Stanford, but across the country, called it Vietnam Summer. A coalition of local groups planned anti-war community education, anti-draft organizing, and the creation of the *Peninsula Observer, a* weekly alternative, but professional tabloid that published until late 1969.

---

23. George Orwell's recounting of the mid-1930s Spanish Civil War, *Homage to Catalonia,* influenced my view of Leninism and Stalinism.
24. See "Port Huron Statement," Students for a Democratic Society, June 15, 1962. http://www.progressivefox.com/misc_documents/PortHuronStatement.pdf

# Chapter 3: Feeling the Draft
## Hell No!

Come on all of you, big strong men,
Uncle Sam needs your help again.
He's got himself in a terrible jam
Way down yonder in Vietnam
So put down your books and pick up a gun,
We're gonna have a whole lotta fun.

"I Feel Like I'm Fixin' to Die Rag,"
~*Country Joe and the Fish, 1966*

Though closely related to the War, the draft struck closer to home. On many issues, I've been a do-gooder, working to help others. However, growing up in the 1960s, I was directly in the target hairs of the Selective Service System (SSS, the American government's draft agency). Across the country, many men decided to stay in school after high school as a way to avoid the draft by qualifying for a II-S student deferment. Most women were close to men with draft worries. It wasn't just the fear of being drafted and sent to Vietnam. The knowledge that the government could control our life choices angered even those who were classified undraftable.

In December 1966, the month I turned 18 and was thus required to register with the SSS, SDS held its national conference in Berkeley. At that meeting SDS took the incredible—nearly treasonous, it seemed—action of voting to challenge the draft. In January 1967 Stanford SDS created the Stanford Anti-Draft Union (ADU).

Because the SSS was using academic performance as a basis for awarding student deferments, in early March, we wrote President Sterling:

> We request you to take steps as soon as possible to end
> university participation in the Selective Service System. We
> ask you to cease computing academic standing, and to withhold
> information on students' grades from the local draft boards, as
> well as to refuse to administer selective service examinations.[1]

We argued against the draft in general and as well against the
particular injustice of sending struggling students off to war.

We circulated two versions of our "We won't go" statement. In
one, draft-age men pledged to refuse induction if called. In the other
they promised not to serve in Vietnam. Signing was not a trivial
decision. Many men were worried about the loss of jobs, scholarships,
deferments, or inheritance. Some were concerned that they might be
blacklisted in the future. There was even the possibility of criminal
prosecution, just for signing. We published more than 160 of them
in a half-page *Stanford Daily* ad on April 25, 1967,[2] and eventually
we collected over 400 pledges. Male and female medical students
circulated their own statement, and men ineligible for the draft and
women signed support petitions.

The Anti-Draft Union traveled to the induction center in
Oakland, where we picketed and leafleted. Sometimes activists
who had been called in for pre-induction physicals circulated fliers
inside. Occasionally such behavior was enough to get the resister
exempted from the draft as a trouble-maker.

At times, I found the early morning encounters depressing. The
busloads of potential draftees were not looking forward to military
service, but they were passive, alone, and apparently apolitical.

1. Richard Bogart and Gary Coutin, letter to President Sterling, March 3, 1967.
http://a3mreunion.org/archive/1967-1968/67-68_anti-draft/sadu/files_
sadu/67-68Draft_SADU_to_Sterling.pdf
2. "We will not fight in Vietnam," *Stanford Daily,* April 25, 1967. https://
archives.stanforddaily.com/1967/04/25?page=4&section=DIVL258#issue
See also, "We Won't Go," Stanford Anti-Draft Union. http://a3mreunion.
org/archive/1967-1968/67-68_anti-draft/sadu/files_sadu/67-68Draft_
SADU_We_Wont_Go.pdf

Our task seemed futile, despite occasional gestures of agreement or offers of marijuana. In retrospect, however, it was successful, as part of a larger effort. Not only did induction refusals become a daily occurrence at the Oakland center, but many of those who nevertheless went into the Army eventually resisted in other ways.

Our leaflets contained information about alternatives to the draft as well as anti-war polemics. We reprinted a Selective Service memo entitled "Channeling."[3] In this document, the draft system's architects explained that the draft not only brought men into the military, but it also forced others into schools and careers that they might not have otherwise chosen, but that the SSS considered good for the country.

Early one morning, passing out fliers to a couple of busloads of draftees in San Jose, headed for Oakland, I handed a flier containing the line, "Rich men make war; poor men's sons get drafted" to a rich man's son. The father and son were offended, but in general the statement was accurate. Elite Stanford students could more easily avoid the draft. Poor kids didn't even know that there were options.

To help individual draft-age men, I became a draft counselor. I studied Selective Service System regulations, read memos from the Central Committee for Conscientious Objectors and groups in Canada, and compared notes with other counselors. I tried to let potential draftees know what their alternatives were. I told them what might convince a draft board that they were physically or morally unfit, qualified for Conscientious Objector status, or politically dangerous. Some anti-draft groups felt that helping someone dodge the draft was impure, that it just merely led to another man being called up. I countered that it made it harder for the system to function and it could be the first step in outright resistance.

I prided myself in offering *political counseling.* I suggested that the best way to avoid being drafted was to stop the war, or at

---

3. "Channelling [sic], A Reprint of an Official Selective Service Memorandum," Stanford Anti-Draft Union, original date July 1, 1965. http://a3mreunion.org/archive/1967-1968/67-68_anti-draft/sadu/files_sadu/67-68Draft_SADU_Channeling.pdf

least to shut down the draft. I believe that this sense of collective resistance caught on, strengthening the anti-war movement as a whole.

I counseled for about two years, gaining an appreciation for how much the threat of the draft shaped people's lives, prompting educational and family choices, emigration, and humiliation. Eventually, many schools and colleges, including Stanford, provided their own paid counselors. These people were much more knowledgeable of the latest in draft policy, but they did not engage in political counseling.

The Anti-Draft Union worked in cooperation and competition with another anti-draft group, the Resistance. The Resistance began locally, from small groups at Stanford and Berkeley. David Harris was its most articulate spokesman. Like the ADU, it encouraged induction refusal. Many of its "members" signed the ADU "We Won't Go" statement. Unlike the ADU, however, it invited arrests, court tests, and imprisonment. It did not counsel draft dodging. Rather it discouraged the acceptance of student and other deferments and instead encouraged men to turn in or burn their draft cards.

The Resistance was more dramatic and newsworthy than the ADU. More Resistance men went to jail. While working toward the same ends, the ADU and Resistance had a blurry philosophical difference. Most Resistance resisters took their stands as individuals, absolving themselves from responsibility for the killing in Asia and hoping to set an example for others. The ADU saw its work as strategic, working with less committed men to stop the draft and the war. Some of us rejected the idea of "volunteering for jail." Looking back, the two approaches were complementary. Only anti-war activists knew the difference between the moralists and the politicos.

In the spring of 1967, a "nationwide" petition, asking Congress to debate the draft, blitzed the campus. It was initiated by Allard Lowenstein, a former Stanford professor and administrator who later won renown for sparking the drive to dump LBJ. But I didn't support it; in vain I argued that it undercut the growing "We won't go" pledge by giving men something

**Fig. 3.1. Resistance leaders David Harris and Paul Rupert burn draft documents in White Plaza, November 14, 1968.**

less to do. In retrospect, it may have been helpful, encouraging signers to gradually increase their commitment to the anti-war/ anti-draft cause.

Anti-Draft Union activists who returned home to places like Montana in the summer of 1967 took the ADU message with them, and those who stayed in the Palo Alto area formed the Vietnam Summer Draft Project. In Palo Alto we stepped up counseling and spent many evenings handing out fliers at the downtown Baskin-Robbins ice cream parlor.

We felt we were making progress in college-town Palo Alto, but in the spirit of SDS organizing efforts in Newark and Chicago, we tried organizing in nearby Sunnyvale, home of the giant Lockheed Missiles and Space Company. However, we were clearly outsiders. We leafleted homes and shopping areas, but the only people who showed up at our meeting in Fair Oaks Park were three plainclothes Sunnyvale policemen.

## Stop the Draft Week

We took part in sit-down demonstrations at local draft boards and small protests at the Oakland Induction Center, but throughout the Bay Area, activists wanted to do more. People from campus SDS chapters, the Resistance, civil rights activists, and pacifists started meeting at the SNCC[4]-affiliated *Movement* newspaper office in San Francisco's Mission District. We came up with a plan for massive street demonstrations to shut down the Induction Center for a week in October.

Organizers soon divided. A group of doctrinaire pacifists, led by Peninsula bookstore owner Roy Kepler, refused to have anything to do with militant confrontation. They proposed to stage a symbolic sit-down in front of the Induction Center, and then either walk to paddy-wagons or let the police carry them away when placed under arrest. SDS and SNCC activists, on the other hand, did not wish to submit voluntarily to arrest. We proposed to take over the streets of downtown Oakland and refuse to disperse. This tactical dispute, grounded in principle, was inherited from the Civil Rights Movement, and it continued through the end of the Vietnam War. We militants were willing to engage in passive resistance, but often, in our view, it was not enough.

Though some enmity developed between "pacifists" and "militants," the two groups worked out an arrangement. The pacifists would conduct their sit-down on Monday, October 16, the same day as a nationwide draft card turn-in organized by the Resistance, and on Tuesday the militants would stage a massive mobile "mill-in."

To publicize and organize the mill-in, the Stop the Draft Week Steering Committee met several times that summer. We went beyond SNCC national leader Stokely Carmichael's

---

4. SNCC was the civil rights group, the Student Non-Violent Coordinating Committee, but by then it had shed its civil-disobedient orientation.

popular anti-draft slogan, "Hell no! We won't go!" With great bravado, we declared "Hell no! Nobody goes!" We planned not just to protest, but to shut down the Induction Center.

The mobile mill-in was a new tactic, at least for the U.S. It meant mobilizing so many people in downtown Oakland early in the morning of October 17, 1967 that the Selective Service System could not bring in its busloads of inductees. Expecting that the Oakland police and other law enforcement agencies would attempt to disperse our crowd, we studied local geography[5] and developed detailed plans to retreat orderly in the face of police charges.[6]

The Steering Committee organized a number of monitors, responsible for leading groups of people to intersections that needed to be blocked. The Stanford contingent not only trained a number of monitors, but we organized affinity groups—clusters of people who would stick together for the duration of the demonstration. (Remember, we didn't have mobile phones to coordinate our activities.) We tried to get all demonstrators from the Stanford area to join affinity groups in advance. We collected medical masks and Vaseline to protect ourselves against tear gas, Army surplus helmet liners to protect our heads from billy clubs, and a few spray cans of paint to illustrate the demands of the protest. Some of us prepared decorated plywood shields, also to fend off police batons. In addition, we taught as many people as possible what to expect from well trained, as well as poorly trained, riot police.

---

5. My roommates and I went so far as to draw a map of downtown Oakland on the living room wall of our rented house in East Palo Alto. In this narrative I refer to roommates. I lived in a rented house at 2357 Oakwood Drive from the summer of 1967 to the summer of 1972, when I moved to Mountain View. We had four living spaces. Many young men and women, most of whom were politically active, cycled through the deteriorating structure while I was living there.

6. See, for example, "What Stop the Draft Week Is All About," October, 1967. http://a3mreunion.org/archive/1967-1968/67-68_anti-draft/stdw/files_stdw/67-68Draft_STDW_All_About.pdf

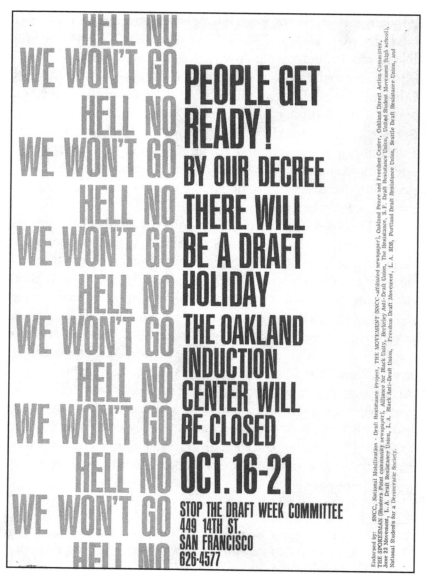

**Fig. 3.2. First poster promoting October, 1967 demonstrations at the Oakland Induction Center.**

The greatest danger, we believed, was panic. So we taught people faced by a line of advancing riot police not to run, but to turn around and walk away, chanting "Walk! Walk!" in unison.

**Fig. 3.3. Second poster promoting October, 1967 demonstrations at the Oakland Induction Center.**

Not long before W-Week, we held a monitors' practice run in the area, trying out our walkie-talkies, practicing our codes, and scouting the premises. Working out of Lafayette Park, we were pleased to learn that some of the aging denizens of the park had been members of the Industrial Workers of the World. However, in general we had little contact with the predominantly black West Oakland community.

At our planning sessions there were two monitors whom nobody knew. One we welcomed at first, because he supplied us with walkie-talkies and a citizens' band transceiver. But we couldn't find anyone to vouch for them. To vet them, Lee Felsenstein, the computer pioneer-to-be who led our communications team, asked both of them to deliver sealed envelopes, supposedly containing secret codes, from Berkeley to my house in East Palo Alto.

One envelope arrived in a crudely re-sealed envelope. The other looked good, until we realized that the arriving envelope was slightly smaller than the ones Lee had shipped. We concluded that they were spies, and on October 17 Lee called them aside on phony business. We were right. Both turned out to be Oakland policemen. They testified at the Oakland Seven trial, during which seven mill-in organizers were charged with conspiracy.

Organizers at Stanford, San Francisco State, and smaller Bay Area colleges knew that they would have to work hard to mobilize large numbers of people to show up in Oakland at 6:00 am, particularly since the Induction Center was located inconveniently across the Bay. Furthermore, three leading Stanford anti-war professors—the Grove's Mancall, Political Scientist Charles Drekmeier, and Dean of the Chapel B. Davie Napier—urged Stanford students to stay home. Their "Urgent" flier warned, "There is a very great chance that serious violence will erupt this morning at the Oakland Induction Center."[7] Still, we brought hundreds of demonstrators, largely in chartered buses.

---

7. B. Davie Napier, Mark Mancall, and Charles Drekmeier, "Urgent–Read This," October, 1967. http://a3mreunion.org/ archive/1967-1968/67-68_anti-draft/stdw/files_stdw/67-68Draft_ STDW_Urgent.pdf I believe this undated flier was handed out on Tuesday, October 17, but it could have been circulated on Friday.

Nearby Berkeley, with its growing history of large protests, would have an easier time bringing protestors out. But they had something else going for them: the state's anti-student, right-wing governor, Ronald Reagan. Berkeley organizers reserved Pauley Ballroom at the UC Berkeley student union, to gather demonstrators the night before the Tuesday confrontation, essentially daring the governor and the university administration to cancel the reservation. And that's exactly what they did. The off-campus draft demonstration all of a sudden became an on-campus free speech issue, just under three years after similar restrictions triggered the groundbreaking Sproul Hall sit-in. Stop the Draft Week thus became a *cause célèbre*.

Meanwhile, the first day of Stop the Draft Week was a resounding success. About 200 men, including 19 from Stanford, turned in their draft cards at a rally at the Federal Building in San Francisco.[8] According to the *Stanford Daily,* at least 19 Stanford faculty and students were arrested peacefully at the Oakland Induction Center, along with more than 110 others, including Joan Baez. The *Daily* reported that 150 to 200 people from Stanford were in the supporting picket.[9]

The Berkeley rally and peaceful Monday activities set the stage for Tuesday. Thousands of people gathered in the streets of downtown Oakland, encircling the Induction Center. From the police staging area in a parking garage kiddy-corner from the Center, a police official read an order to disperse: "In the name of the people of the state of California, I order ..." The protestors responded immediately, loudly, and self-righteously, "We are the people! We are the people!"

Soon the police launched into the crowd, tossing tear gas grenades and swinging their clubs. Most demonstrators, prepared for mobile action, pulled back easily, chanting "Walk!"

8. Kirk Hanson, "Stanford Students Surrender Cards in Draft Protest," *Stanford Daily,* October 17, 1967, page 1. archives.stanforddaily.com/1967/10/17?page=1&section=MODSMD_ARTICLE1#article

9. Geoffrey Stevens and Peter Baldo, "19 Stanford Students, Profs Arrested At Oakland Sit-In," *Stanford Daily,* October 17, 1967, p. 1. archives.stanforddaily.com/1967/10/17?page=1&section=MODSMD_ARTICLE4#article

As planned, demonstrators strategically retreated to nearby intersections, building small barricades and blocking traffic. Stanford's affinity groups performed well, but the police were eventually able to clear a path for inductee buses, late in the morning.

However, those who sat down to block the induction center doors were beaten badly, as were members of the press. Bloodied professors and hippies don't normally make big news, but bruise a reporter and you've got police brutality all over page one. That police miscalculation gave us better reporting than we would have received otherwise.

As a Steering Committee member directly involved in communications, I sat in our "command center" in a second-story hotel room that morning, a block from the Center. Veteran SDS leader Jeff Segal seemed to be in charge. With the citizens' band radio provided by one of the police infiltrators, I was supposed to connect with a dozen or so monitors with walkie-talkies.

The command center was a complete failure, because we couldn't see much of what was going on in the streets below. That is, we didn't know where police lines blocked the movement of protestors. Furthermore, we had no chain of command. That is, some of the walkie-talkie operators had little influence over the surrounding demonstrators. To overcome this disadvantage, two Steering Committee leaders in the streets improvised, coordinating actions by systematically circling the area in opposite directions.

Though we were uncomfortably safe—compared to our comrades in the streets—in the hotel room, we were unnerved when someone—perhaps the hotel manager—opened the door to our room. But instead of police or FBI with a warrant, the uninvited guests were network TV reporters and camerapersons. They used our window to film the demonstrations while interviewing one of our leaders. After the buses made it through the crowd, the action died down. I spotted my sister, still a UC student, in the street, so I descended to catch up with her.

In the course of my draft counseling, I had found a few anti-war men scheduled either for induction or pre-induction physicals that day. I supplied them with leaflets to pass out on the buses or inside the Center. Declaring a "draft holiday," the flier predicted, "When you arrive in Oakland you may be confronted by an angry crowd. We are not angry at you. We are angry with the draft."[10] I later heard, but was unable to confirm, that one of the inductees set off a stink bomb inside.

The Steering Committee never had made plans beyond October 17, because we didn't know what to expect that day. But the publicity for the "week" worked so well that a large number of people showed up in Oakland Wednesday morning. We felt obliged to supply monitors to keep people out of trouble. Meanwhile, we raised bail and planned for Friday.

The real decision to go back Friday, October 20 was made, I believe, at a huge Berkeley rally mid-day Tuesday, by those who were awake and in Berkeley. The Stanford organizers scheduled a noon campus rally on Thursday, and we recruited more students for Friday. We tried to organize newcomers into affinity groups, but most went up on their own.

At the Thursday rally, proponents of "non-violence"—that is, not actively resisting the police—pushed for a vote on tactics. The crowd voted for non-violence, but since few had been in Oakland Tuesday they didn't fully understand the alternative. Furthermore, there was no way a vote of hundreds at Stanford would influence a regional demonstration of thousands. Fortunately, those advocates of non-violence who went up to Oakland seemed satisfied, after the fact, with the level of militancy.

Friday was the biggest day of the week. We estimated that there were 10,000 protestors; the press said fewer. In any case, it was a show of force by anti-war militants. We blocked the streets with bodies and barricades, delaying the buses for hours.

---

10. "You are Lucky, Today is a Draft Holiday," Stanford Anti-Draft Union, October 17, 1967 http://a3mreunion.org/ archive/1967-1968/67-68_anti-draft/stdw/files_stdw/67-68Draft_ STDW_Lucky.pdf

When Highway Patrolmen and police from throughout the Bay Area cleared intersections, we fanned out, without panic, to block access streets.

We abandoned our radio communications, relying on ground-level contact. So I was in the streets, speaking on the ADU bullhorn. It wasn't very loud, but it gave me authority. Even though few of the demonstrators knew me, or even who I was, I was a leader by virtue of that 4-watt amplifier and horn. I sometimes wonder if a police agent with a bullhorn could have turned the crowd around. Actually, my role was quite limited. People knew the plan. I just tried to let them know what was happening elsewhere, and to prevent panic when the police charged.

The Alameda County grand jury eventually indicted seven people—the Oakland Seven—for conspiracy to commit misdemeanors at the Induction Center. Six were members of the steering committee. One was a Berkeley campus leader who got involved just a few days before the action. The district attorney did not press charges against organizers from Stanford or San Francisco State or any of the female members of the steering committee. Attorney Charles Garry mounted a spirited defense. Despite the testimony of the two police infiltrators, all seven were acquitted.

Though the buses eventually delivered the draftees to the Army, and the war did not end, we considered Stop the Draft Week an enormous success. That week—Stop the Draft Week in Oakland, demonstrations against Dow Chemical at the University of Wisconsin, and the Saturday, October 21 march on the Pentagon—marked the national evolution "from protest to resistance." It wasn't an escalation to violence. It was a move from civility to physical disrespect.

Stop the Draft Week was the climax of anti-draft activities. The Anti-Draft Union continued to collect "We Won't Go" signatures, support resisters, and counsel, while more and more men joined the Resistance by turning in or burning draft cards. The pacifist coalition carried out another sit-down at the induction center. We unsuccessfully tried another mass barricade.

### My Version of "Alice's Restaurant"

My personal interaction with the Selective Service System was never newsworthy, but my March 1968 "Guide to Draft Counseling" illustrates how I counseled draft-age men.[11] From the start, I was committed to neither serve in the U.S. military nor go to prison. Furthermore, I was uncomfortable with the idea of a student (II-S) deferment, though that discomfort was magnified by the recognition that it would extend my draft eligibility from age 26 to age 35. A key element of my counseling and personal strategies was to delay processing as much as possible in the hope that demand for draftees would eventually fall.

In January 1967, soon after my 18th birthday and draft registration, I applied for conscientious objector (CO) status. This category was built into the draft to respect the First Amendment rights of men who belong to religious sects that eschew warfare, such as the Quakers. I've never considered myself a violent person. For example, I've never owned or fired a real gun. Nevertheless, I was not a Quaker, but a Jew, and by the time my Draft Board considered my application Israel had just conquered large amounts of Arab territory. They turned me down.

Following normal procedure, in September 1967 I went down to Los Angeles to appear in person. When I walked into the draft board's conference room, I pulled off my black gloves, unlocked my brief case, and opened it to pull out my forms and correspondence. This seemed to startle one of the draft board members, whom I imagined to be a retired Army officer. They turned me down. So did the appeals board.

Even though I was enrolled at Stanford, I did not request a student deferment. That put me in line for a pre-induction physical. I delayed it, quite legally, by transferring it to the Bay Area, where I then lived. I "called in sick" once, delaying it further. When I finally showed up, I handed out leaflets opposing

---

11. Lenny Siegel, "Guide to Draft Counseling," Stanford Anti-Draft Union, March, 1968. http://a3mreunion.org/archive/1967-1968/67-68_anti-draft/sadu/files_sadu/67-68Draft_SADU_Guide.pdf

the Army and the draft. I wrote, "If the NLF [National Liberation Front] has the support of the Vietnamese people because it helps them, why doesn't the U.S. Government support the Viet Cong."[12] I wanted to influence the other draftees, but I also wished to convince the Selective Service that I was more trouble than I was worth.

My allergies, supported by a letter from my doctor, earned me a trip to the Army's Letterman General Hospital at the San Francisco Presidio, where I waited for a few hours to see an unsympathetic ear-nose-throat specialist. The whole experience gave me a bad sinus headache, but no exemption.

In the spring of 1969, the first academic quarter when I was not allowed to register for classes, I was expecting a draft notice. So when the April Third Movement blockaded SRI's counterinsurgency offices,[13] I made no attempt to conceal my identity when I retrieved a police-fired tear-gas canister and threw it into the building. I turned myself in along with other demonstrators who were not arrested the day of the protest.

My draft notice arrived within a week, and I gleefully wrote the SSS that I had been arrested for misdemeanors, and I supplied documentation. I awaited trial for a year, and after pleading *nolo contendere* I received a year of probation. I had another physical in October 1970, at which I passed out another leaflet.[14] Sometime in that period I was classified 1-Y, temporarily unfit to serve. Finally, in June 1972 I received notice that I was classified 4-F: I was permanently unfit to serve. I had no further personal contact with the SSS.

---

12. Lenny Siegel, "Brothers," November 19, 1968. http://a3mreunion. org/archive/1967-1968/67-68_anti-draft/sadu/files_sadu/67-68Draft_ SADU_Brothers_2.pdf
13. See Chapter 6.
14. Lenny Siegel, "Brothers," October 1, 1970. http://a3mreunion. org/archive/1967-1968/67-68_anti-draft/sadu/files_sadu/67-68Draft_ SADU_Brothers.pdf

So like Arlo Guthrie, who in his talking song "Alice's Restaurant" told how his littering arrest kept him out of the draft, I stayed out of the Army and prison by spending an hour in jail for "disturbing the war."

# Chapter 4: Student Power

There's a time when the operation of the machine becomes so odious—makes you so sick at heart—that you can't take part. You can't even passively take part. And you've got to put your bodies upon the gears and upon the wheels, upon the levers, upon all the apparatus, and you've got to make it stop.

~ *Mario Savio, University of California at Berkeley, 1964*

The 1960s Movements at Berkeley, Stanford, and universities across the country weren't just about civil rights or the Vietnam War. Campus conflict was intensely personal for so many of us because the people who ran the universities saw them as institutions to conduct research in support of the activities of the government and major corporations and to grind out graduates who would easily slide into predetermined roles in those institutions. At least, that's what we activists concluded.

At the same time, elite universities were designed to give upper class and meritorious youth the tools they needed to lead and govern. Thus, they included coursework and faculty members that encouraged independent thought. In my view, this fundamental contradiction evolved into a battle for control of the universities. At Stanford, women undergraduates sought the same right to live off campus that men had; non-white students demanded more non-white admissions and scholarships; non-radical students pursued academic reform. And the Left pursued a multi-year campaign to halt Stanford's fueling of the military-industrial complex. To us, all these efforts were part and parcel of the same struggle for decision-making power at the university.[1] The 1967-68 academic year illustrated that underlying conflict.

Nationally, the most significant way that the military, allied federal agencies, and military contractors used universities was by recruiting graduates and other matriculating students. Consequently, SDS and other activist groups targeted recruiters when they came to campuses. For example, the same week as Stop the Draft Week, thousands of University of Wisconsin students protested a visit by representatives of napalm manufacturer Dow Chemical.

## Confronting the CIA

Less than a week after the massive October 20, 1967 Stop the Draft Week mobilization in Oakland, my housemate and fellow physics undergraduate Rick Bogart wrote President Sterling, on behalf of Stanford SDS, asking that the "anti-social" Central Intelligence Agency (CIA) be denied access to Stanford's new Placement Center, located in the building that just months before was home to the Experiment. Vice-President and Provost Richard Lyman wrote back, on behalf of the university administration:

> I can think of nothing more antithetical to the values that a university seeks to cherish than to deny access to any person or group because of disagreement with their views. How would you react to a request by those who strongly differ with the goals of your own organization that it be banned from the campus.[2]

---

1. My belief that the Movement should make structural, rather than quantitative demands, was reinforced by French Leftist André Gorz's *Strategy for Labor.* When you demand power, you either achieve your specific objectives or you learn how the inequitable distribution of power is an obstacle to achieving those ends.
2. Richard Bogart, Letter to President Sterling, October 25, 1967. a3mreunion.org/archive/1967-1968/67-68_cia/files_67-68_cia/67-68CIA_Letters.pdf

Though at a gut level Lyman's response seem disingenuous, it forced us to think through what we meant when we advocated freedom of speech. For many of us, the answer was simple. We would be glad to have the representative of the CIA debate its role in the world. But we found private interviews unacceptable. We believed that the function of free speech was to limit the grip of those in charge, powerful men who had plenty of opportunities to be heard, but many others on campus still believed that restricting the CIA would undermine the university's tradition as a free marketplace of ideas.

My friends and I replied that you couldn't have a free marketplace where the Board of Trustees and the warfare state owned all the stock. The Trustees, acting through administrators such as Sterling and Lyman, determined which departments got large budgets, which buildings got built, and in the final analysis, which professors were hired and fired. Over time, by creating a self-perpetuating faculty, they set the ideological tone of the university. Professors who got too far out of line were forced out.

If one looked at Stanford from the outside, one did not see an ivory tower of knowledge-seeking intellectuals. Rather, one saw a carefully designed technological research factory, equaled by few institutions anywhere. Just as important, Stanford trained an elite of professionals and managers for a society based upon social, economic, cultural and political inequality. Enabling Dow, the CIA, and the Pentagon to absorb these trainees, unchallenged, was not an exercise of free expression; it was a perpetuation of the financial and social control of creative ability. This was not the same as providing opportunities for the dwindling number of pro-War students and faculty to express their beliefs, an exercise that I considered a valid form of free expression.

On Monday, October 30, SDS activists handed out fliers advertising a noon rally. Back in those days there were no mobile phones; no social media. E-mail was at best a twinkle in some technologist's eye. We had to rely on mimeographed pieces of paper. Our best spot for reaching large numbers of undergraduates was where White

Plaza funneled past the Experiment/Placement Center to the Engineering Corner of the historic sandstone Quad. Some us got pretty efficient at handing sheets to pedestrians and bicyclists as they moved past in multiple directions.[3]

We held rallies at the far end of White Plaza, on the side of Dinkelspiel Auditorium. The Associated Students had a sound system that student groups could use, but I learned early in my Stanford education that rally sponsors had to supply their own 100-foot extension cord to connect to an outlet at the back of Dinkelspiel. It wasn't long before I stored one in the trunk of my car, along with a bullhorn.

At the rally, outside experts described the CIA's roles in overthrowing foreign governments. Learning from the *Daily* that the administration had moved the interviews from the Placement Center to Encina Hall, the main administration building on campus, we made plans to demonstrate at Encina early the next morning.

At 8:00 Tuesday morning, November 1, only a handful of demonstrators met in White Plaza to march the fraction of a mile to Encina Hall. We learned a lasting, but inconsistent lesson: Don't expect many college students to show up at a campus demonstration before noon, unless they arrived the night before. As the morning progressed, more people gathered. One group climbed through a window to an empty room near the recruiter, sang, and danced. I stayed on the walkway below, seemingly out of trouble, and used our bullhorn to make announcements and lead chants.

That day, for the first time in my experience, Stanford invoked its "demonstration policy," guidelines that changed many times over the years. Its intent was clear, to stifle disruptive demonstrations, but its precise meaning and implementation were cloudy. The Dean of Students filed charges against eleven students for their actions that day. I was one of them, not because

---

3. There is a pretty good clip of this about 55 minutes into *Fathers and Sons,* the 1968-69 documentary about Stanford SDS. See Don Lenzer *et al., Fathers and Sons,* Public Broadcasting Laboratory, 1969. a3mreunion.org/archive/video/fathers_and_sons.html

I engaged in any disruptive activity, but because the Associate Dean knew me from anti-draft rallies.[4] We were brought before the all-student Judicial Council in January 1968.

The Council, which included a few students who were sympathetic to, but not active in SDS, cleared some of us unanimously and failed to convict the rest on a split vote. But the trial, like many to follow, was more than a question of judicial outcome. We used it as educational theater. I wore my trench coat and black gloves. Our defense was simple. We said we should be found guilty of not driving the CIA from campus. We listed the reasons why the CIA did not belong at Stanford, or for that matter, anywhere. I personally said I should be found guilty because I did not go into Encina Hall.

Meanwhile, students on other campuses were doing similar things. Activists at Columbia University, where SDS researchers uncovered direct faculty collusion there with the CIA, had also been put on trial for a demonstration against CIA recruiters. So I was excited to drive, along with SDSers from Stanford and San Jose State University, to the SDS National Conference that December at the University of Indiana in Bloomington, Indiana. I remember three things about the Conference. First, New Leftists still seemed to hold leadership positions. Second, I played touch football with a group that included SDS co-founder Tom Hayden. And third, I connected with a young activist researcher doing similar things at Columbia to what I was doing at Stanford. His name was Ted Gold, and I was dismayed a couple of years later when I learned that he was one of the "Weathermen" who died in a New York City townhouse explosion in March 1970.

The 1967-1968 academic year marked, for me, the beginning of tensions at Stanford between the New Left, represented by the original SDS, and Old Left tendencies. H. Bruce Franklin, an articulate young English professor, had

---

4. Associate Dean of Students Willard Wyman was a young, soft-spoken liberal who believed, "The university is the best thing America has produced." His job was to get to know campus activists. He appears a few times in *Fathers and Sons*.

been a Movement leader before I came to Stanford, spearhead-
ing, so I was told, the campaign against napalm. My freshman
year he was at Stanford in France, and when he returned in the
fall of 1967 he identified himself as a Maoist and seemed determined to form the kernel of a Marxist-Leninist revolutionary
party. He helped organize the Stanford contingent to Stop the
Draft Week and took part in the CIA demonstration.

He formed a small organization call the Peninsula Red
Guard, named after the groups that led the Cultural Revolution
in China. The local Red Guard appeared initially to be a study
group, but from what I could tell it adopted an organizational
strategy transplanted from China in the 1930s. Bruce wanted
to form a "United Front Against Imperialism," led by his Red
Guard. He stimulated the formation of an umbrella organization
of the Stanford Left, called, appropriately, the Stanford
Community of the Left. The first few meetings of this coalition
attracted hundreds, but soon it faded away.

An SDS loyalist at the time, I was frustrated about
being drawn into a coalition that did little more than SDS did
on its own. But in retrospect, Bruce may have been right, for
the wrong reasons. Many potential activists are turned off by
the personalities and cliques of existing groups. It turned out,
over the years, that it made sense to play "fruit basket upset"
periodically. In any case, the Movement was driven to unity by
the missteps of the Stanford administration.

But before I tell the story of the Old Union sit-in of May
1968, it's important to know what was going on in the world at
the time. The Vietnamese National Liberation Front and North
Vietnamese launched the surprisingly effective Tet Offensive
at the end of January 1968. Anti-war Presidential candidate
Eugene McCarthy, backed by many "clean for Gene" student
idealists, nearly upset President Lyndon Johnson in the March
New Hampshire Democratic Primary. This prompted Robert F.
Kennedy, the brother of assassinated President John F. Kennedy,
to join the Democratic Presidential race, also attracting support
from anti-war students. At the end of March Johnson announced
that he was halting his re-election campaign, paving the way for

a three-way California primary contest in June, as Vice President Hubert Humphrey took the baton-pass from Johnson. Kennedy won that vote, but he was assassinated at his victory party in Los Angeles.

Throughout 1968, fueled by mass protests, Czechoslovakia underwent a period of decentralization and democratization, until reversed by the Soviet invasion in August. In early May, French students touched off protests that threatened to overthrow President Charles DeGaulle and the Fifth Republic.

Closer to home, Martin Luther King, Jr. was assassinated on April 4, triggering riots across the U.S. and campus unrest and negotiations at Stanford. This was one of the first major mobilizations of Stanford's Black Student Union, and we in SDS did what we could to provide support. Across the country Columbia University students staged a strike and sit-ins that were broken up violently by the New York Police Department at the end of April. At Northwestern University, black students took over the university's main financial building in response to campus racism.

Against this backdrop, on May 2 Stanford's all-faculty Interim Judicial Board (IJB) found seven students guilty of violating the Demonstration Policy and recommended that they be suspended.[5] The remainder of the original defendants, including me, had not been re-charged because there was no evidence that we had done anything. The verdict outraged not only activists but student government leaders, because it stripped them of what little power they had. It was also, on its face, double jeopardy.

---

5. The IJB verdict shared the May 3, 1968 *Stanford Daily* front page with a report on the police assault on Columbia protestors. Michael Sweeney, "IJB Finds Demonstrators Guilty; Ask Suspensions," and A.M. Rosenthal (New York Times), "Students Versus Police." archives. stanforddaily.com/1968/05/03?page=1&section=MODSMD_ ARTICLE4#articleandarchives.stanforddaily. com/1968/05/03?page=1&section=MODSMD_ARTICLE3#article

The campus reaction surprised me, since many liberal anti-war students thought we had denied the CIA its free speech. At first, one of my roommates, who was one of the seven, and I felt the whole thing was a tempest in a teapot. We didn't want to stage a confrontation over the issue of judicial procedure and student power. The CIA and Vietnam, we felt, were much more important issues.

We did not immediately comprehend how local and global issues were intertwined. Looking back, they always were. To many students the likely suspensions were merely a smaller version of the hypocrisy that the Vietnam War represented. Those in authority did not support the democratic ideals that they had brought us up to believe in.

We also drew support from students who abhorred the use of force. When SDS acted against the CIA, these students opposed SDS. But when the administration acted against SDS, they opposed university officials. This sizable chunk of the student population rarely became active, but at the time they established a political climate on campus that made it easier for their activist friends to take action.

Student government politicians were angry at the Dean of Students and Interim Judicial Board for their action. The suspensions, over-riding the Student Judicial Council, had collapsed their sandcastle. Some student government leaders were sympathetic to SDS, but I considered most of them opportunists. They wanted to lead large numbers of students, but they never embraced any cause long enough or deeply enough to generate their own following. They latched onto the SDS activity to establish themselves as alternative, more responsible, leaders of dissatisfied students. The alliance helped us, though. It brought us added legitimacy and support.

## In Even-Numbered Years, the Old Union

Over 100 students rallied in front of the President's office in the Inner Quad on Friday, May 3, to demand that student judicial power be reinstated and that the seven not be suspended.[6] President Sterling quickly rejected the demands, and he scheduled a meeting of the all-faculty Academic Council for Wednesday afternoon, May 8. Sunday night about 200 of us met in Tresidder Union to plan action. I proposed a sit-in, while others suggested we first educate the student body about what was happening. Some emphasized the need for non-violent action, but in the wake of Stop the Draft Week there was disagreement about what that meant. In the end, we resolved our differences. We voted to occupy a building if we didn't have to break in, elected a tactics committee to choose a building and work out details, and scheduled a noon Monday rally in White Plaza to launch the sit-in. Activists and the administration alike assumed that we would try to occupy the Old Union, the three-story student services building adjacent to White Plaza.

The noon rally May 6 was the largest I'd ever seen at Stanford, with perhaps a thousand participants. At least three hundred were prepared to occupy the Old Union.[7] Not only had supporters shown up in large numbers, but the tension of an expected confrontation brought hundreds more onlookers. The official tactics committee had planted some women students in Old Union restrooms, but Stanford police—really just security guards—escorted them out, closed the building, and locked the doors and windows, and they chained the front doors closed as an added deterrent.

Fortunately, a few of us, experienced as Stop the Draft Week monitors, had formed an alternate tactics committee. We were concerned that the Old Union would be locked by the time we arrived. Some had already reconnoitered the building, finding a utility tunnel—a secret passage into the building's basement. When we saw the chains on the front doors, I ran down to Memorial Auditorium, where I had a work-study job in the

6. Dan Snell, "Sterling Rejects Demands As Students Vote Action," *Stanford Daily,* May 6, 1968, page 1. archives.stanforddaily. com/1968/05/06?page=1&section=MODSMD_ARTICLE1#article

7. "Student Demonstration Today," Student Press Committee, May 6, 1968. http://www.a3mreunion.org/archive/1967-1968/67-68_old_union/files_67-68_old_union/67-68OldUnion_Release.pdf

campus theater workshop, and borrowed, without authorization, a bolt-cutter. I passed it to three members of our committee, who waited quietly in the tunnel.

When protestors moved over to the Old Union, they found it locked. A few of us forced our way into a back door when it was opened, presumably to let an employee leave. I'm sure that if we had done this by the front door, the "violence" would have alienated many demonstrators. Our little band of extremists would have been castigated for violating the rules of the majority.

But the assembled crowd did not see what we did. We moved through the building, ascending in the elevator. A guard spotted us and chased us out through a locked, but unchained side door. Our tunnel-hidden comrades took advantage of the diversion and walked through the front lobby, calmly cutting the chains and opening the main doors. This is what the demonstrators, onlookers, and reporters saw. As far as they were concerned, we had peacefully entered the building.

We thus learned two key lessons: First, never be seen forcing one's way into a building. Second, never trust moderate leaders to do the necessary tactical preparation.

To many people, the term "sit-in" implies a tight group of demonstrators, barricaded in a building, shouting slogans to those outside. At Stanford, this was rarely the case. As hardcore activists entered the building, we welcomed undecided and curious observers. We quickly broke down into discussion groups. One large group debated the whole thing with the Associate Dean of Students, the "nice guy" who in error had fingered me for the CIA protest.

With our own locks and the university's chains, we chained the front doors open, inviting bystanders to view our friendly, peaceful activity. We were comfortable with this approach, because we knew it would be both politically and practically difficult for the administration to call in real police. In the first few hours, we had met a key test of any confrontation: We had involved a new group of protestors not already committed to militancy. The sitters-in included large numbers of liberal anti-war students wearing McCarthy and Kennedy buttons.

In my retrospective that summer, "Lessons of the Stanford Sit-in," I explained our open-building strategy:

> It permitted various levels of commitment. The sit-in took place during most mid-terms, yet students could leave to go to class or to study. We could leave to shower or to eat (such activities don't make one any less revolutionary). Of the 650 who eventually signed a statement of participation, only about 200 slept-in over the two nights. Often only a handful stayed in the building as rallies, meetings, and seminars were held in the grassy courtyard.[8]

We did not ignore our own security, however, since there was always a chance we might be attacked by counterdemonstrators or police. We established watchdog committees on every floor. We noted potential escape routes and the availability of potential defensive weapons, such as fire hoses.

We held a series of mass meetings in the lobby, with our PA system pointed outside so others could hear. At each meeting, we would debate whether to stay or leave. A parade of professors who professed sympathy for our goals urged us to end the sit-in, arguing that the faculty as a whole would do nothing to help us while under pressure. But we knew otherwise: The faculty as a whole only took positive action when pressured by the Movement.

We decided to stay in the building past its normal 5:00 pm closing time. We were already "preventing" business as usual because the administration had shut down all the offices in the

---

8. Lenny Siegel, "Lessons of the Stanford Sit-In," p. 4. http:// a3mreunion.org/archive/1967-1968/67-68_old_union/files_67-68_ old_union/67-68OldUnion_Lessons.pdf I don't remember writing this. I must have sent it to other SDS chapters. Five decades later, I find it amazing or strange that I was already formulating "lessons learned" at age 19.

morning. We agreed to stay in the hallways, with one exception. Everyone was comfortable with me operating the mimeograph machine in the basement, to produce fliers. That was educational.

Our meetings were all open, so they attracted people who did not support the sit-in. We developed a novel voting procedure, utilized a year later at the larger occupation of the Applied Electronics Lab. We asked, before major votes, for those who were sitting-in to raise their hands or stand up to identify themselves. Then, only those could vote. This discouraged opponents from interfering with our democratic process, and it encouraged demonstrators to confirm their participation.

The first evening, student-body President Cesare Massarenti, originally a supporter of the protest, called a campus-wide meeting in the Old Union Courtyard, and against the wishes of other sit-in organizers he put everything up for a vote. As many as 2000 students attended. Opponents of the sit-in from the fraternities showed up in force. While 70% to 80% of those present voted to support sit-in demands and amnesty, 60% to 70% voted in favor of ending the sit-in.

**Fig. 4.1. May 6, 1968 mass meeting in the Old Union courtyard during the sit-in protesting the suspension of anti-CIA demonstrators.**

Trapped by the vote, most of the demonstrators left the building for Memorial Auditorium, where Provost Lyman had convened his own mass meeting. I had earlier gone to Mem Aud and found Lyman's presentation boring. I returned to the Old Union only to find most of the demonstrators headed to hear Lyman. Fewer than fifty of us remained, disheartened.

However, Lyman displayed the arrogance characteristic of university administrators. He rejected the student demands, and he failed to respond to a demonstrator's announcement that the sit-in was over. In response to his patronizing attitude, 500 people returned to the Old Union, more committed than before. We grooved to two rock bands and kept a lookout for assaults by student supporters of the administration.

Around 3:00 am, when most of us were asleep in the Old Union hallways, we learned that someone had set fire to the Naval Reserve Officer Training Corps building, located in an isolated wooded area of campus. This upset many students, who felt such a violent incident would limit our support. Some wanted to leave; others started to issue a condemnation.

I was in the faction that did not morally oppose the fire, so we didn't want to condemn it. We argued that a statement by the sit-in would reinforce the speculation that we had something to do with it. Steve Weissman, a Stanford graduate student who had been a leader in Berkeley's Free Speech Movement and was now the preeminent leader of the sit-in,[9] kept saying that a press statement denying involvement would be just like saying, "I didn't get your daughter pregnant." I still do not fully understand the analogy, but we did not issue a statement.

We weathered the fire, and early the next morning protestors fanned out to the dorms and campus entrances to pass out leaflets that I had mimeographed in the basement. We had established a Stanford sit-in tradition, ignored rarely over several years. Occupied buildings served as base areas from which to organize the campus.

---

9. Weissman was a mentor to some of us SDS undergraduates, helping us learn how to organize and conduct research. His critique of corporate liberalism had a lasting impact on us.

The second day of the sit-in some, if not all, offices in the building re-opened, even as we remained in the hallways. Some of the student government leaders arranged, on their own, for a "negotiation" with Lyman. Experienced negotiators among us, such as Weissman, warned that the other side would attempt to strike a deal with our negotiators, and then to maintain their leadership the negotiators would try to impose their solution on the group. We decided to send representatives, but not people who had a lot of influence among occupiers. We ended up selecting two women, with the purpose of encouraging female leadership. But we were also making the sexist assumption that these women were not influential over the group.

Tuesday night David Packard, one of the founders of Hewlett-Packard and a member of the Board of Trustees, made a condescending appearance. He tried to talk us out of the sit-in, and I'm pretty sure that he patted Weissman on the head. Enough of us knew about Packard's connections to the military industrial complex—he later became Richard Nixon's Deputy Defense Secretary—that he was not taken seriously.

We knew that Lyman had called a faculty meeting for Wednesday afternoon because he thought a vote by the faculty would carry a lot of weight. We agreed. We asked sitters-in to lobby faculty members they knew, but we also planned an event that as far as I know was unique to Stanford's sit-in tradition. We declared a "faculty open house" for mid-day Wednesday. I remember this as my idea, but I think Bruce Franklin, who knew the faculty as well as anyone, pushed it.

We fliered faculty mailboxes Wednesday morning, inviting them to visit the Old Union or its courtyard.[10] I recall some of our protest-hardened, counterculture undergraduate women, dressed up in what must have been the frocks they wore to their admission interviews, serving tea to the professors. The open house was enormously successful. Many professors, not

---

10. See Concerned Students, "Dear Faculty Member," May 8, 1968. http://www.a3mreunion.org/archive/1967-1968/67-68_old_union/files_67-68_old_union/67-68OldUnion_Letter.pdf   There must have been another notice with the specifics of the Open House.

66

just sympathetic ones, engaged in "rational dialogue" with us. We convinced them that we were not all that dangerous. Many walked through the building, noticing how peaceful and clean the occupation was.

The ongoing struggle at Columbia University also strengthened our position. The Columbia Administration's hardline against sit-ins only brought continued disruption and a bloody reputation.

When Lyman sought a vote of confidence from the Academic Council later that afternoon in nearby Dinkelspiel Auditorium, this body of august scholars rebuked him, voting 284 to 245 to support the essence of our demands: Do not suspend the CIA demonstrators; reform judicial procedures; do not punish those who were sitting in. Some of the professors who bucked the administration reportedly suffered reprisals, such as frozen salaries, for years to come.

Professor Franklin returned to the Old Union, flashing a "V" sign, bringing cheers from our concurrent meeting. But many of us, including members of Franklin's own Red Guard, were skeptical. The faculty vote had no force of law. Nevertheless, activist leaders quickly realized that most people wanted to leave. Chances were slight, they believed, that the Administration would ignore the faculty vote that it had sought.

I encouraged Weissman, who was chairing our meeting, to allow debate to continue. The more people who were able to speak against leaving, the stronger and more likely to return we would be if Lyman crossed the faculty majority. We voted to leave, cleaned the building, and left. Phil Taubman wrote in the *Stanford Daily:*

> Fifty-six and one-half hours after they walked into the Old Union with only themselves for support, over 650 student demonstrators peacefully departed last night with an unprecedented vote of support for their demands by the Stanford faculty.[11]

---

11. Philip Taubman, "Sit-In Ended As Academic Council Supports Amnesty, No Suspensions," *Stanford Daily,* May 9, 1968, page 1.

We distributed a one-page mimeographed report after leaving the Old Union. In response to Provost Lyman's claim that the proposal endorsed by the faculty majority would encourage future disruptions, we stated:

> Yet such demonstrations would not occur if there were an equitable division of power and responsibility within the university community. The present system is not equitable and cannot fail to create crisis situations like the events of this past week. At present, power and responsibility for decision rests with the trustees and administration. Future militant responses by students can be avoided if the Board of Trustees and administration are willing to accept equitable distributions of power.[12]

Few people discussed Vietnam at sit-in general meetings. Economic and political theory were scarcely mentioned at rallies or in our leaflets. But during the sit-in, SDSers and others with a left-wing perspective organized small discussion groups. We did not insist that the sit-in accept Marxist or New Left ideologies. But participants knew that the leaders did.

I felt effective in such discussions, not because I knew theory well (I didn't), but because I thought I could present ideas in language that the students understood. Immediately after the sit-in, I privately criticized Bruce Franklin for his Marxist jargon. Surprisingly, he agreed, explaining in terms he understood, that Mao had promoted "mass line."

The school year was nearly over. Sit-in moderates, preparing for their summers, almost magically began to ask the hard core of activists what to read—about U.S. foreign policy,

---

https://archives.stanforddaily.com/1968/05/09?page=1&section=MODSMD_ARTICLE1#article

12. I don't think I wrote that paragraph, but it represented the kernel of the New Left ideology that I had embraced: People have a right to control the institutions that affect their lives. "Report to the Community," May 9, 1968. http://a3mreunion.org/archive/1967-1968/67-68_old_union/files_67-68_old_union/67-68OldUnion_Report.pdf

the nature of capitalism, etc. The Old Union sit-in, despite its narrow demands for student power, irrevocably altered the political attitudes of most of its participants.

We didn't do much more organizing that spring. I had to make up three physics mid-terms that I had missed during the sit-in. When the faculty had voted that students not be punished for their participation, they had included the right to make up classwork without penalty. So I holed up in the Physics Library and studied. Much to my surprise, it turned out that all of the other students in my physics classes, except me and my roommate, normally spent almost all of their time in the Physics Library. This was my first full recognition that many people on the Stanford campus were primarily engaged in academic pursuits. Most of the time most students were simply students. Any organizing strategy had to recognize that.

There was a corollary: Just as Vietnamese guerillas had to time their actions to the wet and dry seasons of the Southeast Asian countryside, Stanford activists had to recognize the seasonality of the academic year. Each year there was substantial turnover of both the undergraduate and graduate student body. It took months to educate new students to campus issues and to build dynamic tension. By spring quarter there would be opportunities for major challenges to university leadership.

Provost Lyman, as his follow-up, scheduled a question-and-answer session with students in Tresidder Union. To his dismay, many of those who attended were SDS members or sympathizers. I recall that an undergraduate friend of mine asked him if he supported "revolution." Lyman glibly replied that "Revolution can mean many things, such as a revolution in women's clothing," referring, I think, to an advertising slogan. He was right.

# Chapter 5: Golden Spike

Come you masters of war
You that build the big guns
You that build the death planes
You that build all the bombs
You that hide behind walls
You that hide behind desks
I just want you to know
I can see through your masks

*~Bob Dylan, Masters of War, 1963*

Richard Lyman's "Time of Troubles" went global in 1968. Student-led protests overwhelmed France, Mexico, Japan, and other countries. A new, progressive world order seemed possible. In August, the whole world watched the Chicago police brutally repress predominantly young protesters at the Democratic National Convention. Though most Stanford activists were locally focused, a number of Stanford students took part in the Chicago demonstrations.

In the Bay Area, SDS and other campus activists mobilized support for the Oakland-based Black Panther Party, subject to escalating repression and assaults from local police and the FBI. In Palo Alto the Red Guard joined forces with the drug and counter-culture-dominated Free University to demand a place in downtown Palo Alto for rock concerts and other events. In Berkeley, sit-ins and a class boycott supported a proposed class that would have included a series of lectures by Eldridge Cleaver, author and Black Panther leader. Tension was building at San Francisco State University, where demands by black and other Third World students led to a lengthy student strike starting November.

In October 1968 at Stanford, students had the opportunity to hear a range of progressive speakers, including Cleaver; Senator and former Democratic Presidential candidate Eugene McCarthy;

Columbia University strike and SDS leader Mark Rudd; Columbia professor and black power leader Franklin Williams; guerilla ex-Catholic-priest Art Melville, fresh from Guatemala; leaders of the United Farm Workers; Daniel Berrigan, a priest convicted of napalming draft records in Catonsville, Maryland; and the Communist Party's presidential candidate.[1]

Stanford SDS began the year in San Francisco by protesting Hubert Humphrey's visit to the Mission District on September 26. Election night, November 5—when Richard Nixon defeated Humphrey for the Presidency—we staged a "People's Party" in Lytton Plaza, in downtown Palo Alto, site of several summertime confrontations over the right to rock. Working with groups from local high schools and community colleges, we organized a rock dance with a minimum of overt political content.

Meanwhile, the Resistance organized an "Electoral Wake," a candlelight march, featuring Joan Baez, from Stanford to another spot in Palo Alto, where several men were to burn their draft cards. At first I had viewed plans for this action to be competitive, but since several committed card-burners were also in SDS, it was not difficult to combine the two events. Once the draft cards were nothing more than smoldering ashes, most of the people at the Electoral Wake, including most of campus SDS, walked the few blocks to Lytton Plaza, in the streets.

They never left the streets, and the combined crowd of several hundred blocked University Avenue, downtown Palo Alto's main thoroughfare, adjacent to Lytton Plaza. The candles, carefully placed on the street's centerline, made a breath-taking sight. Youths lit bonfires in the street, and pretty soon the Fire Department came and the police cleared the street. A few demonstrators may have

---

1. I mention these speakers as a sign of the times. In subsequent sections I am listing only a small fraction of the guest lecturers who visited Stanford in that era.

thrown rocks, and a few cops may have swung their clubs wildly at demonstrators, but all in all there was very little violence. It was a good showing of disgust at the national electoral farce.

Several people were arrested during or as a result of this demonstration. Once they went to trial, we could not dominate as we did at campus judicial proceedings. Still, I remember one line of questioning at the trial. Grad student Art Eisenson testified that a firefighter had climbed up on a fire engine to make an announcement. When the Assistant District Attorney challenged him, he changed his story slightly: "It was either a fireman or someone dressed as a fireman."

## We Demand

The real story of the 1968-69 school year, however, was our sustained drive against war research at Stanford and SRI. It began in the summer of 1968 when the Stanford Board of Trustees announced that Kenneth Pitzer would replace retiring Sterling as university president, after refusing to seriously consider student input, even from student body officers. Working with the *Peninsula Observer*, we quickly researched Pitzer's past and published a flier on his background.[2]

Pitzer, a chemist, had been President of Rice University, in Houston, since 1961. From 1949 to 1957, he had been research director at the Atomic Energy Commission (AEC). Not only was he a "vigorous advocate" of hydrogen bomb development; he testified at 1954 McCarthyite (Joe, not Eugene) hearings at the AEC's Personnel Security Board against J. Robert Oppenheimer, one of the "fathers of the atomic bomb." As we reported, Pitzer testified that Oppenheimer had "dragged his feet" on H-bomb (thermonuclear)

---

2. "Goods on Pitzer," *Peninsula Observer*, August 26, 1968. http://a3mreunion.org/archive/1968-1969/68-69_president_pitzer/files_68-69_president_pitzer/Goods_on_Pitzer.pdf

development.[3] At the time of his appointment to Stanford, Pitzer was also on the Board of the Rand Corporation, the military's own non-profit think tank. But Pitzer was not scheduled to arrive until later in the fall term.

As the start of school approached, we published the 50-page *Through the Looking Glass: A Radical Guide to Stanford,* again with the help of the *Observer.* This orientation booklet discussed students' survival needs, presented SDS analysis of Pitzer and the Trustees, documented the Stanford complex's participation in the Southeast Asian War, and introduced several activist groups on campus.[4]

This pamphlet is the first of many documents that I produced or helped to produce over the next five decades describing the local jobs-housing imbalance.

> The 1600 Stanford undergraduates and 5200 grad students who live off campus face a housing shortage of crisis proportions.... Yet this is not an isolated student problem. The housing market is just as tight for the poor and the lower-middle class workers brought to the Peninsula to work in the electronics, aerospace, and other war-based industries.... The University then reaps higher profits and enhances the value of its land by building high-cost housing and setting up industrial parks.[5]

*Through the Looking Glass* was so successful that the next year the administration published its own guide for incoming students and plagiarized my section on local transportation.

---

3. *ibid.* "In the Matter of J. Robert Oppenheimer," Transcript of Hearing before Personnel Security Board, Atomic Energy Commission, April 12-May 6, 1954, pp. 697-709. http://a3mreunion. org/archive/1968-1969/68-69_president_pitzer/files_68-69_ president_pitzer/Oppenheimer_Testimony_1954.pdf
4. *Through the Looking Glass: A Radical Guide to Stanford, Stanford SDS,* Fall, 1968. http://a3mreunion.org/archive/1968-1969/68-69/ files_68-69/68-69_Glass_p1-50.pdf
5. *ibid.,* pp. 10-11. I do not remember whether I wrote these paragraphs.

Just before frosh arrived on campus for orientation, we held two important SDS meetings. At the first one we decided to focus our activities for the school year on "getting Stanford out of Southeast Asia" or "getting Stanford out of imperialism." More than fifty students, nearly all veterans of the May sit-in in the Old Union, attended the second. This was incredible, since school was still days away, and SDS meetings the previous school year rarely drew so many participants.

The second meeting essentially mobilized undergraduate activists to take part in the official frosh orientation program. This wasn't too hard to do, since most of those officially involved in that program had become SDS sympathizers during the Old Union sit-in, and it was too late for the administration to replace them.

I wasn't too close to this loose group of undergraduate organizers, though most, like me, were in their junior year. They were on the whole WASPs (white Anglo-Saxon Protestants), alienated by conflict and emotional intensity.[6] They were typical Stanford undergraduates. I learned from them that it was possible, meeting with small groups of students in dorms, to build the Movement's base of support.

On other campuses, such as Berkeley, organizers could rely on administration intolerance or police brutality to catalyze mass student activity. At Stanford we faced a more sophisticated administration, so we had to rely on grassroots, research-based organizing. In later years, many students who began to see themselves as revolutionaries wrote off other Stanford students, who like these revolutionaries, did not fit the archetype of the oppressed person. But if one was a Stanford student organizer, one's logical primary constituency was the student body. I learned from my WASP friends that you could work with students if you did not look down at them, even though some of them later lost interest in organizing their fellow students.

---

6. David Pugh described this 15 minutes into *Fathers and Sons*. See http://a3mreunion.org/archive/video/fathers_and_sons.html

On the heels of the Old Union Sit-In, the Chicago Democratic Convention, and global news about student rebellions, many students arrived back on campus in the Fall of 1968 with great expectations. Several hundred people attended the first SDS meeting of the academic term. However, many drifted away, uncomfortable with our rhetoric and often intense internal disagreements. Still, we had a critical mass and high visibility.

I wrote, the following summer:

> Our strategy was simple. We would use direct action to focus on the issues, and we would use our educational activities to involve more people in action. Fall quarter this meant symbolic, non-confrontational demonstrations and dorm discussion groups.... The problem was that despite our documented analysis most members of the Stanford community trusted the men responsible for making the major decisions governing the university—the Stanford Trustees.[7]

We adopted the demand:

> WE, the members of Stanford SDS and concerned members of the Stanford community, DEMAND that Stanford University, its wholly owned subsidiary, the Stanford Research Institute, and all members of the university community immediately halt all military and economic projects and operations concerned with Southeast Asia.[8]

---

7. "The April Third Movement," *Maggie's Farm,* Fall, 1969, page 40. a3mreunion.org/archive/1969-1970/69-70/files_1969-1970/69-70_Maggies_Farm_parts_1-7.pdf
8. Because of the work of SRI and some Stanford professors in Thailand, we did not limit ourselves to Vietnam or even Indochina. http://www.a3mreunion.org/archive/1968-1969/68-69/files_68-69/68-69_Demand.pdf

**Fig. 5.1. With a gold-painted spike, SDS nailed its demand that Stanford Get Out of Southeast Asia to the Board of Trustees' office door, October 8, 1968.**

On October 8 we marched to the Board of Trustees office in the Inner Quad and nailed the demand to the door, *a la* Martin Luther. To mix the symbolism, we painted the nail gold to commemorate the golden spike that railroad tycoon Leland

77

Stanford hammered in 1869 to connect the transcontinental railroad—now in the Stanford Museum (Cantor Arts Center). Stanford, who had also served as California governor, founded the university with money he extracted from U.S. taxpayers and farmers, on land stolen from Indians, while exploiting Chinese laborers.[9]

The *Stanford Daily* polled a cross-section of the student body, and to no one's surprise it found that 23.5% supported the SDS demand and 4% (500 students) would take part in an SDS demonstration at SRI.[10] We did not view this as a failure, but as a challenge. We would be using the next several months to engage in both actions and education to build support for our proposals. Furthermore, we had no intention of giving up even if a clear majority came down against us, because people, such as peasants in Southeast Asia, affected by a Stanford or SRI decision to continue war and counterinsurgency studies did not have a chance to vote. Still, we realized the more support we amassed the more likely we were to achieve our objectives.

To get SRI out of Southeast Asia, we demanded that the university exercise more control over its subsidiary. The acting university president, Robert Glaser, appointed a student-faculty committee to reconsider the relationship between Stanford and SRI. Its assigned purpose was *not* to review SRI's war and counterinsurgency work, so we published a poster-sized critique, called the "Street Wall Journal." Still, two SDSers got themselves appointed to the committee and participated assiduously in its proceedings.

Since SDS and its allies spent a great deal of our time attacking the Trustees, the university administration must have thought it would undermine our organizing if they sent some

---

9. To its credit, Stanford University now hosts an informative, moving project telling the story of Chinese Railroad Workers in North America. See https://west.stanford.edu/projects/chinese-railroad-workers-north-america-project

10. Thomas C. Dawson and Marshall Schwartz, "SDS To Protest SRI," *Stanford Daily,* October 14, 1968, p. 1. https://archives.stanforddaily.com/1968/10/14?page=1&section=MODSMD_ARTICLE1#article

leading Trustees to campus living groups to eat dinner and talk with students. We mimeographed brief biographies of each of the guests, and we fanned out to welcome the Trustees.

I was among the few SDSers who went to Delta Tau Delta, one of the leading athletic fraternities on campus. The students who grabbed David Harris, when he was student body president, and sheared his long hair were Delts. We sparred politely with Bill Hewlett, the other founder of Hewlett-Packard. We didn't instantly convert any frat brothers to radicalism, but they learned that SDSers did more than rant and rave at rallies. On our part, we learned that the Delts had heads, not just footballs. They thanked us for coming.

In some other dorms, where we had done outreach earlier, SDS actually dominated the dialogue, even performing guerrilla theater (a political skit) in one. The second night, after debating Trustee Roger Lewis, head of leading Defense contractor General Dynamics, at Toyon Hall, I thanked him in the name of the Vietnamese people for the under-performing F-111 aircraft.

Our detractors always used to complain that the Movement got too much publicity. Students who did not break the rules, critics explained, did not get news coverage. But neither did we get coverage of our day-to-day work that made the demonstrations possible.

We combined our election protest, described above, with our campaign against war research. We held a rally in which SDS'ers impersonated the presidential candidates. I played George Wallace. Our makeshift "Gorilla Band" performed parodies such as:

*Yankee Doodle went to war, riding an F-111*
*Dropped some napalm on some gooks and sent them*
*all to heaven*

Then about a hundred of us marched over to the section of campus which housed most of the physical science and electrical engineering labs and classrooms. The Gorilla Band exorcised the building originally known as the Applied Electronics Laboratory (AEL). It housed the electronics research administration offices and the Systems Techniques Laboratory, home of most of Stanford's classified (secret) war research. I had been pressing for some kind of action there ever since I learned about Stanford's war work my freshman year. There was a sign at the top of its stairway warning that one needed a security clearance to enter the second floor. While the election-day visit was non-confrontational, it identified AEL as a site for possible direct action in the future.

**Fig. 5.2. SDS marches to the Applied Electronics Laboratory, election day, November 5, 1968, to exorcise the building.**

Meanwhile, earlier in Fall quarter, a team of filmmakers headed by Don Lenzer, had approached SDS, proposing to follow us around to produce a documentary. They were sympathetic, and some us even got together with them to sing folk songs. We agreed, on the condition they give us a copy of the finished film.[11] It contains great footage, showing among other things, the

---

11. *Fathers and Sons*, Public Broadcasting Laboratories, running about 90 minutes, was broadcast first in April, 1969, during the April

continuing internal debates within SDS. Many of us criticized the film for its focus on four male undergraduates, both because it ignored the role of women but also because it seemed to cast an anti-war, anti-imperialist Movement as largely a rebellion against parents.

In fact, many SDS members were opposing their parents, for their parents were members of the ruling class that dominates American society. Our movement included a Rockefeller, a Bechtel, a Katzenbach, and a Laird. David Pugh, whose father was a vice-president of timber multinational Weyerhauser, was featured in *Fathers and Sons.* Privately he told the story of how, on an obligatory family vacation in Aspen, he called Robert McNamara an imperialist while riding up the ski-lift.

At an upper-class campus such as Stanford, it wasn't too difficult to win over the sons and daughters of the ruling class. The ideals they had been taught did not match the values that their fathers, uncles, and grandfathers made policy by. Half-seriously, at some point I started calling our organizing "child stealing." Among the most active members of the April 1969 AEL sit-in were daughters of the leaders of the on-campus right-wing Hoover Institution. Indeed, I believe the reason that Bruce Franklin was the subject of attacks by right-wing trustees, faculty, and alumni is that he was viewed as a Pied Piper, leading their children astray.

Harvey Hukari, the long-haired leader of our right-wing opponents on campus, cleverly turned our power-structure research on the Trustees around and "exposed" the ruling-class roots of SDS members. We non-elite SDSers were proud, however, since we had won them over. How could our nation's leaders fight a war and repress their own population to preserve their wealth and position, if there was no one willing to inherit it. More pointedly, I always wondered if the actions of Bill Graham,

---

Third Movement. We transferred our somewhat degraded 16mm-film copy to VHS then DVD then to YouTube. It can now be viewed at http://a3mreunion.org/archive/video/fathers_and_sons.html
The events in the film are not in chronological order.

a Stanford SDS member who was arrested during Stop the Draft Week, influenced his mother Katherine when she decided to print the *Pentagon Papers* in the *Washington Post.*

Pitzer was scheduled to begin his presidency on Monday, December 2, during "dead week," the week before finals when the *Daily* doesn't publish. So SDS organized a series of events it called Pitzer Week, including a touch football "bowl" game and an inaugural ball. We also considered a welcoming sit-in in his office in the Inner Quad. *Fathers and Sons* captured one of the meetings where SDS debated whether to confront Pitzer or engage in dialogue. In the end we planned a hybrid, and that's essentially what happened.

On Tuesday at least 50 of us marched to Pitzer's second-floor office and milled around inside without disrupting anything. When Pitzer showed up, most of our group met with him outside. According to the *Daily*, at least 150 people gathered.[12] Meanwhile, I and a handful of others remained upstairs chanting, at times, "Ho, Ho, Ho Chi Minh! NLF is gonna win."

When a student asked Pitzer if he supported U.S. imperialism, SDS member Ralph Moss, wearing a paper-bag mask with Pitzer's photo, emphatically replied affirmatively, adding, "The dirty Yankee imperialist system is going to go down to bloody defeat ..." The real Pitzer's answer was more qualified. He uncomfortably expressed his opposition to the war and American domination of other peoples, but he made no promises to change anything at Stanford. He said, "SRI has its own pattern of government." After about an hour the SDSers who had been talking to Pitzer joined us in his office where we remained until closing time.[13]

---

12. "Sit-In Greets Pitzer," *Stanford Daily,* December 6, 1968, p. 1. archives.stanforddaily.
com/1968/12/06?page=1&section=MODSMD_ARTICLE5#article
13. This confrontational dialogue was captured in *Fathers and Sons,* about 48 minutes into the documentary.

## January, 1969

In January 1969, President Richard Nixon nominated electronics tycoon and Stanford Trustee David Packard to be Deputy Secretary of Defense, and Stanford SDS continued its campaign to get Stanford and SRI out of Southeast Asia.

Back in those days, at the beginning of each quarter, students reported to Encina Pavilion to register for classes and pay fees. We used "IBM" punched cards. Outside the Pavilion, campus groups, including SDS, set up literature tables to greet and recruit students. Among our handouts was a two-page SDS Strategy Proposal that Fred Cohen, Marc Weiss, and I had prepared over the holidays.[14] We proposed a mix of education, organizing, and action in support of the Southeast Asia demand we had nailed to the Board of Trustees' door in October.

In particular, we proposed to deliver an ultimatum to the Trustees at the Board's mid-January meeting on campus. We suggested adding specifics to the demand we had nailed to the Trustees office door. We wrote, "Our presentation should disrupt the normal deliberations of the Board." Following that we proposed a mix of activities leading to an unspecific "Rad Day" of confrontation.

SDS never adopted our plan. In fact, during this period many SDSers prepared other position papers.[15] I wrote up a structural proposal for SDS. I mention this because I proposed

---

14. In March, Ed Montgomery, the *San Francisco Examiner's* FBI-connected reporter wrote a front page exposé about a confidential memo for "top echelon" SDS members in which SDS leaders plotted to disrupt the Trustee meeting. Ed Montgomery, "How SDS Plotted Stanford Violence," *San Francisco Examiner*, March 4, 1969, p.1. a3mreunion.org/archive/1968-1969/68-69/files_68-69/68-69_Strategy_Proposal.pdf
http://a3mreunion.org/archive/1968-1969/68-69_jan14_trustee/files_68-69_trustee_meeting/68-69-3-4_sf-examiner.pdf
15. See 1968-1969: Position Papers, April Third Movement Historical Archive. http://a3mreunion.org/archive/1968-1969/68-69_position_papers/68-69_position_papers.html

that one of SDS's officers be titled the Bureaucrat, responsible for lists, accounts, purchasing, printing, mail, etc.[16] This position was tailor-made for me. SDS had plenty of articulate members, and the Movement relied on a series of charismatic leaders. However, I was never charismatic. Still, I was able to exercise leadership as the Bureaucrat. In fact, ever since that time I have volunteered to take responsibility for such tasks in most of the organizations I have founded or joined.

The position papers, at least ones I've preserved, were all over the map. One group wanted immediate militant action. Someone else wrote that SDS was undemocratic and needed to better incorporate personal liberation. Some writers felt that SDS was floundering, and that we needed to shift our emphasis from the Golden Spike demand or at least broaden our program. The most important take-away: SDS was not a disciplined organization marching in lock step.

I focus here on David Pugh's "Prayers to the Rain-Gods this Winter" because in some ways it closely matches what we ended up doing.[17] David advocated more participation in the campus-wide academic reform debate, around the Study of Education at Stanford; further pursuing the creation of alternative political science seminars; and demanding the creation of an interdisciplinary Department of Radical Studies. He argued, "It's clear that our original demand was too general to relate to." He suggested that we circulate a petition that would include eight specific demands, based on the original demand to get Stanford and SRI out of Southeast Asia. Those demands closely resembled what we took to the Board of Trustees.

---

16. Leonard Siegel, "Structural Proposal for Stanford SDS," January, 1969. See 1968-1969: Position Papers," April Third Movement Historical Archive. http://a3mreunion.org/archive/1968-1969/68-69_position_papers/files_position_papers/68-69Positions_Structural_Proposal.pdf
17. David Pugh, "Prayers to the Rain Gods This Winter," January, 1969. http://a3mreunion.org/archive/1968-1969/68-69_position_papers/files_position_papers/68-69Positions_Prayers_to_the_Rain-Gods.pdf

Somehow, despite differences within SDS, we planned a demonstration at the Trustees' on-campus meeting January 14, 1969. Some of that drama is documented at the end of *Fathers and Sons*. That morning we circulated fliers inviting people to meet with the Trustees at 12:30 pm at the Bowman Alumni House. We audaciously wrote, "Today there will be an open meeting of the Stanford Board of Trustees." Our flier included nine specific demands, similar to Pugh's list. Notably, like Pugh, we did not say anything about classified (secret) research. We just opposed military electronics research.[18]

When about 100 of us arrived at the Alumni House, the Trustees were out to lunch at the nearby Faculty Club. We occupied their conference room, and we engaged in internal debate about what to do next. *Fathers and Sons* captured some of that discussion. Each time I watch that segment, I am struck by how many articulate, informed, opinionated people we had in our Movement. We decided that our goal was to open the Trustee meeting, not to *disrupt* it.

The Trustees decided to stay at the Faculty Club, and they voted unanimously not to open their meeting. Associate Dean of Students Wyman told us, "If they're going to have an open meeting, they'd like to publicize it so that all the students at Stanford could participate equally." So eventually we made our way to the Faculty Club courtyard and hallway, just outside their lunch room. In what became the concluding scene in *Fathers and Sons,* I read our demands over my bullhorn, an act that university officials considered disruptive. Eventually, one of our number found his way into the room and pushed open the door to the hallway. After a quick shoving match we entered the room. One administrator, Fred Glover, accused me of pushing

---

18. "You're Invited," January 14, 1969. http://a3mreunion.org/archive/1968-1969/68-69_jan14_trustee/files_68-69_trustee_meeting/68-69-1-14_Invited.pdf

him over, but Dean of Students Joel Smith noticed that I actually caught Glover and prevented him from crashing to the floor.[19] We tried to talk to the Trustees, but they fled.

**Fig. 5.3. I read the SDS demands to the Trustees. This is what ended my academic career.**

Our militant action sent shudders throughout the campus. We had committed the crime of disrespect. Conservative students launched a petition. People were most upset because some SDSers ate the Trustees' desserts: éclairs. I didn't get any. I did drink a few drops of gin remaining in a gin bottle. It has been a long-standing complaint of mine that my college education was ended because people thought I ate one of the Trustees' éclairs, when I didn't.

---

19. I believed in force, not violence. Thirty years later, when I was being interviewed by the Defense Investigative Service because I served on a Defense Science Board task force, the investigator asked if I believed in the overthrow of the U.S. Government by force or violence. Thinking it a multiple-choice question, I responded "force." He was not amused.

**Fig. 5.4. As demonstrators forced our way into the Trustees' lunchroom, I was sandwiched among Presidential Assistant Fred Glover, Dean of Students Joel Smith, and News Service head Bob Beyers.**

Whenever we engaged in militant activity that upset a portion of the Stanford community, we would publish fliers and pamphlets, hold rallies, and conduct dorm meetings. Unsympathetic students would say, "I'm not going to listen to you because you disrupted. Why did you do it?" So we stepped back from our militancy and carefully explained our position at a teach-in, debate, and rallies. About 30 right-wing students disrupted one of those rallies.[20] But they never got much traction, because they were unable to answer our critique of the Southeast Asian War and Stanford's role in it.

---

20. Marshall Kilduff, "Conservatives Disrupt SDS Old Union Rally," *Stanford Daily,* January 30, 1969. archives.stanforddaily.com/1969/01/30?page=1&section=MODSMD_ARTICLE1#article This event was included near the beginning of *Fathers and Sons,* out of chronological order.

**Fig. 5.5. Inside the Trustees' lunchroom at the Faculty Club. The student to my right was the one who identified himself as Emiliano Zapata.**

Our militant action sent shudders throughout the campus. We had committed the crime of disrespect. Conservative students launched a petition. People were most upset because some SDSers ate the Trustees' desserts: éclairs. I didn't get any. I did drink a few drops of gin remaining in a gin bottle. It has been a long-standing complaint of mine that my college education was ended because people thought I ate one of the Trustees' éclairs, when I didn't.

Whenever we engaged in militant activity that upset a portion of the Stanford community, we would publish fliers and pamphlets, hold rallies, and conduct dorm meetings. Unsympathetic students would say, "I'm not going to listen to you because you disrupted. Why did you do it?" So we stepped back from our militancy and carefully explained our position at a teach-in, debate, and rallies. About 30 right-wing students disrupted one of those rallies. But they never got much traction, because they were unable to answer our critique of the Southeast Asian War and Stanford's role in it.

**Fig. 5.6. SDS entered President Pitzer's office on January 28, 1969 to invite him to a rally the following day. Characteristically, I was holding a clipboard.**

In the wake of the Old Union Sit-In, the university had created a new policy on disruption as well as a new trial court, the faculty-student Stanford Judicial Council (SJC). Once the delegated faculty member declared the protest a disruption, Associate Dean of Students Willard Wyman collected the names of the protesters in the faculty club. He knew many of us. Others voluntarily identified themselves. David S. said his name was "Emiliano Zapata," the Mexican revolutionary popularized in American film.

By February, twenty-nine of us—almost all undergraduates—were brought before the Judicial Council, headed by Law Professor Jack Friedenthal. Law School lecturer Doron Weinberg conducted our defense, which blended a discussion of the day's events, challenges to the way the disruption policy was enforced, and the underlying reasons

89

for the protest.[21] SDS'ers who were not on trial disrupted the proceeding with a guerilla theater skit about "Jumping Jack Free-for-All and his kangaroo court." One evening marijuana brownies were shared among most of the defendants and student members of the Judicial Council. At one point, David S. was sitting with the defendants, and one of the officials—perhaps Friedenthal himself—pointed at him and called out, "That's him. That's Emiliano Zapata." He was never identified and charged.

The SJC found us all guilty. We were given suspended suspensions. Most of us were fined $50 each, to be paid to the Martin Luther King, Jr. Scholarship Fund.[22] The SJC also found mitigating circumstances:

> That the failure of the University administration and the Board of Trustees to develop and maintain methods for the orderly exchange of views with the student body regarding issues relevant to the University was a contributing factor of the disruption.[23]

---

21. See "Stanford 29 Speak," Stanford Students for a Democratic Society, March, 1969.
http://www.a3mreunion.org/archive/1968-1969/68-69_jan14_trustee/files_68-69_trustee_meeting/68-69-1-14_Stanford29.pdf
22. During our judicial process, the Black Students Union was pursuing its own demands on the university. A group of black students destroyed property in the Stanford bookstore as part of their protest. Madelyn Spatt, "Militant Blacks Raid Bookstore, Pitzer's Absence Causes Fury," *Stanford Daily,* February 21, 1969, p. 1.
https://archives.stanforddaily.com/1969/02/21?page=1&section=MODSMD_ARTICLE2#article
23. "Statement of the Proceedings," Stanford Judicial Council," February 27, 1969, p. 15.
http://a3mreunion.org/archive/1968-1969/68-69_jan14_trustee/files_68-69_trustee_meeting/68-69-1-14_Statement_of_Proceedings_complete.pdf

Some on campus felt that SDS had failed. In an early March editorial, "SDS Strikes Out?" the *Stanford Daily* opined:

> The options facing SDS are thus not very wide or pleasant from a radical outlook. All would not be lost, however, if SDS had any support or respect among the broad base of Stanford students. Judicial hang-ups and judicial legitimacy would only be a temporary roadblock to SDS if they had effectively built a movement at Stanford. They have not built a movement, largely because their tactics have been insensitive to most student and faculty opinion. SDS believes in revolution. Somewhere along the line, they forgot to muster support.[24]

President Pitzer considered the SJC verdict a success. In a March 10, 1969 letter to Trustee Tom Pike, he argued that campus discipline was more effective than the use of outside police and the criminal justice system:

> if internal judicial mechanisms operate and internal sanctions are enforced, disrupters are brought to justice more promptly and punished more effectively than is possible through the external legal system. Those arrested at San Francisco State and at Berkeley are promptly released on bail to return to the campus and continue agitation as heroes in the eyes of many fellow students. In contrast, the S.D.S. leaders recently convicted by the S.J.C. at Stanford drew virtually no support at a recent rally.[25]

---

24. Editorial, "SDS Strikes Out, *Stanford Daily,* March 3, 1969, p. 2. https://archives.stanforddaily. com/1969/03/03?page=2&section=MODSMD_ARTICLE10#article
25. Kenneth S. Pitzer, "Letter to Thomas P. Pike," March 10, 1969. http://a3mreunion.org/archive/1968-1969/68-69_president_pitzer/files_68-69_president_pitzer/Hesburgh_letter.pdf . I find it interesting how closely Stanford's administration was following events at other campuses.

We knew better. The following day was the turning point for the SDS campaign to get Stanford out of Southeast Asia.

**Fig. 5.7. The March 11, 1969 student-trustee forum in Memorial Auditorium was a turning point for the Stanford Movement.**

## "Ours!"—The March 11 Trustee Forum

Despite discomfort on campus about SDS's rhetoric and militant tactics, there was growing support for better communications between the Trustees and students. In response, Pitzer created the University Advisory Committee, made up of five students, five faculty, and five trustees, with Pitzer as chair. When SDS and its allies reserved Dinkelspiel Auditorium March 11 for an open meeting of the Stanford Community, inviting the Trustees—who were scheduled to meet on campus that day—the student members of the Advisory Committee countered by arranging a forum in larger Memorial

Auditorium the same afternoon. The five Trustee participants who agreed to take part included Hewlett-Packard founder William R. Hewlett and Charles Ducommun, who ran his own manufacturing business but also served on the Lockheed Corporation's Board of Directors. The seven student panelists included three SDS members, Resistance leader Paul Rupert, and a young Republican. Doron Weinberg, the law lecturer who had represented the Stanford 29, served as moderator.

Mem Aud nearly filled that day. The bulk of the audience was undecided, not knowing whether to believe the radicals narrative about the Trustees, the campus, and the War.

Opening up for the students, Paul Rupert encapsulated how the world view of activist students differed from the establishment Trustees. He concluded:

> I urge you to lay down your weapons and your defensiveness; if you will not, then please resign and let the community replace you with men who will lead by the strength of their vision and not by their power. Mr. Ducommun, will you lay down your weapons.[26]

Ducommun replied, "I have to answer that categorically NO."

At one point, an undergraduate in the audience, Nick Selby—who was not part of SDS or any other radical faction—asked Hewlett if FMC (originally Food Machinery and Chemical Corporation), where Hewlett sat of the Board of Directors, made nerve gas.[27] Hewlett said no, and he attacked the activists and their sources, saying he had just confirmed

---

26. "Trustees Routed: Transcript of the Meeting," *Peninsula Observer,* March 31, 1969, p. 10.
http://a3mreunion.org/archive/1968-1969/68-69_mar11_trustee/files_trustee_forum/68-69-3-11_Trustees-Routed.pdf
27. Selby ended up joining the April Third Movement, penning a column, "Sit-in Is Normal," in the April 16, 1969 *Stanford Daily,* p.2. https://archives.stanforddaily.com/1969/04/16?page=2&section=MODSMD_ARTICLE14#article

that with FMC's president. Pressed by panelists, however, Hewlett admitted that FMC had built and operated the plant "at the request of the government and they turned that plant over to the government about six months ago."[28]

Toward the end of the meeting, Rupert asked the Trustees to commit to an open Trustee meeting to discuss the forthcoming report and recommendations of the student-faculty committee on SRI's future. Trustee Ducommun said students and faculty would be involved, but when Rupert pressed for an open meeting, Ducommun questioned: "But whose request?" In unison, the audience loudly answered, "Ours!"[29]

The brief interchange about nerve gas production was the turning point for the Stanford Anti-War Movement. Before Hewlett's duplicity, SDS and our allies were considered a vocal minority on the campus. After that, we spoke for the bulk of the Stanford community. Rupert reported:

> The day after I sat on a panel when Stanford SDS held its meeting with five of the university's trustees, a student hasher [someone who earns money toward school expenses by serving food] in a dormitory stopped me. "You guys were fantastic," he said. I thanked him. He continued, "You know, I'm no radical or anything—I mean I don't belong to SDS or the Resistance. In fact, I'm on the football team.

---

28. "Trustees Routed," p. 10. Nationwide there was a growing movement against the development and potential use of chemical and biological weapons, for both moral and practical reasons. In response to that movement, at Stanford and elsewhere, President Nixon and Congress sharply reduced the CBW program in late 1969. One of the proponents of this move was Defense Secretary Melvin Laird, whose niece was active in the Stanford anti-war movement. Closing the circle, in 2011 I visited the Newport Chemical Depot in Indiana, the plant that Hewlett was referring to, as part of a National Academies of Sciences committee overseeing the demolition of the inactive plant.
29. "Trustees Routed," p. 13.

94

> I went to that meeting and I tried to do it with an open mind, but you guys were right. Those trustees shouldn't be running this place."
>
> In a sense, that sums up the March 11 meeting. Five powerful and legitimate trustees came before the people they ruled, most of whom were trying to keep an "open mind" or were still angry at SDS for breaking into the last trustees' meeting. But by meeting's end, the rulers had lost control of their audience, and the people were demanding an open meeting.[30]

Rupert noted that this decisive point grew out of the campaign, a mix of research, education, and action, that I've described in this and earlier chapters.

I learned a decade or so later that the March 11 Trustee Forum was also a turning point for Bill Hewlett. Hewlett's frustration emerged immediately. Shortly after the nerve gas interchange, he told Jeanne Friedman, the only woman on the student panel, to "Shut up." His frustration lasted. I was active in Mountain View politics in the late 1970s and early 1980s. I got to know Bill's son Walter, who was an investor in a company seeking a cable television franchise from the city. He told me that his father had become more rigidly conservative after an event at Stanford where he had been "set up." The students and moderator he had faced were not representative of the student body. I told Walter that was true at the beginning of the meeting, but not the end.

As the Winter 1969 quarter drew to an end, some SDS members got together with other campus activists, as well as the United Student Movement in Palo Alto High Schools, to form the SRI Coalition, focusing on the SRI portion of the SDS

---

30. Paul Rupert, "You Guys Were Fantastic," *Peninsula Observer,* March 31, 1969, p. 9.
http://a3mreunion.org/archive/1968-1969/68-69_mar11_trustee/files_trustee_forum/68-69-3-11_Fantastic.pdf

demands. I saw it as an unnecessary challenge to the leadership of SDS, but it proved successful in broadening the base of our campaign and bringing new talents and leaders to the fore. It circulated a petition, the initial version of which was signed by numerous faculty and non-SDS student leaders, urging "that SRI be brought under closer control by the University community and that no further Chemical-Biological Warfare or counter-insurgency contracts be accepted by SRI."[31]

---

31. "Stanford Research Institute Coalition," March, 1969.
http://a3mreunion.org/archive/1968-1969/68-69_sri_coalition/
files_68-69_sri_coalition/68-69_SRICoalition_Petition.pdf

# Chapter 6: "Research Life Not Death"— The April Third Movement

> It isn't nice to block the doorway,
> It isn't nice to go to jail,
> There are nicer ways to do it,
> But the nice ways always fail.
> ~*Malvina Reynolds, It Isn't Nice, 1964*

My old Stanford friends look back at the spring, 1969 April Third Movement, particularly the nine-day Applied Electronics Laboratory (AEL) sit-in, as the zenith of the Stanford Movement. We acted forcefully, with the demonstrated support of most of the Stanford community. Individual activists blossomed, utilizing a wide variety of skills. We built community and many lasting friendships. And we won one of our most important demands.

It was also a turning point in my life. Not only is this when I was called up for induction into the U.S. armed forces, but it is when my academic career ended. It's an outcome that I accepted at the time because I believed—mistakenly, it turned out many years later—that the careers I was preparing for would force me to work for the military industrial complex.

On spring quarter Registration Day, the Stanford 29 offered to pay our fines to the Black Panther Party instead of the Martin Luther King Jr. Scholarship Fund. Pitzer refused, choosing to stick with the SJC recommendation. The *Daily* reports that 27 of us received pink "hold cards" in our registration packets. Some of us burned them. Eventually, some of the 29 settled with Stanford and continued to receive degrees there. Others never went back. A handful of us never graduated from any college.

I lost my scholarship, but for some amazing reason—probably federal rules—I was paid the equivalent of the work-study money I would have earned if I had successfully enrolled. The Director of Financial Aid wrote me:

> Since you have been suspended on an interim basis from the University, you are no longer eligible for employment under the College Work-Study Program. It is assumed by the Provost's Office that you will need funds equivalent to your earnings to maintain yourself. For this reason, the University will pay you an equivalent amount for the period of your interim suspension...[1]

April began with great expectations, and with no schoolwork many of my friends and I had time on our hands. Several organizations—essentially the SRI Coalition—called for a mass meeting in Dinkelspiel Auditorium at 4:00 pm on April 3, 1969.[2] Eight hundred people attended and developed a list of demands building upon the earlier platforms of SDS and the SRI Coalition. We demanded an open Trustee meeting on campus the week of April 21. President Pitzer agreed to bring our demands to the Trustees at their April 8 meeting in San Francisco.[3]

The community meeting added one demand that made me uncomfortable. Though on Election Day we had protested at the Applied Electronics Laboratory (AEL), the building housing Stanford's secret, "classified" research, I always argued that we should oppose research based on its end use. Others, such as Bruce Franklin, felt that we would win more faculty support by proposing

---

1. Robert P. Huff, letter to Leonard Siegel, May 9, 1969.
2. "April 3RD: A Community Meeting on Stanford-SRI," late March or early April, 1969. http://a3mreunion.org/archive/1968-1969/68-69_april_3_meeting/files_68-69_april_3_meeting/A3M4-3_Announcement.pdf
3. Letter to President Pitzer, April 3 Community Meeting, April 4, 1969. http://a3mreunion.org/archive/1968-1969/68-69_april_3_meeting/files_68-69_april_3_meeting/A3M4-3_to_Pitzer.pdf

to end classified contracting, because it was inconsistent with the openness associated with academic freedom. They prevailed, strengthening the argument—five nights later—for a sit-in that shut down AEL, and leading to a recognizable victory in the phasing out of classified research. But it left to future years the ongoing debate over the continuation of unclassified Defense Department-sponsored research on campus.

Actually, I focused my energy on naming our group. We sent our April 4 letter to the Trustees in the name of "The April 3 Community Meeting," but I thought that unwieldy. I proposed and lobbied for "April Third Movement." Appreciating the ring but not the politics of "M2M," the acronym of the Progressive Labor Party's May Second Movement, I suggested that we call ourselves "A3M." On this I prevailed. I also ordered campaign buttons that stated, "Research Life Not Death" and "Keep SRI"—the latter referring to our demand that SRI be brought closer to the university so its war research could be constrained.

Among radical students, few thought the demands would be won easily, if at all. Our strategy might be considered "revolutionary reformism." The demands seemed reasonable, and it was conceivable that some would be implemented. However, they clashed with the real interests of the Trustees and many of the faculty. Our actions would either achieve our stated objectives or expose those interests.

On April 8, about 100 students gathered for a vigil in the Old Union Courtyard. The *Daily* reported that the demonstration began with the song, "It Isn't Nice," by Malvina Reynolds.[4] About forty of us carpooled to the San Francisco financial district, where we picketed outside the Trustee meeting. President Pitzer kept his promise to present the A3M demands. He condemned the war and the draft, asking the Trustees to show their concern. But he did not

---

4. Barbara Hyland, "Separate Vigils Attract Small Student Turn-outs," *Stanford Daily,* April 9, 2019. archives.stanforddaily.com/1969/04/09?page=1&section=MODSMD_ARTICLE2#article

endorse the A3M program.[5] The Trustees responded by asking SRI not to accept new CBW contracts while its relationship with the university was being resolved.

That night, the Up Against the Screen film series, organized by members of SDS and the Resistance, showed the revolutionary feature film *Battle of Algiers* in Memorial Auditorium.[6] Directed by Gillo Pontecorvo, it is considered one of the most influential political films in history.[7] Its showing had been scheduled long before anyone knew what might be happening in April, but it raised the political temperature on campus. The film series organizers kept the film for a week, projecting it again on the wall of AEL during the nine-day sit-in.

Wednesday night, April 9, an overflow crowd of as many as 1000 people gathered again in Dinkelspiel Auditorium in the expectation that they would launch a sit-in. President Pitzer, speaking from a floor microphone, counseled patience. Jeanne Friedman, the graduate student whom Bill Hewlett had told to "shut up" on March 11, made a motion to occupy AEL. I followed, urging, that it was "a night not to talk but to act."[8] On the other side, popular anti-war theology professor Robert McAfee Brown argued that the proposed sit-in would be counterproductive.

---

5. K.S. Pitzer, "Remarks to the Trustees of Stanford University in Opening Discussion of the Future Relationship of Stanford Research Institute to the University," April 8, 1969. http://a3mreunion.org/archive/1968-1969/68-69_apr8_trustee/files_68-69_april_8/A3M4-8_from_Pitzer.pdf

6. "Up against the Screen: The People's Theater," The Resistance and S.D.S., Spring, 1969 http://a3mreunion.org/archive/1968-1969/68-69/files_68-69/Peoples-Theater-1.pdf and a3mreunion.org/archive/1968-1969/68-69/files_68-69/Peoples-Theater-2.pdf

7. *The Battle of Algiers.* criterion.com/films/248-the-battle-of-algiers

8. "Students Sit In at AEL; Two-Thirds OK Action at Mass Meeting," *Stanford Daily,* April 10, 969, p.4. archives.stanforddaily.com/1969/04/10?page=1&section=MODSMD_ARTICLE1#article I don't remember saying that at this particular meeting, but it's the kind of thing I always said.

This was a dramatic escalation of student tactics. The previous year we sat in the Old Union, partially disrupting student services. In AEL, we would be directly throwing a wrench in the gears of the war machine. Though federal officials, the Trustees, and administration feared that we would rifle through classified documents, that was impractical—they were under lock and key—and senseless. There was nothing we could do with highly technical electronic warfare research. In the end 700 participants voted to occupy AEL. Later they voted not to set an end-date.

Student Body President Denis Hayes sought to tamp down the growing militancy. He next proposed that A3M commit to harming no person, not damaging property, and keeping the doors open.[9] Some regarded his proposed guidelines to be moral imperatives. Others viewed them as tactical exigencies. The most militant of us were not worried that the guidelines would keep us from forcing our way into the building. We had a key, supplied willingly by an AEL employee who was part of the Movement. Hayes' motion passed unanimously, and the resulting tone was central to the popularity and success of the sit-in.

## AEL and Classified Research

The Applied Electronics Laboratory was not a research group, but a building, constructed in 1957 with funds donated by Hewlett-Packard founders William Hewlett and David Packard. Once the vote was taken, a number of us rushed across campus to AEL in the hope of arriving before any guards were deployed to prevent our entry. As we gathered around the door, it magically opened. The *Daily* said it was jimmied.[10]

Maybe four hundred demonstrators occupied the building that night, bringing sleeping bags and other personal articles. Over the life of the sit-in, people slept in hallways, on the roof, and in the ivy. There was a violinist, folk-dancing, and guerilla

---

9. "Dennis [sic] Hayes Motion, April 9, 1969. http://a3mreunion.org/archive/1968-1969/68-69_apr9_meeting/files_68-69_april_9/A3M4-9_Motion_3.pdf
10. "Students Sit In at AEL," p.1 archives.stanforddaily.com/1969/04/10?page=1&section=MODSMD_ARTICLE1#article

theater. Some instructors convened classes in the building. Protestors shared food—ranging from hot stew to peanut butter sandwiches—and hot cider and coffee from a makeshift kitchen. Thirteen protestors fasted. We offered childcare. We kept the doors open and mopped the halls.

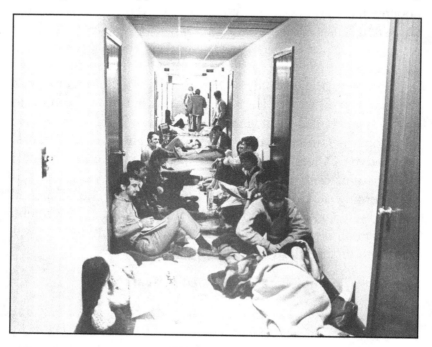

**Fig. 6.1. The AEL Hallway. This is what democracy looks like.**

We built a sense of community that many students felt missing from their conventional Stanford experience. Political positions evolved in small group discussions. Participants developed their understanding of the action by defending it to hostile faculty and students.

Almost every day, in open meetings in the AEL courtyard broadcast on campus radio station KZSU, we would debate whether to end the sit-in. Moderate students and faculty members argued that we couldn't achieve any progress toward meeting our demands as long as we occupied the building.

It was clear, however, to the majority that the only reason our demands were taken seriously was that we were willing to back them up with direct action that put ourselves at risk.

Hundreds of onlookers would gather around the edge of the courtyard, and at first they attempted to vote in our meetings, against the sit-in. Following our practice from the Old Union sit-in the previous spring, we solved that by requiring anyone who wished to vote to identify himself/herself as one of the protesters by signing our Solidarity Statement: "I am sitting-in at the Applied Electronics Laboratory. Wish you were here." By the time we left the building, about 1400 people had signed.[11]

**Fig. 6.2. At AEL, we made our decisions in public.**

---

11. This is perhaps the most significant document that I cannot find in my archives. I'm guessing that I destroyed it well after the end of the sit-in to protect the identity of participants.

We decided to stay at AEL, but not to occupy additional war-research buildings. We demanded that the Trustees meet openly to consider the recommendations of the SRI Study Committee, due out on April 14. Some of our debates were heated, but we restored our cool by breaking out into small discussion groups.

Recalling our success with the Old Union sit-in a year earlier, we used AEL as a base from which to educate and organize. We circulated fliers and newsletters throughout campus departments and residences. We leafleted Palo Alto shopping centers and churches. In cooperation with high school counterparts, we organized lunchtime rallies at all three Palo Alto high schools. At two campuses, our speakers were forced off campus, but at Palo Alto High School Fred Cohen addressed one third of the student body.[12]

We did our best to engage with SRI employees. On April 14:

> At SRI, about 200 researchers and Coalition members met in a parking lot at noon and talked in small groups for more than four hours. When they arrived, Coalition members found tables and chairs set up for their use and refreshments being served. They were met with an apology that there was no "lawn" available for the meeting. This was in reference to a false report in the *San Francisco Examiner* Sunday that the Coalition had planned a "lawn-in"—a mass rally—outside SRI yesterday.[13]

I learned forty years later that one of the SRI employees that A3Mers met with, on a different day, was Doug Engelbart. Englebart's research, sponsored by the Defense Department's

---

12. Felicity Barringer, "Coalition Seeking Support From Area Communities," *Stanford Daily,* April 14, 1969. https://archives. stanforddaily.com/1969/04/14?page=1&section=MODSMD_ ARTICLE2#article

13. By Marshall E. Schwartz, "Sit-In Rejects Resolution To Leave If Senate Acts," *Stanford Daily,* April 15, 1969. https://archives. stanforddaily.com/1969/04/15?page=1&section=MODSMD_ ARTICLE6#article

Advanced Research Projects Agency, was largely responsible for the emergence of interactive computing. Just four months earlier, at a computer conference in San Francisco, Engelbart demonstrated the first computer "mouse" to the world. Apparently, Engelbart was somewhat sympathetic to the Movement.

One of the most remarkable achievements of the April Third Movement was the emergence of a spontaneous, effective organizational structure. Experienced activists and first-time protestors brought their skills, from baking bread in coffee cans to running offset printing presses. We had a small coordinating committee that set the times for general meetings and, as the name implies, tried to coordinate everything that was going on at AEL. But the heart of the Movement was the fifteen or more working committees.[14] These ranged from Women's Liberation to Publications to Dorm and Department Organizing, which had dozens of active volunteers. With most students suspending much of their normal schedules, sitters-in had time to devote to the Movement. And in general the coordinating committee encouraged the committees to act independently.

When we entered the building, we found a print shop in the basement. In that print shop, we found a pile, perhaps boxes, of a 55-page copyrighted pamphlet, "Sex/Family Life Education and Sensitivity Training—Indoctrination or Education?" Apparently, some of the AEL employees were doing an unauthorized print job on the side.[15] To us, this justified our taking over the print shop.

Volunteer Movement printers ran the equipment in the AEL basement pretty much around the clock. These were people whose off-campus print shops contained posters proudly declaring, "Freedom of the press is guaranteed to those who can run one." They printed a daily newsletter, *Declassified*, which

---

14. "Committees, Collectives," April, 1969. http://a3mreunion.org/archive/1968-1969/68-69_ael_sit-in/files_68-69_ael_sit-in/A3MAEL_Committees.pdf

15. "AEL Publishes Anti-Sex Lit," *Unclassified*, April 10, 1969, p.2. http://a3mreunion.org/archive/1968-1969/68-69_declassified/files_68-69_declassified/A3MDeclassified_v1_n1.pdf This first edition of *Declassified* was actually titled *Unclassified*.

**Fig. 6.3. Small-group discussion in the AEL Courtyard. The man with his hands in his pockets is FBI informer Thomas Mosher.**

contained news of the day, a daily biographical summary of a Stanford trustee, and research reports on Stanford and SRI.[16] They published pamphlets on SRI and AEL. They published dozens of fliers, with print runs in the thousands. *Declassified* reflected the views of A3M as a whole, but it was editorially independent.

At one point, a visitor sabotaged one of the presses.[17] Our printers quickly fixed it. In addition, the Movement actually hired a professional repairer to come in and fix one of the machines. At the end of the sit-in, I estimated that we had used 750,000 sheets of paper, most of which we found in AEL.

---

16. See *"Declassified* by Edition," April Third Movement Historical Archive. a3mreunion.org/archive/1968-1969/68-69_declassified/68-69_declassified.html
17. "Printing-Room Sabotage," April 13, 1969. http://a3mreunion.org/DisturbingTheWar/dtw-files/sabotage-4-13-1969.pdf

Strangely enough, criticisms of the Movement for seizing the presses and stealing paper never gained any traction. We made the point that we were protecting the equipment, not damaging it, so we were compliant with our no-property-damage pledge, and our uses were educational. Toward the end of the sit-in, the authors of one A3M statement wrote, "We believe our occupation of AEL and use of printing facilities here has helped the community understand the issue of military research on campus and the need for action."[18]

One of our most successful committees was the April Third Movement News Service. While the *Stanford Daily* independently covered the Movement, most of the outside world, plus many on campus, received their information from the university's media relations office, called the Stanford University News Service. From 1961 to 1989, the News Service was headed by Robert W. "Bob" Beyers.

Beyers was an unusual flack. On the one hand, he was a political liberal. During 1964 he traveled to Mississippi to help organize Freedom Summer media relations. He was a principled journalist, accurately describing controversial news. I think he was the first person I ever saw with what looked like a laptop computer, perhaps with a limited display, furiously taking notes at meetings where I spoke. Even during the April Third Movement his press releases confirmed the Movement's claims about Stanford and SRI's military research, and during AEL they described support statements that protestors were receiving from throughout the campus. Furthermore, over my years of hostile research on Stanford and the Trustees, Beyers always made his files available to me.

On the other hand, he was a sophisticated university loyalist. He testified to the Trustees that Stanford should sever SRI from the university. He built trust with the press by

---

18. "Message from the April 3 Movement to the Stanford Community," April 17, 1969. http://a3mreunion.org/archive/1968-1969/68-69_ guidelines/files_68-69_guidelines/A3MGuidelines_Message_to_ Community.pdf

accurately reporting on the university's critics, but he usually led his releases with explanations from administration spokesmen. When he died in 2002, one of his former team wrote:

> Beyers was the inventor of the preemptive press release. If something bad were going to happen, Beyers put out a full news release before the press found out. His theory was that by getting it out first, you defused the story. A potential scandal that could clang around in the media for a week or month would go away in a few days if the university took the fun out of reporting it. It worked every time. One result was that our office was trusted implicitly. When we put out a press release, reporters believed every word. We never lied. We never obfuscated. We never weaseled. And reporters knew it.[19]

Activists, on the other hand, began calling Beyers "Bobby Bias." One-time *Daily* editor Michael Sweeney went so far as to attack Beyers for "domestic counterinsurgency," because he suppressed news of the April 18, 1969 student vote supporting the sit-in.[20] (See below.) Concerned that Beyers was shaping the image of the Movement, A3Mers recognized the importance of establishing direct contact with the outside press, so we set up the Movement News Service.

In the end, Beyers' loyalty to the administration was not reciprocal. In 1989 he was fired for honest coverage of a scandal about Stanford's unusually high indirect cost recovery on Federal research projects.

---

19. Joel Shurkin, "Bob Beyers Left Legacy of Candor and Courage," *National Association of Science Writers*, Winter 2002-03. https://www.nasw.org/sites/default/files/sciencewriters/html/win0203tex/beyers.htm

20. Michael Sweeney, "'Ugly, Sometimes Fierce'—Beyers' Counterinsurgency," *Stanford Daily*, April 21, 1969. https://archives.stanforddaily.com/1969/04/21?page=2&section=MODSMD_ARTICLE10#article

On Sunday afternoon, April 13, we reprised the faculty tea party that led to the 1968 Old Union sit-in success. The *Daily* reported that 100 faculty members, plus hundreds of others, attended.[21] This event showed how peaceful the sit-in was, and it showed how we militants also believed in rational dialogue. I believe we came across as thoughtful, informed, and even persuasive.

The evening of Tuesday, April 15, we celebrated in candle-light the wedding of Marc Sapir and Carrie Iverson. Paul Rupert, perhaps the best known leader of the sit-in and a recent divinity student, officiated. Recalling the confrontation with the Trustees on March 11, he asked the assembly, "By whose authority are these people being married?" Once again, the crowd shouted, "Ours!"[22]

The same night we were visited by Bobby Seale, chairman of the Black Panther Party, and SDS national co-founder Tom Hayden. Seale placed the Stanford struggle in its national and international context, but he said that it was too soon for students to pick up helmets and clubs to prevent the resumption of war research at AEL.[23] Hayden repeated the Yippie line, "Kill your parents." Though the crowd included many ruling-class offspring and daughters of leaders of the right-wing on-campus Hoover Institution, that suggestion was not particularly well received.

In the wake of the punishment of the Stanford 29 and the trials of election-night demonstrators, sit-in participants knew that they ran the risk of both arrest and suspension. Despite warnings by sit-in opponents that occupying a building with classified records would trigger action by U.S. Marshals, I've never seen evidence that such a response was seriously on the

21. Marshall Schwartz, "Sit-In Continues as Trustee and Faculty Respond to Demands: Names to Be Taken," *Stanford Daily,* April 14, 1969, p. 3. https://archives.stanforddaily.com/1969/04/14?page=1&section=MODSMD_ARTICLE1#article
22. Susan Sward, "Pair Married in AEL Courtyard," *Stanford Daily,* April 16, 1969, p. 1. https://archives.stanforddaily.com/1969/04/16?page=1&section=MODSMD_ARTICLE4#article
23. "Can't Fight Fire with Fire," *Declassified,* April 16, 1969, p. 1. http://a3mreunion.org/archive/1968-1969/68-69_declassified/files_68-69_declassified/A3MDeclassified_v1_n7.pdf

table. The first night, Stanford police—little more than security guards—mingled with protestors, chatting through the night. Negotiations between protestors and the administration led to the continuing presence of campus police, unarmed and out of uniform.

Stanford had never brought in police or sheriffs to break up a sit-in. There were good reasons. Police action at San Francisco State had paralyzed the campus. The first day of AEL, 400 police battled hundreds of students at Harvard (the Stanford of the East), and the result was headlined in the *Stanford Daily* on April 11.[24] Governor Reagan urged Stanford to call in police, but Provost Richard W. Lyman, later a strong advocate of police intervention, stated, "The results of using off-campus methods to end disorder elsewhere have not been especially happy or encouraging."[25]

Pitzer, in the wake of what he considered the successful prosecution of those of us who had entered the January 14 Trustee meeting, chose to rely on campus judicial proceedings. In many ways, interruption of one's college education was more punitive than criminal arrest. On the first full day of the sit-in, Pitzer declared it a violation of the University Policy on Campus Disruptions. On April 13, we voted to give our names, when confronted by faculty name-takers, as "April Third Movement" with the address "AEL." Our flier asserted:

> If the administration chooses to select victims on the basis of faculty investigation, instead of prosecuting ALL THOSE WHO SIGN THE STATEMENT OF SOLIDARITY, there will be

---

24. Associated Press, "Police Battle Students At Harvard Sit-In," *Stanford Daily,* April 11, 1969. archives.stanforddaily. com/1969/04/11?page=1&section=MODSMD_ARTICLE2#article
25. "About 250 Supporters of the April Third Movement...," Stanford University News Release, April 15, 1969.
http://a3mreunion.org/archive/1968-1969/68-69_stanford_releases/ files_68-69_stanford_pr/A3M_PR_Stanford_April_15(2).pdf

a vicious breach of justice.... [The community meeting] also suggested that calling the faculty cops a bunch of mother-fuckers was not the best tactic ..."[26]

**Fig. 6.4. April, 1969. A key feature of the AEL sit-in was our round-the-clock operation of the building's print shop.**

26. "Answer to Faculty Investigators: Name? 'The April Third Movement,' Address: 'AEL,'" April 13, 1969.

Despite meetings of the Professor Friedenthal's SJC kangaroo court, designed to hold AEL demonstrators accountable, other more militant demonstrations soon eclipsed AEL. I don't recall whether any students were punished for the AEL sit-in. I don't even know if I was, because I received SJC summons for a series of activities, whether or not I took part. That is, in the phrase from the movie *Casablanca*, I was a "usual suspect."

Despite continuing criticism from the administration and faculty leadership, the AEL sit-in continued to gather support. Dorms, fraternities, and graduate student associations issued statements. Eighty-five staff at the Stanford Linear Accelerator Center signed a statement of support. An AEL research associate wrote, "Therefore I must do whatever I think will be effective and consonant with my own values, both within and without the law, to stop military research at Stanford."[27] Typically group support statements reported overwhelming support for A3M's demands, lesser but majority support for the sit-in, and a donation of money.

My favorite, looking back, was a letter supporting our demands from 27 members of Delta Tau Delta, the same "jock" fraternity that attacked David Harris and shaved his head in October 1966.[28] The times, indeed, "were a-changing." One AEL veteran, Allan Wernick, recently recalled:

> A young, clean-cut man approached the open mic at an evening meeting, wearing an open-collar shirt and slacks. He announced that he was president of Delta Tau Delta. Everyone was quiet. He stated that while

---

27. R.W. Lee, "A Personal Position Statement," April 15, 1969, p. 2 of PDF. http://www.a3mreunion.org/archive/1968-1969/68-69_ael_support/files_68-69_ael_support/A3MAELSupport_letters.pdf The collection of support statements is posted at http://www.a3mreunion.org/archive/1968-1969/68-69_ael_support/68-69_ael_support.html

28. Delta Tau Delta letter, p. 4 of PDF. http://a3mreunion.org/archive/1968-1969/68-69_ael_support/files_68-69_ael_support/A3MAELSupport_Misc_3.pdf

the Delts did not endorse the tactics, they endorsed the demands and were donating $500 to the strike fund. The crowd erupted in sustained cheers.[29]

There was one more gesture of support that I found personally fulfilling. My parents were visiting the Bay Area, and one night, to the surprise of no one in my family, they proudly joined the sit-in.

The day the sit-in ended, study body president Denis Hayes conducted a ballot in Frost Amphitheater, in which over 3,000 of Stanford's 11,000 students voted. Overwhelming majorities opposed chemical and biological warfare research, counterinsurgency studies, and war-related research. The vote against classified research was "only" 2120 to 1045. Most telling, a majority—1633 to 1468—said they were willing to sit-in if the Trustees did not respond positively by May 14 to Stanford community concerns about SRI research.[30]

On April 13, *Declassified* reported, "This is now the longest occupation of a university war research building in the history of the world."[31] The sit-in was peaceful and in most instances, even civil. Many of us spent hours talking to building employees. However, we disrupted the work of not

---

29. Personal e-mail, October 16, 2019

30. "More than 1500 Stanford students...," Stanford University News Release, April 20, 1969. http://a3mreunion.org/archive/1968-1969/68-69_stanford_releases/files_68-69_stanford_pr/A3M_PR_Stanford_April_20.pdf As Michael Sweeney pointed out, the *Daily* published the results more rapidly than the Stanford News Service. "Slim Student Majority Backs Possible Sit-In," *Stanford Daily,* April 19, 1969. https://archives.stanforddaily.com/1969/04/19?page=1&section=MODSMD_ARTICLE4#article But the *Daily* headline was misleading. The majority took a stronger position: They said that they would "participate in" a sit-in. See below for Stanford's official poll of student and faculty views on these subjects.

31. "AEL Occupation in 4th Day," *Declassified*, April 13, 1969. http://a3mreunion.org/archive/1968-1969/68-69_declassified/files_68-69_declassified/A3MDeclassified_v1_n4.pdf

only researchers conducting classified research but a total of 150 people who worked in the building. After the sit-in, *Electronic Warfare* magazine reported, "The [AEL] staff (which included several Old Crows) was forced to operate out of a conference room (whose location was more-or-less secret) in an adjacent building with borrowed typewriters."[32]

**Fig. 6.5. Mass meeting of student body, April 18, 1969, the day the April Third Movement left AEL.**

AEL researchers asserted that we cost the university $5,000 to $6,000 each day.[33] We never attempted to gain access to classified documents, and Movement researchers who reprinted unclassified materials said they returned everything. On the other hand, electronic warfare researchers asserted that we

---

32. The Association of Old Crows is the American professional and social association of electronic warfare specialists. At the time, their magazine was titled *Electronic Warfare*. "Radicals Vilify AOC," *Electronic Warfare*, 1969. http://a3mreunion.org/archive/1968-1969/68-69_ael_sit-in_ael/files_68-69_ael_ael/A3MAEL-AEL_Vilify_AOC.pdf

33. "Leaders of the April Third Movement...," Stanford University News Service, April 17, 1969. http://a3mreunion.org/archive/1968-1969/68-69_stanford_releases/files_68-69_stanford_pr/A3M_PR_Stanford_April_17.pdf

permanently removed documents, and a U.S. Senate Committee printed a claim that we damaged property worth $10,000 and cost the university $90,000 in salaries and overhead.[34]

Though most protestors knew that labs inside AEL were doing secret research for the U.S. military, they did not initially know what projects were underway. In fact, even when they saw titles or summaries of research projects, few understood how that research was being used in Southeast Asia. So on April 14 A3M researchers published a quickly assembled 17-page pamphlet, with a bright red cover of stolen glossy cover stock, entitled "The Goods on AEL." It drew upon documents found in AEL offices and background articles from the military-contracting trade press that I and perhaps others had been collecting. Its subhead, "Declassified by the April 3rd Movement," was a misleading joke. It drew upon no classified information.

The pamphlet explained:

> Stanford has been and remains extensively involved in defense contracting. The bulk of this work is concentrated in the Electrical Engineering Department which currently holds about 2.2 million dollars in classified contracts.... One branch of this is the Systems Techniques Lab (STL) located in the Applied Electronics Lab (AEL). STL at this time holds six classified contracts totaling over one million dollars.... Most of this classified research is in the area of what is known as electronic warfare.[35]

---

34. "Radicals Vilify AOC." http://a3mreunion.org/archive/1968- 1969/68-69_ael_sit-in_ael/files_68-69_ael_ael/A3MAEL-AEL_Vilify_AOC.pdf "Riots, Civil, and Criminal Disorders: College Campus Disorders," Second Interim Report of the Senate Committee on Government Operations Permanent Subcommittee on Investigations, March 23, 1971, p. 9. http://a3mreunion.org/archive/1968-1969/68-69_us_senate/files_68-69_us_senate/A3MUSSenate_Senate_Report_1-12.pdf

35. "The Goods on AEL: Declassified by the April 3rd Movement," p. 1. http://a3mreunion.org/archive/1968-1969/68-69_ael_sit-in_ael/files_68-69_ael_ael/A3MAEL-AEL_Goods_on_AEL.pdf

"The Goods on AEL" explained how electronic warfare included techniques for monitoring, jamming, deceiving, and even destroying enemy communications and radar systems. It cited the January 1, 1968 issue of *Aviation Week*, "Electronic warfare is emerging from the air campaign over North Vietnam as a recognized ingredient of victory in war." That is, technology developed at research labs such as STL was used to undermine North Vietnam's air defenses and enable the U.S. bombing of that country.

The pamphlet also demonstrated how STL research project descriptions were sanitized when reviewed by the faculty's Committee on Research Policy. All mentions of specific military applications were removed. Even project titles were changed. For example, "Applied Research in Electronic Warfare Techniques" became "Applied Research in Electromagnetics." "Goods" includes a hand-edited page of a technical paper, in which one of the principal investigators deleted an entire paragraph that mentioned electronic countermeasures. In later years, student research teams showed how even unclassified research proposals that professors presented to the university community differed from their submissions to the Department of Defense.[36]

Both David Pugh and Marc Weiss credited the pamphlet as a key to our success in eliminating classified on-campus research. In Pugh's 2018 oral history, he reported, "We printed 10,000 copies for the undergraduates and the graduate students, five thousand for each, with a few hundred extra for the faculty."[37]

Weiss, in his 2018 interview, recounted:

> It was so dramatic when the faculty committee was meeting at the Law School to determine what to do about the SDS demands related to on-campus

---

36. See Chapter 9.
37. "David Pugh," Interview with David Pugh conducted by Vanessa Ochavillo, 2018. The Movement Oral History Project (SC1432). Department of Special Collections & University Archives, Stanford Libraries, Stanford, Calif., p. 38. historicalsociety.stanford.edu/publications/pugh-david

research, to classified research, and so forth. And we went marching into the meeting and distributed copies of "The Goods on AEL," which completely blew the mind of all the professors when we proved that everything that we'd been saying all along was true. It had a big impact. And then because of "The Goods on AEL," they voted to end classified research on campus because they realized that some of the professors that were doing it, like William Rambo, could not be trusted when he kept saying that [AEL's secret research] had nothing to do with the Vietnam War.[38]

Reinforcing the impact of the carefully researched pamphlet, occupiers found a certificate attesting to STL head Professor William R. Rambo's charter membership in the Association of Old Crows (AOC), the fraternity of electronic warfare specialists.[39] Displaying a crow emitting lightning bolts, it noted Rambo's "sincere interest and dedication to the advancement of the art of electronic warfare." An anonymous A3M songwriter even wrote a song of condemnation, "Rambo, Black Crow."[40]

We publicized background information that I had collected on AOC from its magazine, *Electronic Warfare*. The Old Crows Latin motto translated as "They shall not see." Students were

38. Interview with Dr. Marc A. Weiss conducted by Vanessa Ochavillo, 2018. The Movement Oral History Project (SC1432). Department of Special Collections & University Archives, Stanford Libraries, Stanford, Calif., pp, 43-44. historicalsociety.stanford.edu/publications/weiss-marc

39. "Association of Old Crows." http://a3mreunion.org/archive/1968-1969/68-69_ael_sit-in_ael/files_68-69_ael_ael/A3MAEL-AEL_Old_Crows.pdf I was amused, as I searched in 2019 for information on the AOC, that the initials now stood for Alexandria Ocasio-Cortez, not the Association of Old Crows.

40. "Rambo, Black Crow," *Declassified,* April 17, 1969, p. 6. http://a3mreunion.org/archive/1968-1969/68-69_declassified/files_68-69_declassified/A3MDeclassified_v1_n8.pdf

shocked at what appeared to be a glorification of warfare. After the sit-in *Electronic Warfare* published its own report on the April events: "Radicals Vilify AOC."[41]

I would be remiss, however, to characterize Rambo as a right-wing warmonger. He had supported peace candidate Eugene McCarthy for President in 1968. He earned his wings during World War II. I've found sources that say he worked at Harvard's Radio Research Laboratory—where Frederick Terman was—during World War II, and that he served as a radar operator on combat aircraft fighting against Nazi Germany. Most of us in A3M supported that war retrospectively. Still, following Terman's precepts of university-industry cooperation, he was a co-founder of Applied Technology, a manufacturer of electronic warfare equipment located in the Stanford Industrial Park.

The handwriting was clearly on the wall for classified research on the Stanford campus. As early as April 3, Pitzer had told the student legislature "that he personally would be happier if there were no classified research on campus."[42] The Committee on Research Policy, headed by Law Professor William Baxter, held an emergency 2½ hour meeting on April 14, attended by an estimated 260 people.[43] But it didn't take action.

The following night, however:

> The Academic Senate last night called for the drafting of new policy guidelines "which prohibit research which involves secrecy of sponsorship or results."

41. "Radicals Vilify AOC." http://a3mreunion.org/archive/1968-1969/68-69_ael_sit-in_ael/files_68-69_ael_ael/A3MAEL-AEL_Vilify_AOC.pdf

42. "Increase in University's Strength May Result from Recent Actions," *Campus Report,* April 9, 1969, p. 3. http://a3mreunion.org/archive/1968-1969/68-69_campus_report/files_68-69_campus_report/A3MCampusReport_April_9_p1-3.pdf

43. Douglas Anderson, "Committee Explains Research," *Stanford Daily,* April 15, 1969, p. 4. https://archives.stanforddaily.com/1969/04/15?page=4&section=MODSMD_ARTICLE21#article

> The vote for a "significant change" in present policy
> came with a single dissent after four and a half hours'
> discussion.[44]

The Movement viewed this as a promise. When we left AEL a few days later, we threatened to return if the faculty reneged. On April 24 Dean Joel Pettit announced that the Engineering School was phasing out classified research, and in a six-hour meeting the Academic Senate enacted a "sweeping ban on secret research at Stanford" affecting all twelve classified research programs.[45]

After the sit-in, most of the STL researchers moved their secret electronic warfare work to SRI, where they were allowed to continue. We still viewed this as a victory. However, we immediately issued a statement challenging objectionable unclassified research, such as SRI's research into the dissemination of chemical and biological agents and counterinsurgency studies.[46] We knew all along that 1400 protestors at Stanford, even along with our allies on other campuses, could not reverse national policy. But we were chipping away at the military industrial complex in a way that showed a growing number of people that we needed to continue and expand our struggle.

At the start of the AEL Sit-in, we set up a committee to develop a vision of what research policy at Stanford and SRI should look like. Our Review Board and Guidelines Committee, made up largely of people from science and engineering departments—some of whom had worked on the March 4, 1969

---

44. Mark Weinberger, "Senate Asks Curbs On Secret Research," *Stanford Daily,* April 16, 1969, p. 1. archives.stanforddaily.com/1969/04/16?page=1&section=MODSMD_ARTICLE5#article
45. "Academic Senate Bans Secret Research," *Stanford Daily,* April 25, 1969. archives.stanforddaily.com/1969/04/25?page=1&section=MODSMD_ARTICLE1#article
46. "Proposals for Controlling Research and Stanford and SRI," April 24, 1969. http://a3mreunion.org/archive/1968-1969/68-69_guidelines/files_68-69_guidelines/A3MGuidelines_Proposals_for_Controlling_Research.pdf

Convocation on Science and Society—produced "Guidelines for Research at Stanford and SRI." This 8-page document makes as much sense today as it did in 1969.

Building on the April Third Movement demands, the Guidelines expressed appreciation for SRI's interdisciplinary approach to many areas of study. It called for closer cooperation between Stanford and SRI, not just to limit SRI's military work, but to get better research results. Furthermore, the authors observed:

> It is the pattern of funding of research, and not the demand for community guidelines which is the great threat to academic freedom today. Scholars today are encouraged to do the work of the powerful at the expense of the poor.[47]

The Guidelines called upon the Peninsula scientific community to focus its "energy and influence to the redirection of scientific funding away from those areas of science which destroy life and increase oppression."[48] They called for a broad-based Stanford-SRI Review Board to oversee and perhaps terminate or block contracts not meeting community standards, such as those put forward in the A3M demands. They proposed publication of existing and proposed research project descriptions, as well as the deliberations and decisions of the Review Board.

Guidelines committee members did not just talk the talk. Several pursued scientific careers according to the ideals put forward in the document. Most notable was Lee Herzenberg, who along with her husband Len ran the Herzenberg Lab in the Medical School's Genetics Department. Since Len's death in 2013, Lee has steered the ship alone. The Herzenbergs are best known for the development of Fluorescent Activated Cell Sorting (FASC), around the time of the April Third Movement. FASC was

---

47. "Guidelines for Research at Stanford and SRI," April 14, 1969, p. 3. http://a3mreunion.org/archive/1968-1969/68-69_guidelines/files_68-69_guidelines/A3MGuidelines_Guidelines_for_Research_p1-8.pdf
48. *ibid.*, p. 4.

the first commercially available method of separating cells by type. It made possible many of the advances in medical research and therapy that we take for granted today. The Herzenberg patents also earned Stanford hundreds of millions of dollars.

None of us expected the AEL sit-in to go on forever, but we were so used to "moderate" opponents trying to end it prematurely that we never laid out conditions for departure. However, on April 18, we decided to quit while we were ahead, in response to three decisions by others. First, President Pitzer declared that AEL would be closed for a week. For demonstrators, that meant they would not have to sleep in hallways, the roof, or in the ivy to stop war research for that period. It was a tantalizing proposition. Second, as noted above, the Academic Senate had already "promised" to eliminate on-campus classified research. And third, Student Body President Hayes had announced that he was convening a mass meeting of the study body for 1:00 pm in Frost Amphitheater that day.[49] Requirements and rules for the meeting were provided for in the Associated Students constitution.

That summer I wrote:

> By the ninth day the sit-in reached an impasse. It was clear that we could force no more than a phase-out of classified research—and the faculty had promised that. Fears of arrest were growing. So when Pitzer announced the closing of the building, many welcomed the excuse to leave. We threatened to return if the faculty backed down on its stand against classified research, but most of us hoped that we would not have to.[50]

---

49. "General Meeting of the Student Body Called for Tomorrow, Friday, 1:00, in Frost Amphitheater." http://a3mreunion.org/archive/1968-1969/68-69_apr18_meeting/file_68-69_april_18/A3M-4-18_Meeting.pdf

50. "The April 3rd Movement," *Maggie's Farm: A Radical Guide to Stanford*, Fall, 1969, p. 41. a3mreunion.org/archive/1969-1970/69-70/files_1969-1970/69-70_Maggies_Farm_parts_1-7.pdf

After an early morning vote, we left about as quickly as we arrived. We grabbed our sleeping bags, mopped the floors, and used the basement press to print the last edition of Declassified from within the building. The unidentified authors wrote:

> The Applied Electronics Laboratory was the birthplace of a movement and its community.... The most intensive educational campaign in Stanford history will continue. We will continue to coordinate our efforts in learning and teaching about what kind of place our University must become.[51]

At Frost Amphitheater some 8,000 people, according to the Stanford News Service, heard speakers debate our issue. This was the same meeting where students voted support for A3M, as described above. Members of the Black Student Union, not highly visible during the sit-in, took the stage and demanded that SRI research serve the predominantly black residents of nearby East Palo Alto.

When an undergraduate asked:

> "How do you know that these people want to be liberated?" Lincoln Malik, a graduate student from Iraq, and member of the April 3 Coalition, answered for the Third World and the crowd's emotion reached a peak during his fiery speech. Several times they broke into wild applause and he received an enthusiastic ovation. Malik said that the desire of the Third World peoples to free themselves was shown by the struggles in Vietnam and Latin America.[52]

---

51. "We're Gonna Get There," *Declassified*, April 18, 1969, p. 1. http://a3mreunion.org/archive/1968-1969/68-69_declassified/files_68-69_declassified/A3MDeclassified_v1_n9.pdf
52. Michael Kuhl and Kim Thorburn, "Rally Airs Research," *Stanford Daily*, April 19, 1969, p. 1. archives.stanforddaily.com/1969/04/19?page=1&section=MODSMD_ARTICLE1#article This was an unusual Saturday edition. See also "'We should look inward to find moral concerns ...,'" Stanford University News Service, April 18, 1969.

## Refocusing on SRI

In late October, 1968, acting university president Robert Glaser had named a twelve-person committee and charged it with studying the university's relationship with SRI. He was following the age-old playbook of deflecting demands for action with a study. My SDS colleagues and I wrote, "The *Daily* and some faculty members said this would take the wind out of SDS's sails."[53] Little did they know that the committee's reports would be released in the midst of the longest sit-in against campus war research in world history.

We had immediately questioned the scope of the SRI Study Committee, known as the "Scott Committee" after its chairman, Law Professor Kenneth Scott. We added:

> For SDS the real issue is America's foreign policy and Stanford's relationship to it, not intramural questions of nomenclature and organization within the university. Consequently, SDS actions will be about the effects of U.S. foreign policy, and those who profit from those policies.[54]

We called for the prompt release of information about all of SRI's military contracts.

The Scott Committee met regularly with little fanfare throughout the academic year. It issued a collection of reports on April 14.[55] There was a majority report, advocating divestiture with restrictions on future research, signed by seven committee

a3mreunion.org/archive/1968-1969/68-69_apr18_meeting/file_68-69_april_18/A3M-4-18_Press_1.pdf

53. "SRI, Stanford, and SDS," October, 1969, p. 1. http://a3mreunion.org/archive/1968-1969/68-69_sri_study_com/files_68-69_sri_study_com/68-69SRIStudy_SRI_Stanford_SDS.pdf

54. *ibid.*, p. 1.

55. "Report of the Stanford-SRI Study Committee," April 11, 1969, *Campus Report Supplement,* April 14, 1969. http://a3mreunion.org/archive/1968-1969/68-69_sri_study_com/files_68-69_sri_study_com/SRI_Final_Report_Cover_Letter-p52.pdf

members. Scott and Provost Richard Lyman penned their own recommendation for divestiture, emphasizing the potential revenue from sale but opposing restrictions. History Professor Barton Bernstein and the two SDS members on the committee, undergraduate Anne Bauer and graduate student Harry Cleaver wrote separate minority reports backing the April Third Movement demands. Curiously, copies of the minority report did not make it to SRI, for consideration by its employees, until A3M activists chased them down.[56]

Both the majority report and the Bauer-Cleaver dissent contained background information about SRI. The majority devoted pages to SRI financial statements. Cleaver and Bauer listed SRI counterinsurgency projects, but they also listed reports growing out of research on the development of an Anti-Ballistic Missile (ABM) system. They placed the military work in the context of SRI's endeavors to establish the Bay Area corporate elite's hegemony over the Pacific Basin economy.

While the seven-person majority provided cover for the university administration's preferred option of divestiture, they professed sympathy for A3M's concerns about the nature of SRI research:

> Approximately $6½ million or 10% of SRI's total work is in research in chemical-biological warfare, counter-insurgency, or work that directly supports the war in Vietnam. It is our firm opinion that much of this research should not be carried on either at the University or a University-affiliated research institute. All components of such morally objectionable research should be phased out as soon as possible; no new research projects should be sponsored that are clearly morally objectionable.

---

56. "Half a Report Is Stranger Than None," *Declassified*, April 17, 1969, p. 4. http://a3mreunion.org/archive/1968-1969/68-69_declassified/files_68-69_declassified/A3MDeclassified_v1_n8.pdf

> There must be a prohibition of research in chemical-
> biological warfare, of much work in counter-
> insurgency and of much work that supports the war
> in Vietnam. But it needs to be clearly stated that such
> a prohibition on morally objectionable research can
> be prescribed and maintained whether or not SRI is
> placed on sale or maintained under University control.
> The question of the organizational relationship does
> not depend in any way on the moral question about
> objectionable research.[57]

They favored the establishment of a review committee to oversee the restrictions.

Scott and Lyman considered such restrictions impractical,
and one of the seven, student Patrick McMahon, stated that his
support for divestiture rested on the conduct of a legal review that
would ensure that research restrictions were legally enforceable.
He added, "If there is doubt, my support goes to the Bauer and
Cleaver minority recommendations, favoring closer ties." The
committee's internal vote count meant little, however, because
the ultimate decision was up to the Stanford University Board of
Trustees. McMahon also called upon the Trustees to conduct an
open decision-making process.[58]

The outside press seemed to think that the anti-war
movement simply wanted Stanford to be rid of SRI, to wash
its hands of research that we considered objectionable. But
after the AEL sit-in and the 8,000-person community meeting,
the majority of the student body supported the A3M demand
for retention, repeated in the SRI Study Committee Minority
Reports. On Saturday, April 19, the *Daily* editorialized, "Unless
we speak forcefully, the trustees may agree with those who are
urging them to sell SRI. If SRI is sold, the consequences will be
tragic for this campus—and the world."[59]

---

57. "Report of the Stanford-SRI Study Committee," p. 18. http://
a3mreunion.org/archive/1968-1969/68-69_sri_study_com/
files_68-69_sri_study_com/SRI_Final_Report_Cover_Letter-p52.pdf
58. *ibid.*, p. 32.
59. Editorial, "SRI," *Stanford Daily*, April 19, 1969, p. 2.

125

On April 28 the university released results of its official poll, based upon a complicated questionnaire formulated by a student-faculty team headed by Communications professor Nathan Maccoby. It showed overwhelming student support for A3M's SRI demands, with faculty opinion split. The response rate was high, with 44% of the student body and 55% of the faculty filling out questionnaires. The month of intense activity had made people throughout the sprawling campus aware of the issues we had raised.

A whopping 68.2% of the student body and 35.6% of the faculty favored bringing SRI under closer control of the university community. The student body expressed strong support for restricting counterinsurgency research and studies related to the Southeast Asian war, and overwhelming majorities backed restraints on chemical, biological, and radiological warfare research.[60]

Following the AEL departure, A3M set up shop on the top floor of the University Clubhouse, adjacent to the Old Union and White Plaza, where the Campus Ministry was located. We had use of a mimeograph machine and phone lines.

Monday, April 21, A3M led tours to campus buildings that were potential targets for future demonstrations. More important, after a noon rally I led a march of nearly 100 people to the Stanford Industrial Park, site of SRI's counterinsurgency research office, the Regional Securities Study Center at Hanover Street and Page Mill Road. Along the way we described the military work being done by private companies on Stanford land.[61]

---

archives.stanforddaily.com/1969/04/19?page=2&section=MODSMD_ARTICLE6#article

60. See "Two Thirds of the Student Body...," Stanford University News Service," April 28, 1969. http://a3mreunion.org/archive/1968-1969/68-69_university_polls/files_68-69_university_polls/A3MPolls_Press_1.pdf and "A Majority of the Stanford Community...," April 3 Movement News Service, April 29, 1969. http://a3mreunion.org/archive/1968-1969/68-69_university_polls/files_68-69_university_polls/A3MPolls_Press_2.pdf

61. "Students March on SRI," *Stanford Daily,* April 22, 1969, p. 1.

Student voters at Frost Amphitheater had called for a Day of Concern, so Tuesday, April 22 was filled with panel debates about Stanford, SRI, and war research, plus a noon performance in White Plaza by the San Francisco Mime Troupe. Hundreds attended each event. In addition, the faculty Academic Senate discussed SRI for three hours, without coming up with a recommendation.

More meetings and debates continued for another week. Thirty-five hundred people signed our petition calling for an open meeting of the entire Board of Trustees. Instead, on April 30 five Trustees heard public testimony from SRI leadership, faculty, and students representing diverse perspectives. When the Trustees refused to explain what standards they would use to determine the future of SRI, A3M supporters walked out of both the Forum room at the Undergraduate Library and Memorial Auditorium, where a full house watched the hearings remotely.

Several hundred A3Mers gathered outside Mem Aud to discuss the Movement's response. We later moved to the Large Lounge at Tresidder Union. Many of us proposed a sit-in that went beyond the AEL occupation, which moderates viewed as an educational exercise, to what seemed to be more coercive tactics. I prepared a handout attempting to answer, "Politically, how do we stand to gain from a sit-in?"[62] I argued that we needed to take decisive action before the Trustees took their anticipated vote on divestiture. We needed to cost the Trustees by threatening the stability of the university and its relationship to the military industrial complex.

Recalling that we didn't have the capability of bolding, italicizing, or enlarging text, I concluded in capital letters:

---

archives.stanforddaily.com/1969/04/22?page=1&section=MODSMD_ARTICLE1#article

62. Lenny Siegel, "Why?" April 30 1969. http://a3mreunion.org/archive/1968-1969/68-69_encina_sit-in/files_68-69_encina_sitin/A3MEncina_Why.pdf This is one piece of literature that I don't remember writing, but it is signed, "L. Siegel".

I THEREFORE PROPOSE THAT WE SHUT DOWN THE BUSINESS FUNCTIONING OF THE UNIVERSITY, AS WELL AS THE NEWS MANAGER'S OFFICE. THIS CAN BE DONE BY OCCUPYING AND CONTROLLING MOST OF ENCINA HALL, KEEPING THE BUSINESS STAFF FROM THEIR JOBS, AND FORCING THE TRUSTEES TO USE FORCE OF THEIR OWN IF THEY WANT TO RE-OPEN THE OFFICES WITHOUT MEETING THE DEMANDS OF THE STANFORD COMMUNITY.

In the crowded Tresidder Lounge, the Movement debated whether to sit in again. It was tense. Indeed, it was acrimonious. The *Daily* reported that about 10:45 pm we voted 450 to 280 to occupy a building.[63] But we still had to decide which one.

At that point, one of our members from the Music Department reported that nearby Dinkelspiel Auditorium, site of our April 3 and April 9 meetings, was open. What happened next is an anecdote that I often repeat to illustrate the temperamental contradictions of the Stanford Movement. In the midst of a heated meeting planning one of the most militant group actions in the history of Stanford activism, we entered darkened Dinkelspiel only to find the Stanford Opera concluding a dress rehearsal of *The Rape of Lucretia*. Without instruction, we filled the auditorium quietly. When they finished, we spontaneously applauded. Then we went on to argue for a couple more hours.

We decided to move on Encina Hall, home to most of the university's business offices and the academic Food Research Institute. We had keys to the latter, and with my handy bolt-cutters I snapped the padlock on the roll-up fire door separating the Institute from the administrative offices.

---

63. Michael Sweeney, "April 3rd Movement Seizes Encina Hall; Policy of Summary Suspensions Invoked," *Stanford Daily,* May 1, 1969. https://archives.stanforddaily.com/1969/05/01?page=1&section=MODSMD_ARTICLE1#article

Little did I know that there was a confrontation underway simultaneously at the front entrance. Two or three dozen members of the right-wing Young Americans for Freedom (YAF) were blocking the door. Not realizing that we were already inside, one of our militants kicked between Harvey Hukari's knees and shattered the front glass. The YAFers scattered, clearing the way for A3Mers to enter the building.

That single instant, the sound of breaking glass doomed the sit-in. Hundreds of people who had marched down from Dinkelspiel stood outside, bewildered. But the breaking of windows also broke a barrier. Within a year window-breaking on campus was routine.

A few hundred of us occupied the building for several hours, voting to encourage the payroll staff to come into work. We also renamed the building the Huey P. Newton Institute for the Study of Racism, Imperialism, and Capitalism, after the jailed Black Panther leader. We agreed to engage in "no violence toward any person," but we also agreed "that there are certain types of information in this building that in the interests of democracy and the free flow of information, should be made public." That turned out to be paper records of faculty and administration salaries, which demonstrators removed from the building.[64]

Provost Lyman saw an opportunity to break Stanford's taboo on bringing in outside police to break-up demonstrations, and he convinced Pitzer to call in the County sheriffs. Their riot squad arrived around 7:00 am the morning of May 1, and in a hurried meeting we decided to leave. Lyman later considered this one of the highlights of his career at Stanford.[65] As I see it, it set the precedent for the use of police the following Spring to break up a peaceful sit-in (no broken windows, no file-rifling, no disruption of university activities) in the Old Union Student

64. "Encina Renamed," May 1, 1969. http://a3mreunion.org/archive/1968-1969/68-69_encina_sit-in/files_68-69_encina_sitin/A3MEncina_renamed.pdf
65. Kathleen J. Sullivan, "Richard W. Lyman, Stanford's Seventh President, Dead at 88," *Stanford Report,* May 27, 2012. https://news.stanford.edu/news/2012/may/richard-lyman-obit-052712.html

129

Services Building. This drove the Movement to hit-and-run tactics, such as throwing rocks through hundreds of plate glass windows on campus and on-campus street battles between students and police.

Immediately, the administration obtained a temporary restraining order against three dozen demonstrators and 500 Jane and John Does, on the path to winning court approval for a permanent injunction.[66] Initially, suspended students were banned from campus, except to attend judicial hearings, but that restriction was later relaxed. Shades of Emiliano Zapata from January, one of the named defendants was Wilbur Arroyo, the name of a dorm on campus.

Five decades later, I am surprised and disappointed (it's called subpoena envy) that I was not initially a named defendant, particularly because I spent time in jail in 1970 for violating the injunction. Today, browsing through the affidavits, I see that one witness spotted me outside Encina hall and two others received my "Why" handout, but no one fingered me inside Encina. Also in the affidavits, it's clear that Bob Beyers and his News Service staff considered themselves part of the university administration, not neutral reporters. But we knew that.

Moderate activists who eschewed coercion saw the injunction as over-reach by the administration. It brought the divided Movement back together. We pointed out that it was issued *ex parte*. That is, "defendants were given no notice that an order dealing with and regulating their political speech and conduct would be sought."[67] The night of May 1 we packed Cubberley Auditorium for another energetic meeting, and process servers showed up to deliver copies of the restraining order to defendants and a number of Does. Julia Harvey, a long-time Stanford employee involved in the nascent campus union

66. "A3M: Encina Injunction," April Third Movement Historical Archive. http://a3mreunion.org/archive/1968-1969/68-69_encina_injunction/files_68-69_encina_injunction/A3MInjunction_Complaint.pdf
67. "Smash the Injunction," *Declassified*, May 12, 1969, p. 8. http://a3mreunion.org/archive/1968-1969/68-69_declassified/files_68-69_declassified/A3MDeclassified_v1_n13.pdf

movement, brought down the house when she suggested that we do what labor unions have always done when confronted with an injunction: "Smash it."

The April Third Movement was declared dead by its critics. But spurred on by the extremity of the court injunction against it, the movement resolved to rebuild, learning the lessons of the Encina debacle.

Ever since the first mass meetings, the April Third Movement had a major organizational flaw. Most business and discussion was conducted in large meetings. Most people were afraid to speak at these meetings, or they could not express themselves well. The more militant and radical students dominated the meetings, both through experienced leadership and exuberant, intimidating shouting. During AEL we had broken up into small discussion groups during large meetings, but we had merely scratched the surface of creating our own democracy.

The most important result of the Encina sit-in, in terms of the development of the movement, was the formation of affinity groups: small groups of ten to twenty people who met together and worked together on a continuing basis. We slowly rebuilt our strength by talking out the questions that had divided us. And, working on a class boycott and political carnival, we recreated much of the community which had bound us together at AEL.[68]

We formed at least 14 affinity groups, each with one or two dozen participants, most with creative names such as "Yossarian," "Ugly Americans for Freedom," and "Big Bill Hewlett's Fragmentation Bomb."[69] The affinity groups held discussions and staged low-key demonstrations. One group fasted. Another built a plywood geodesic dome in White Plaza,

_____

68. I wrote these three paragraphs in the summer of 1969. See "The April 3rd Movement," *Maggie's Farm*, p. 42. http://a3mreunion.org/archive/1969-1970/69-70/files_1969-1970/69-70_Maggies_Farm_parts_1-7.pdf
69. "The April Third Movement Lives! And Affinity Groups Prove It," May, 1969. http://a3mreunion.org/archive/1968-1969/68-69_april_third/files_68-69_april_third_movement/A3M_Affinity_Groups.pdf

on a lawn that some of us called "Agitators' Grass." We called for a class boycott for the two days leading up to the Trustees' May 13 meeting in San Francisco where we expected them to determine SRI's future. We won the support of many on campus who decried the Encina sit-in, such as the new Associated Students' Council of Presidents. One of A3M's moderate members wrote in *Declassified:*

> The class boycott on Monday will serve three functions: (1) it will focus attention on the demands of the April 3rd Movement through educational opportunities such as speakers; (2) it will provide an opportunity for everyone on the campus to peacefully express his concern with the research questions; (3) it will demonstrate to the Trustees our solidarity in the eleventh hour of the SRI question and make them realize that the educational atmosphere has been disrupted not by the boycott or by sit-ins but by the presence of unacceptable research and unresolved issues on our campus.[70]

The *Daily* reported that 47 faculty members from 18 departments canceled classes. The boycott also made a large dent in attendance in the classes that met:

> The A3M estimated attendance on the first day of the boycott in large humanities and social sciences classes at about 40% of normal while classes in the sciences had attendance of about 70% of normal. In classes having mid-term examinations, the attendance was about 100%. In Economics I, however, with an enrollment of 300 students and an average attendance of about 250, only 60 to 70 students appeared in class yesterday morning.[71]

---

70. Tori Block, "Boycott," *Declassified,* May 12, 1969, p. 3. http:// a3mreunion.org/archive/1968-1969/68-69_declassified/files_68-69_ declassified/A3MDeclassified_v1_n13.pdf

71. Jenny Matthews, "Movement Awaits Trustees' Action," *Stanford Daily,* May 13, 1969, p. 1.

The first day of the boycott we staged a carnival in White Plaza, attended by about 1000. This included music, guerrilla theater, speeches, and carnival games organized by affinity groups. These included "'Hit the Heavies,' where students threw tennis balls at targets representing the Board of Trustees, and 'Smash the State,' where three sledge hammer blows on a used car sold for 25¢."[72]

**Fig. 6.6. It didn't make headlines, but much of our Movement's activity consisted of people sitting in circles, talking, listening, and thinking.**

On Wednesday, May 13 the Board of Trustees voted to terminate SRI's formal relationship with the university, with no restrictions on research. They noted that SRI had already decided not to conduct research "dealing directly with the development of weapons of biological or chemical warfare," but that language

https://archives.stanforddaily.com/1969/05/13?page=1&section=MODSMD_ARTICLE6#article

72. *ibid.*

seemed to leave room for continuation of the meteorological and dissemination studies that represented SRI's piece of the nation's CBW program.[73]

Student leaders who had criticized A3M's tactics were outraged, and they saw the outcome as an opportunity to push for increased student power within the university establishment. The Associated Students Council of Presidents issued a statement:

> Today the Board of Trustees as it is presently constituted signed its own death warrant. By its unwillingness to listen and examine potentially creative ideas related to SRI the Board demonstrated its collective inadequacy. Men who know little of universities and education should not be making final decisions for this institution.[74]

A3M called one more mass meeting, this time in spacious Memorial Auditorium. The Movement was going to take action. It was just a question of what and where. After breaking out into affinity groups for discussion, the Movement reconvened in Memorial Church. After more discussion five hundred or so voted overwhelmingly to once again take direct action against military research: to disrupt operations at SRI's counterinsurgency center, at Hanover and Page Mill in the Stanford Industrial Park. Though on Stanford land, this facility was beyond the boundaries of the academic campus.

We arranged for the presence of white-coated medics. We activated our legal aid committee and asked participants to write its phone number on their skin in case they ended up needing bail. Using the representative structure of the affinity groups, we selected a secret tactics committee. We did not publicly disclose the details of our demonstration,

---

73. Trustees' Statement on SRI," *Stanford Daily,* May 14, 1969, p. 1. archives.stanforddaily.com/1969/05/14?page=1&section=MODSMD_ ARTICLE4#article

74. Craig Wilson, "Trustees to Terminate SRI Relationship," *Stanford Daily,* May 14, 1969, p. 1. https://archives.stanforddaily. com/1969/05/14?page=1&section=MODSMD_ARTICLE1#article

but we created a new affinity group, the "Chickenshit Brigade," for protestors who hoped to avoid confrontation by picketing peacefully on the sidewalk across Page Mill Road.

**Fig. 6.7. One of our April Third Movement affinity groups built a plywood Geodesic Dome on "Agitators' Grass" in White Plaza, May 12, 1969.**

Late that night, some 200 of us marched to the Hanover facility for what the *Daily* called a "practice run." Reportedly, persons unknown broke a window and a glass door and set a fire in a refuse container. Demonstrators spontaneously blocked traffic. SRI President Charles Anderson and his wife drove by to see what was happening, only to be recognized and surrounded by 75 protesters. Protestors sang "Solidarity Forever" and then chanted "Free Charlie." The *Daily* reported that I persuaded the crowd to let them leave.[75]

75. Marshall Schwartz and Lynne McCallister, "A3M Plans Action At SRI-Hanover, Reconnoiters Site in Practice Run," *Stanford Daily,* May 14 [sic], 1969. The masthead says May 14, but the paper reported on events of the night of May 15.
https://archives.stanforddaily.com/1969/05/15?page=1&section=MODSMD_ARTICLE5#article

I do not remember the Anderson incident. I'm guessing that as a member of the tactics committee I felt obligated to enforce our promise not to attack people. As we normally did, we established ground rules. We had announced in advance, that we would not initiate violence.

Around 6:00 am on Friday, May 16, Palo Alto police, security guards, and reporters arrived. Demonstrators marched over from the campus in affinity groups, carrying signs such as "SRI Kills." Some protesters blocked the intersection in earnest, flattening tires on an empty school bus as well as a klunker of a sedan apparently brought in from a wrecking yard. There were confrontations with motorists, but notes I've inherited say that some of the demonstrators let a cement truck through so the cement wouldn't harden. We attempted to explain our protest to motorists, but only a fraction expressed support. Most drivers found a way out. At the time, our disruption caused what was one of the largest commuter traffic jams in Palo Alto history. Now that level of congestion is normal.

Demonstrators improvised barricades on Hanover Street with ping-pong tables, dumpsters, sawhorses, construction materials they found nearby, and even a downed tree. Meanwhile dozens of demonstrators linked arms, singing "We Shall Overcome," to prevent what appeared to be an SRI counterinsurgent from entering the building. It turned out, however, that he was a counterdemonstrator dressed in a suit. It seemed that most people who normally worked in the Hanover offices had been warned not to come in that morning.

For a couple of hours, things quieted down. One demonstrator painted "No academic freedom to kill Thais" on the front of the building. Right-wing leader Harvey Hukari stood atop a VW microbus with a bullhorn reciting his power structure research on the parents of SDS members. One of our graduate students, Steve Smith, shouted back, "But what does it mean?" Other right-wingers, wearing their blue buttons, took photos of demonstrators, setting off some minor fistfights. It was my job to break them up, because we had promised not to initiate violence.

**Fig. 6.8. A determined A3M Affinity Group marches up Hanover Street toward SRI's Counterinsurgency Offices. May 16, 1969**

Most of the decisions about what to do were made within the affinity groups, but we had a tactics committee of four who were responsible for coordinating the action. Based on what we learned from Stop the Draft Week in 1967, we circled the demonstration, checking in with each affinity group. The police and prosecutors never figured out our "command structure." They even asked about it at the jury trials that some demonstrators went through, but only a handful of affinity-group leaders knew who was "in charge." The police thought some motorcyclists

137

with walkie-talkies might have been running the show, but they were from the campus radio station, KZSU.

At around 11:00 am, enough police had gathered from multiple local jurisdictions for them to take action.[76] Wielding batons and launching tear-gas canisters, they marched up Hanover Street. Demonstrators set fire to the barricades and retreated slowly, chanting "Walk, Walk, Walk ..." as we had done during Stop the Draft Week. Affinity groups on Page Mill fired rocks they had collected at the building, breaking most of its windows. A few demonstrators rammed a large pipe into SRI, as well. About 15 people were arrested immediately, mostly from my affinity group, which I had left to serve on the tactics committee.

**Fig. 6.9. Motorists avoid the A3M blockade at Hanover and Page Mill. Hewlett-Packard stands in the background.**

I had come prepared. I slipped a wet bandana across my face to filter the tear gas. I put on my gloves. When a hissing tear-gas canister rolled up, I picked it up and held it high over my

---

76. This was the same week as the much larger People's Park confrontation in Berkeley. I wondered if that diverted manpower that could have been used in Palo Alto.

head to avoid the gas. I wheeled and prepared to thrust it toward a second-story window. However, I saw Jeff Littleboy, part of Bob Beyers' News Service team, standing at that window. I've always bragged how I "found a secondary receiver" and threw the canister through another window, avoiding injury to Littleboy. At any rate, people in the building reported the smell and irritation of tear gas. Another A3Mer claimed that he was the one who tear-gassed the building. Maybe we both did. Littleboy didn't realize that I had spared him, or maybe he would have turned me in anyhow. I found out years later that he signed the police report identifying me as the thrower. The report summarized:

> He saw Siegel approach a yellow canister which had been thrown by police officers in an effort to disperse the crowd, bend over, pick up the canister and throw it through the second story window of the SRI building.[77]

As protesters regrouped and returned to campus, it felt like victory. About 100 of us turned ourselves in, in response to arrest warrants, in the days following the Hanover Street demonstration. I was charged with Penal Code violations, 404, 416, and 594: Rioting to Disturb the Public Peace, Failure to Disperse from an Unlawful Assembly, and Malicious Mischief. Most of us were identified in photos taken by right-wing counter-demonstrators, but it was never clear why their presence was not also unlawful assembly or disturbing the peace.

---

77. Palo Alto Police Department Case Number 69-2898. http://a3mreunion.org/archive/1968-1969/68-69_may16_sri/files_68-69_may_16/A3M-5-16_Police-Report.pdf English lecturer Ed McClanahan recounted a more dramatic version in his barely fictionalized, "Another Great Moment in Sports." In *My VITA, If You Will.* (Washington, DC: *Counterpoint*, 1998.) Renaming me "Norman," he wrote, "So you might say that Norman had been preparing all his life for his Clear Moment, sacrificing hours of reading Marx in the library to work on his forward pass so that he'll be ready when the time comes, planning for that nanosecond in history that will mark the convergence of the hot grenade, the glove, and the plate glass window." (p. 205)

We called our actions, "disturbing the war."

I was not upset by my arrest. As I related in Chapter 3, this was my ticket out of the draft. My arrest postponed my draft induction for a year. I wanted to go to trial, but the DA's office bundled me with a law student whose career depended on me pleading *nolo contendere* (no contest), so I did. I was on probation for a year, furthering delaying the Selective Service Systems interest in me.

Later I heard complaints from people who considered our window-breaking premeditated violence. But we saw it as a response to police violence designed to protect SRI personnel who were engaged in or provided tools for deadly violence in Southeast Asia. It seems to be an American characteristic to view minor crimes against domestic property worse than lethal violence in the Third World.

**Fig. 6.10. Demonstrators let this concrete truck pass when the driver said the concrete would harden, Hanover and Page Mill, May 16, 1969.**

**Fig. 6.11. May 16, 1969 demonstration that for a day closed down SRI's counterinsurgency offices at Hanover and Page Mill.**

The following Monday a massive police presence prevented us from mounting a similar disruption at SRI's larger main offices in Menlo Park, so several hundred of us picketed peacefully. SRI sought and received its own temporary restraining order against trespass and further militant protests. This time I made the initial list. I believe that one student, with the last name Bechtel, had her case separated from the rest of us at the behest of family lawyers.

A few more rallies and picket lines were all A3M could muster, and the Movement withered away into final examinations and the promises of the California summer. SRI vacated its Hanover Street offices, claiming that the move had been long planned.

The Judicial Council continued its proceedings against Encina occupiers. When SJC chair Friedenthal complained that protesters had removed photos, used to identify Encina protestors, from his office, I playfully told the *Daily*, "If the

Judicial Council is interested in replacing the photographs, then I'm sure that members of the April Third Movement would be willing to re-enact the whole sequence of events."[78]

**Fig. 6.12. Preparing for the police sweep on Hanover Street, May 16, 1969.**

I wrote that summer that the April Third Movement was a significant, successful experiment in political action. Masses of middle- and upper-class college students united around issues that directly threatened the American empire. We helped build the clamor against the war and, in particular, chemical and biological warfare.

I concluded:

> But most important, we have built a movement. Students who may easily have been channeled into the niches of corporate anonymity now see social purpose in radical politics. We have found community.

---

78. "Encina Sit-in Photos Missing," *Stanford Daily,* May 23, 1969, p.1. https://archives.stanforddaily.com/1969/05/23?page=1&section= MODSMD_ARTICLE2#article

We are questioning the whole nature of the society in which we live. And we will never forget the lessons we learned during the April Third Movement.[79]

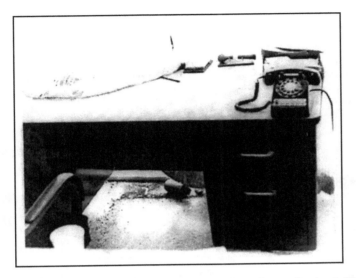

**Fig. 6.13. Expended tear-gas canister under a desk at SRI.**

79. "The April 3rd Movement," p. 43. http://a3mreunion.org/ archive/1969-1970/69-70/files_1969-1970/69-70_Maggies_ Farm_parts_1-7.pdf

# Chapter 7: Beyond SDS—Grass Roots, ROTC, and Cambodia

> This is not an invasion of Cambodia.
> ~*Richard Nixon, April 30, 1970*

In the wake of A3M and similar movements on campuses throughout much of the country in the first half of 1969, Students for a Democratic Society seemed to have established itself as the spearhead of an increasingly anti-imperialist, even revolutionary, predominantly white student movement. However, the national organization imploded. The Movement continued, reaching new heights in the spring of 1970, but my hopes for a growing, cohesive, national New Left front disappeared.

Not surprisingly, SDS was having trouble finding a convention hall willing to host its June, 1969 national convention. Members of the Stanford chapter looked into the Duveneck Ranch in Los Altos Hills, site of a youth hostel owned by progressive Democrats. I even wrote the Stanford administration. Fortunately, both turned us down. The meeting ended up in the Chicago Coliseum.

A group of us, to some degree strange bedfellows politically, arranged to ride to Chicago together in Aaron Mangianello's van. Aaron was a musician, motorcyclist, and at the time Minister of Information of the Brown Berets. I remember his affiliation clearly because our departure for Chicago was delayed until his wife found his Brown Beret. Our entourage included Bruce Franklin, Mary H. of Stanford SDS, and Chris Milton, whose family owned China Books in San Francisco. Several boxes of Maoist literature were strapped to the roof. The van broke down in Davenport, Iowa, so Mary and I left the group and the pamphlets behind and hitchhiked the rest of the way. On the way I figured out that our ride was probably a stolen car. After the convention I flew back to California.

When we arrived, I quickly realized that while most SDSers were in the trenches opposing the war, fighting for justice, and reshaping their universities, a subset were also organizing to take over national SDS. There were three major factions among delegates. The largest was the Worker-Student Alliance, sponsored by the Progressive Labor Party (PL). I reported at the time, "PL had chartered planes (!) to bring its people to Chicago."[1] PL emphasized "working-class politics." Rejecting "nationalism," it denounced the Vietnamese National Liberation Front and the Black Panther Party.

The Revolutionary Youth Movement 1 (RYM1) at the time called themselves Weathermen, after the Dylan lyric, "You don't need a weatherman to know which way the wind blows." RYM1 said its prime task was supporting black and Third World liberation movements, but they had abandoned mass organizing for tactical violence.

Revolutionary Youth Movement 2 (RYM2) included the Bay Area Revolutionary Union, which grew out of Bruce Franklin's Peninsula Red Guard as well as other groups in the region. RYM2, which had many adherents from Stanford SDS, was a more traditional Marxist-Leninist organization. It associated itself with the Chinese Cultural Revolution, but it also had a litmus test of movements and countries to support that included Albania! When I questioned the commitment to Albania, which no one knew much about—except that it was aligned with China in the Sino-Soviet split—I was accused of "big-country chauvinism."

There was no room left in national SDS for people who, like myself, still considered ourselves New Leftists. At the beginning of fall quarter of 1969 I penned a column trying to explain what had happened. It appeared the day after SDS's initial meeting of the term, which drew 300 people. I wrote:

1. Leonard Siegal [sic], "SDS Position Clarified," *Stanford Daily,* October 1, 1969, p. 1. https://archives.stanforddaily.com/1969/10/01?page=3&section=MODSMD_ARTICLE15#article While books have been written about what happened to SDS, I only wrote a column.

It appears now, though, that SDS is experiencing the clumsiness of the teenage movement that grew too fast. The splits and sectarianism in SDS, as well as rampant disregard of reality in many sectors, have just about destroyed SDS's development as a national organization. But the enemies of SDS should not take heart. The Movement is much bigger than any set of initials or organization.

The splits in SDS which crystallized this summer are not simple, and are closely tied to the development of the movement. Stanford SDS, and the radical movement at Stanford, has been relatively free of the divisions which have plagued the organization elsewhere.[2]

Nevertheless, I was deeply disappointed, because I realized that it was much easier for a disciplined group of activists to take over and/or destroy an open, democratic organization than it was for them to come anywhere close to making the government responsive to the needs of average people. To this day, I try to stay away from national organizations, preferring to participate in networks or virtual organizations. I am able to work with people on national issues this way, but it's hard to see a path to national progressive structural change in the absence of a broad-based, democratic, multi-issue non-electoral organization.[3]

Neither group that claimed triumph in Chicago was able to reap the benefits of victory, because they had alienated themselves from the vast majority of student activists across the country. In fact, I believed and continue to believe that the principal shortcoming of

---

2. *ibid.*

3. When I first wrote this, I was supporting Bernie Sanders' presidential campaign, and I'm a member of the group that grew out of his 2016 Presidential campaign, Our Revolution. One of the reasons I supported Bernie was his commitment to grassroots organizing. However, it's hard to imagine his movement staying united when he is no long available to hold things together.

all three national factions was that they turned their backs on the constituency from which they had emerged.

Around this time, a group of us formed the Pacific Studies Center (PSC) with what I recall was a $50,000 donation from Larry Moore, an Old Lefty in Palo Alto who made some money as an electronics entrepreneur. I say "us" advisedly. I think I attended some meetings, but I got a job unpacking, pricing, and shelving books at the Stanford Bookstore. PSC was formed by people who had done research and writing for A3M and its predecessors at Stanford. Initially, it paid "subsistence" salaries of $200 per month to several students and former students.

PSC staff continued to write about Stanford and the War, but based upon our understanding of SRI's interests throughout the Pacific Basin, we branched out to study other parts of Asia and the Pacific. Our counterparts at Columbia and Harvard Universities formed similar research centers, the North American Congress on Latin America and the Africa Research Group, respectively, around the same time.[4]

Working with SDS and other groups elsewhere in the Bay Area, we organized a series of activities culminating with a protest at SRI's International Industrial Conference—a meeting of many of the world's top business leaders—in San Francisco in September 1969. We called it the "Festival of Thieves." As an educational campaign, with groups leafleting factories and working class high schools, it may have had some successes.[5] But as a confrontation, it fizzled. The average anti-war activist was not ready to "Kick the ass of the ruling class." About 500 people showed up, but faced with a show of force by the San Francisco Police Department, we mostly picketed peacefully.

---

4. I didn't become PSC's Coordinator until the spring of 1970, so I'll cover PSC's long-term work later.
5. Northern California Regional Staff, "Stop the Festival of Thieves," *New Left Notes,* August 29, 1969. This was one of the last issues of SDS's national newspaper, published before the Weatherpeople went underground.

In preparation for a new round of campus activism, Stanford SDS published a second Radical Guide to Stanford, titled *Maggie's Farm* after Bob Dylan's song of that name—in recognition of the Stanford's "Farm" nickname. It resembled *Through the Looking Glass,* with the addition of a narrative about what happened on campus the previous year, along with numerous telling photographs.[6]

Fall term at Stanford was dominated by the Vietnam Moratorium, a national movement that declared "no business as usual" one day per month. While to some degree it was a larger repeat of previous national mobilizations, leading organizers saw it as a way to build respectability for the anti-war movement, distinguishing themselves from student radicals and hippies.

The October Moratorium at Stanford was impressive:

> Capping a day of canvassing and marching, 8000 Moratorium participants gathered last night on campus in rallies of unprecedented size. About 80 percent of the student body stayed away from class yesterday, with more than 2000 leafleting in shopping centers, on trains and door to door. More than 5000 students and area residents marched at noon in Palo Alto's largest anti-war demonstration to date.[7]

SDS members participated in the larger events and leafleted tech companies in the Industrial Park.[8]

---

6. *Maggie's Farm: A Radical Guide to Stanford,* Fall, 1969. a3mreunion.org/archive/1969-1970/69-70/files_1969-1970/69-70_ Maggies_Farm_parts_1-7.pdf
7. "Moratorium Protest Sweeps Nation: 8000 Jam Stanford Anti-War Rally," *Stanford Daily,* October 16, 1969, p.1. archives.stanforddaily. com/1969/10/16?page=1&section=MODSMD_ARTICLE2#article
8. See "Dear Fairchild Employee," October 15, 1969 and "Dear Watkins-Johnson Employee," October 15, 1969. http://a3mreunion. org/archive/1969-1970/69-70_vietnam/files_1969-1970_vietnam/69-70Moratorium_to_Fairchild.pdf and
http://a3mreunion.org/archive/1969-1970/69-70_vietnam/ files_1969-1970_vietnam/69-70Moratorium_to_Watkins.pdf

**Fig. 7.1. Vietnam Moratorium mass meeting in Memorial Church, October 15, 1969. Linus Pauling is speaking.**

In November, the national Moratorium plan was for three days. On Thursday, November 13, there would be activities such as leafleting, picketing—Stanford people picketed the South Vietnamese consulate in San Francisco—and rallies such as the faculty-staff "Witness" in White Plaza. Friday would be a class boycott and large local march. Saturday would be a huge peace march in San Francisco, simultaneous with an even larger mobilization in Washington, DC.

I had been disappointed with the downtown Palo Alto march in October. I recalled hearing about the January 1966 march to the Palo Alto Post Office, selected because it was a symbol of the Federal government. Yet here we were in the nation's second largest center of military aerospace and electronics contracting, after the Los Angeles basin. I was determined that the November 14 march go through the Stanford Industrial Park, where we had documentation that numerous local firms were taking direct part in the war effort and even more were part of the military-industrial complex.

I went to just about every group that was part of the local Moratorium coalition. There did not seem to be a formal coalition decision-making structure, so I got all the groups— mostly people I had been working with—to make the same decision.[9] Not everyone saw it as a protest of local companies. Some supported it because it would be seen by lots of industrial park employees.

**Fig. 7.2. Leafleting in the Industrial Park, Vietnam Moratorium, November 14, 1969.**

So on Friday, November 14, 1969, several thousand anti-war protestors marched through the Stanford Industrial Park. Peter Dollinger of SDS gave a speech about local companies and the military, and the press, viewing the surroundings, interpreted the march as a protest against the military industrial complex.

---

9. I used a similar strategy in the 1990s. I was raising money for an environmental conference. I had commitments from U.S. EPA, the Air Force, and the Department of Energy. But the Navy couldn't decide which office would make the decision, so I went to four or five offices and got them all to make the same decision: to contribute funds.

**Fig. 7.3. At a November 14, 1969 Vietnam Moratorium Rally at Hanover and Page Mill, SDS member Peter Dollinger described the military work that was underway in the Stanford Industrial Park and explained the companies' connections with Stanford. This is virtually the same location as the SRI blockade on May 16 earlier that year.**

In the wake of the May mayhem at SRI's offices in the center of the industrial park, companies locked their usually open gates. I learned more than a decade later that as a result one locked-in Defense worker made a life-changing decision. Roy Gordon, with whom I worked on the Nuclear Freeze in the 1980s, was among the locked-in employees. He decided on the spot that he was on the wrong side of the fence, and he and his wife Diane subsequently devoted their lives to peace activism. Stories like Roy's make the hard work of protesting seem worthwhile.

The next day, thousands of people from Palo Alto and Stanford joined one or two hundred thousand other people in San Francisco for the largest Bay Area peace march to date. Stanford students, faculty, and staff filled 23 chartered buses. The march terminated at the Polo Grounds in Golden Gate Park, for a rally featuring the usual parade of speakers and the San Francisco cast of the musical *Hair*. I remember wondering why they were included, but they fit into the just-after-Woodstock aura of peace, love, and rock-and-roll.

Perhaps a half million people paraded in Washington, DC the same day. It would be a long time before as many people returned to the streets to demonstrate for peace, but the peace movement was winning over the American people. Furthermore, according to Daniel Ellsberg of Pentagon Papers fame, the massive marches of the Vietnam Moratorium persuaded President Richard Nixon not to threaten the use of nuclear weapons in Southeast Asia.

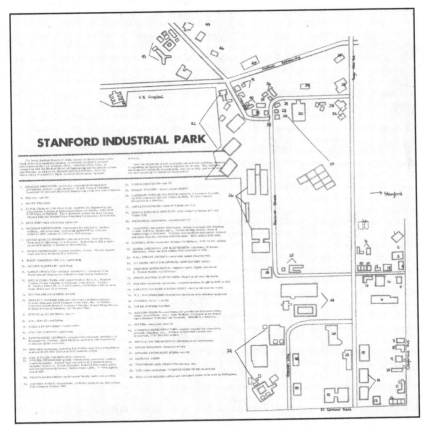

**Fig. 7.4. I created this poster illustrating the military contracting and other work done in the Stanford Industrial Park, produced during the Spring, 1970 Cambodia Strike. In 2016 I showed it to residents of the adjacent College Terrace neighborhood as we pressured Stanford to be more protective of future residents of faculty housing being constructed on Site #1.**

153

While the Movement was never all peace and love, just three weeks after the November Moratorium, an event occurred that many people saw as the end of the innocent hippie era. The Rolling Stones were touring the United States, and they quickly organized a free concert, along with San Francisco bands, Saturday, December 6 at the Altamont Speedway just off a highway leading eastward out of the Bay Area. The venue was not settled until the last minute. The Friday *Stanford Daily* reported that it might be at the Sears Point Raceway in the North Bay.[10]

In the end, 300,000 fans showed up at Altamont. Some of my friends urged me to skip work, but I stayed at my job in the Stanford Bookstore. Four people died at that event. Hells Angels motorcyclists had been asked to provide security, and by most accounts they were violent toward the audience and even some of the performers. Against the backdrop of mass death in Southeast Asia, I never saw Altamont as a watershed moment in the rise of violence. But Winter-Spring of 1970 did turn out to be a time of confrontation.

### The Promise of Stanford's Land

Fast forward to 2018. While serving as mayor of Mountain View that year, I criticized Stanford's plan to add thousands of jobs on its academic campus without providing sufficient new residences to house the new workforce. I explained that I had been working on this issue—the jobs-housing imbalance—on and off for 50 years. Radical student-staff-faculty organizing around Stanford land use issues was interrupted by our need to challenge Nixon's escalation of the Indochina War, particularly the invasion of Cambodia. But we laid the groundwork for the political work I am continuing to this day.

---

10. "Stones?" *Stanford Daily,* December 5, 1969, p. 1 archives. stanforddaily.com/1969/12/05?page=1&section=MODSMD ARTICLE6#article

As soon as we started researching Stanford's participation in the Military Industrial Complex, we knew that Stanford's 8800 acres were an important part of the Stanford story. Trying to find reasonable off-campus housing near campus, we could not avoid recognition of the emerging housing crisis. In fact, in *Through the Looking Glass: A Radical Guide to Stanford,* published by SDS in the Fall of 1968, we devoted 4½ pages, about one tenth of the booklet, to housing. We saw the housing imbalance as a feature of the local war economy.

We explained:

> Encouraged by both Stanford and the Palo Alto Chamber of Commerce, companies profiting from the war have increased their building programs in the area, but low-cost housing for workers hasn't drummed up the same interest. The home-building mortgage market has tightened and interest rates have sky-rocketed with the escalation of the war, and this serves as an added inducement for Stanford to build only expensive homes on its land and for the Palo Alto City Council to freeze out minority groups and low-cost housing.[11]

Coincidentally, about a month later, Acting Stanford President Robert Glaser appointed a Low Cost Housing Committee to explore the housing needs of Stanford and adjacent communities, headed by administrator Robert H. Moulton, Jr. The administrator-faculty-staff-student Committee included Jeanne Friedman, activist grad student Tom Grissom, and Beverly Bogart, a library staff member whose son was my roommate. The Moulton Committee released its report in the *Stanford Daily* on May 12, 1969, as the April Third Movement was boycotting classes and preparing for its assault on SRI.

---

11 "Housing," *Through the Looking Glass,* p. 10. This is a continuation of the quote early in Chapter 5. I believe I contributed to the writing of this section. http://a3mreunion.org/archive/1968-1969/68-69/files_68-69/68-69_Glass_p1-50.pdf

The report highlighted the following conclusions, elaborating on SDS's earlier findings. Plus *ça change, plus c'est la même chose.* That is, the report could have been written in 2021.

> 1. There is a serious shortage of low and moderate rent housing in the Stanford/Palo Alto Area.
>
> 2. The University has helped to produce the area's shortage of low rent housing both because of the housing needs of its students, faculty, and staff, and because its land development programs (primarily the industrial park and the shopping center) have significantly increased demand for local housing.
>
> 3. Land is a key element in any solution to the low-rent housing problem, and Stanford, as the owner of the only large uncommitted parcels of land in the immediate area, is thus conspicuously able to be of help attacking the problem.
>
> 4. The current housing shortage can be alleviated only if a program to develop low and moderate rent housing is given a high priority and the staff and funds necessary to carry out the detailed planning for such a program are made promptly available.
>
> 5. Stanford has a moral obligation to be actively involved in solving problems affecting its community....[12]

Meanwhile, the Committee for Green Foothills, formed by English professor Wallace Stegner and others in 1962, was fighting to preserve Stanford foothills from academic, industrial, and housing development. At the time, one of contested areas was

---

12. Robert H. Moulton, Jr., *et al.*, "Text of Report on Low Cost Housing at Stanford," *Stanford Daily,* May 12, 1969, p. 4. archives. stanforddaily.com/1969/05/12?page=4&section=MODSMD_ ARTICLE17#article

Coyote Hill, a popular scenic spot just above the Industrial Park. Campus radicals identified with the emerging environmental movement, so in general we supported such limits.

At the first SDS meeting in fall 1969, panelist Ned Groth spoke about upcoming issues in "Ecology and Land Use." Covering the meeting but exaggerating our plans, the *Palo Alto Times* headlined, "SDS may charge up Coyote Hill issue."[13]

SDS never charged up Coyote Hill, nor did SDS "charge up the issue." But we did form another campus organization, Grass Roots, to work on Stanford land use issues. In mid-January 1970 I wrote:

> Grass Roots was formed in December, drawing together radicals from the April Third Movement... and a number of people recently radicalized by the media discovery of the "national ecology crisis." Grass Roots hopes to bring an anti-capitalist, anti-imperialist perspective to the "ecology movement," and projects a popular community-based movement demanding large-scale construction of low-income housing in the Palo Alto Area.[14]

Less than a week later, I criticized Grass Roots' initial opposition to industrial development, writing: "Since we live in a society where income distribution depends upon continued industrial development, we must modify this position." I suggested, instead, "Grass Roots shall oppose industrial development which is not accompanied by the construction of enough housing to absorb the new employees brought into the area."[15]

---

13. "SDS may charge up Coyote Hill issue," *Palo Alto Times,* October 1, 1969, p. 1. http://a3mreunion.org/archive/1969-1970/69-70_land_use/files_69-70_land/69-70Land_Coyote_Hill.pdf
14. Leonard Siegel, "House People, Not Profits," p. 1. http://a3mreunion.org/archive/1969-1970/69-70_land_use/files_69-70_land/69-70Land_House-People.pdf
15. Leonard Siegel, "Proposal," January 20, 1970. http://a3mreunion.org/archive/1969-1970/69-70_land_use/files_69-70_land/69-70Land_Grass-Roots-Proposal.pdf

This was an idea five decades before its time. I proposed such a policy in Mountain View in 2014, and it is now being included in the city's precise plans. Other Peninsula cities are considering similar approaches, and most local governments in the area are asking Stanford to fully mitigate its academic employment growth with new housing.

Grass Roots' first demonstration was not an assault on Coyote Hill, but a march down El Camino Real, opposing Dillingham Corporation's plan to building two high-rise office buildings and a hotel on Stanford land at the foot of the Stanford Industrial Park. Two hundred people, mostly Stanford and high school students, took part, led by members of our "Hard Fife and Drum Corps," known as the "hard core." For the parade I dusted off my old snare drum, missing its snares, that I originally received in elementary school. We argued that Stanford was simply seeking to profit off its landholdings, rather than relating to people's needs and promoting environmental conservation. We wanted housing, not an explosion in employment.

**Fig. 7.5. Grass Roots protests Palo Alto Square development, January 12, 1970.**

Around this time, we published a 64-page pamphlet, *The Promised Land,* describing the history of the Stanford corporation's land and the development of Stanford Industrial Complex.[16] Drafted primarily by Paul Rupert, it convincingly linked Grass Roots' housing and environmental concerns with the anti-militarism thrust of the Movement. I probably helped write the section on the Defense Industry. Stanford student Leif Erickson provided the cartoon illustrations. The pamphlet sold for 25 cents.

*The Promised Land* was prescient in its analysis. I cited it in a 2018 letter to the Santa Clara County Board of Supervisors questioning Stanford's General Use Permit proposal:

> Is the housing shortage a small oversight which can be solved easily, or is it grave and persistent, the local outcome of the way in which this area has been developed? Is the ecological crisis simply an abundance of beer cans and auto exhausts, or is it a larger problem, caused by the self-seeking decisions of local land developers and industrialists? Do the people in the area really control local land development through their elected officials, or do the City Councils and Planning Commissions serve the Trustees of Stanford, the directors of major corporations and the real estate kings of downtown Palo Alto?[17]

Meanwhile, April 22, 1970 was the first Earth Day, which among other things propelled former student body president Denis Hayes to national prominence within the environmental movement. Thousands participated at Stanford, where debates between Movement radicals and more centrist environmentalists dominated the program.

---

16. *Grass Roots, The Promised Land: A Grass Roots Report on Mid-Peninsula Land Use,* 1970, http://a3mreunion.org/archive/1969-1970/69-70_land_use/files_69-70_land/69-70Land_Promised_Land.pdf

17. *ibid.,* p. 3.

Among the forty or so organizational booths and tables at the Environmental Fair in White Plaza was "Resource Monopoly," a board game that my friends and I chalked or painted onto the plaza. Instead of Atlantic City streets, the squares on our life-sized board were countries whose resources were subject to exploitation by Yankee imperialists. A business student actually wrote a letter to the *Stanford Daily,* complaining that our crowd was exploiting the three young children who played the game.[18] The children, if I recall correctly, were the kids of radical faculty members.

The *Daily* published my responding letter on April 30, the same day it headlined pitched on-campus battles between police and anti-ROTC protestors. I apologized, explaining the game was targeted at college students and mature adults, people, like the business student, "much closer to playing the game for real."

I wrote:

> What was scary about OUR "exploitation" of kids was how seriously they took the game. It made me think about all the games American kids play just as seriously. In "Monopoly," they learn to be moneygrubbers. In "Yankee Trader," they learn how to conquer the World. Let me suggest that Mr. Van Kuran address [himself] to the "exploitation" of millions of American children by the games they play every day but Earth Day.[19]

My time with Grass Roots left a long-lasting impression with me, but in April 1970 it could not compete for attention with the Indochina War. For example, on April 7 the *Daily* announced

---

18. Pete Van Kuran, "The Real Victim," *Stanford Daily,* April 24, 1970, p. 3. archives.stanforddaily.com/1970/04/24?page=3&section=MODSMD_ARTICLE16#article

19. Leonard Siegel, "Exploitation?" *Stanford Daily,* April 30, 1970, p. 2. archives.stanforddaily.com/1970/04/30?page=2&section=MODSMD_ARTICLE11#article

on page three that a Grass Roots meeting had been cancelled "to allow members to participate in anti-ROTC meetings and demonstrations."[20]

The issues raised by Grass Roots and others obviously did not disappear. In October 1977 the Pacific Studies Center convened a conference and published a pamphlet, *Silicon Valley: Paradise or Paradox.*[21] The same month, a County committee headed by Palo Alto realtor Bob Mang coined, or at least popularized, the phrase "jobs and housing imbalance."[22] When I was appointed to the Mountain View Planning Commission in 1978, I proposed, unsuccessfully, steps to counter the jobs-housing imbalance. Most notably, I called for a moratorium on industrial growth in Mountain View's North Bayshore area, today the home of Google and the workplace of over 25,000 people.

## Offing ROTC

On September 1, 1968, while SDS was preparing its campaign against war research and SRI, several faculty members wrote a letter to the Academic Senate questioning the compatibility of Stanford's three Reserve Officer Training Corps (ROTC) programs—Army, Navy, and Air Force—with the university's academic standards. Among other concerns, they noted that ROTC instructors were not selected by academic departments.

---

20. "Grass Roots," *Stanford Daily,* April 7, 1970, p. 3. <u>archives. stanforddaily.com/1970/04/07?page=3&section=MODSMD_ ARTICLE17#article</u>

21. The term Silicon Valley was for the first time becoming popular. Alan Bernstein, Bob DeGrasse, Rachael Grossman, Chris Paine, and Lenny Siegel, *Silicon Valley: Paradise or Paradox—The Impact of High Technology Industry on Santa Clara County,* Pacific Studies Center, October, 1977.

22. Robert Mang *et al., Housing: A Call for Action,* A Report from the Santa Clara Housing Task Force, October, 1977.

On the surface at least, those opposed to ROTC did not base their concern on opposition to the Vietnam War. But the War was undeniably and consistently in the background, particularly as on-campus anti-war activity grew in magnitude and militancy. And it's likely that the War—be it opposition or the personal risk of combat—was the principal reason ROTC enrollment was steadily declining.

In response, the Senate created a study committee made up of nine faculty and administrators. In early February, a majority of six committee members recommended major changes in the programs, including the phasing out of academic credit for ROTC classes. Other university faculties, including Harvard, Yale, Princeton, Penn, Cornell, and Pomona, had already voted to end ROTC credit. It also recommended an end to the "Punitive Clause," which subjected students who left ROTC to near-immediate military service. The minority suggested less drastic changes.[23]

On February 23, 1969 the Academic Senate voted 25 to 8 to end ROTC credit. In an advisory vote, the student body voted 2106 to 1397 the next day to support ROTC, including the continuation of academic credit. It's my recollection that SDS and its allies were focused on other matters at the time.

On March 11, the same day five Trustees met with the student body in Memorial Auditorium, the Trustees passed a resolution calling ROTC "vital to the continued supply of civilian leadership for the military services."[24] More than 50 professors who opposed the Senate's decision requested a vote of the full faculty. In early May, as the campus was reverberating from the abortive Encina Hall sit-in, the university released the results of

---

23. T.J. Connolly *et al.*, "Stanford University and the ROTC Departments: A Report and Recommendations," Ad Hoc Committee on ROTC, *Campus Report Supplement*, February 11, 1969. http://a3mreunion.org/archive/1968-1969/68-69_rotc_faculty/files_68-69_rotc_faculty/Ad_Hoc_Senate_Com-on_ROTC_1_pp1-14.pdf
24. "Trustees of Stanford University," Stanford University News Service, March 11, 1969. http://a3mreunion.org/archive/1968-1969/68-69_rotc_trustees/files_68-19_rotc_trustees/ROTC_vital.pdf

the full faculty ballot upholding the Senate, 403 to 356. ROTC academic credit was to be phased out, beginning with the 1970 freshman class.

Needless to say, the Defense Department, the Stanford Board of Trustees, and other conservative Stanford alumni were not pleased. The U.S. House of Representatives passed legislation that could have cut off Defense-sponsored research to any university that "would not renew its ROTC contract with the Army, on terms acceptable to the Army."[25] In October Army Colonel S.M. Ramey, head of the Stanford ROTC program, sent a proposal to the university essentially rejecting the faculty's decision.[26] Two weeks later, President Pitzer, following the apparent path of least resistance, unexpectedly showed up at the President's Advisory Committee on ROTC Affairs and urged the faculty to accept Ramey's proposal. On January 16, 1970, Pitzer formally requested a new vote from the Academic Senate, and on January 22, the Senate voted 23-13 to "permit Army ROTC courses to qualify for limited academic credit on a one-year trial basis."[27]

This time, the anti-war movement was paying attention. I don't remember playing a part in that decision, but the historical record shows that I was a visible part of what became known as the Off ROTC Movement. Three groups, including SDS still, called an emergency meeting on January 21, and 100 to 125 people protested outside the faculty Senate meeting, joined by as

---

25. The Senate did not concur, but the pressure was effective. "Washington Growls, Pitzer Jumps," *Stanford Chaparral*, February 16, 1970, p. 15. http://a3mreunion.org/archive/1969-1970/69-70_off_rotc/chaparral/files_1969-1970_off_chaparral/69-70_ROTC_Chaparral_pp_1-24.pdf

26. Col. S.M. Ramey, "Revision of ROTC Institutional and Student Contracts," October 22, 1969. http://a3mreunion.org/archive/1969-1970/69-70_off_rotc/off_rotc/files_69-70_off_rotc/Revisions.pdf

27. "The Stanford Faculty Senate...," Stanford University News Service, January 22, 1970, p.1. http://a3mreunion.org/archive/1969-1970/69-70_off_rotc/faculty/files_1969-70_off_faculty/SenateApproves.pdf

many as 25 counter-demonstrators. After the meeting, the New Stanford Moratorium began circulating a petition demanding complete removal of ROTC from Stanford.

At the New Moratorium meeting on January 23, the Movement for the first time voted to forbid photographs and tape recordings at its meetings. Bruce Franklin argued:

> If any of the decisions at the meetings resulted in actions that were even "mildly illegal," pictures and tape recordings could be used to convict those who attended the meeting on conspiracy charges.[28]

Meanwhile, a group of student journalists, including *Daily* veterans who had been active in the April Third Movement, turned the *Chaparral*, historically the campus humor magazine, into a serious publication. On February 16, it published a 24-page tabloid devoted to criticism of Stanford ROTC. The front cover was graced with a photo in which a protestor dressed as the Grim Reaper lined up, standing at attention with a group of ROTC cadets. The special *Chaparral* issue went beyond the academic criticisms put forward by liberal faculty. It linked ROTC to the Vietnam War, and it documented how students who tried to leave ROTC were punished.[29]

The day after the *Chaparral* publication was also "The Day After" the contempt sentencing for the Chicago 7 defendants and attorneys.[30] Activists across the country took to the streets

---

28. Larry Diamond, "Anti-ROTC Group Adopts Press Ban," *Stanford Daily,* January 26, 1970, p. 1. Remember, at the time people didn't have devices in their pockets capable of photographing, recording, and instantly transmitting discussions. archives.stanforddaily. com/1970/01/26?page=1&section=MODSMD_ARTICLE4#article

29. ROTC Special Issue, *Stanford Chaparral*, February 16, 1970. http://a3mreunion.org/archive/1969-1970/69-70_off_rotc/chaparral/ files_1969-1970_off_chaparral/69-70_ROTC_Chaparral_pp_1-24. pdf

30. These were charges derived from the police riot at the 1968 Democratic Convention in Chicago. By then, Black Panther Party chairman

in protest. At Stanford, 300 to 350 protesters paraded, around midnight, to and down El Camino Real to the Bank of America building, which housed the local FBI office. Bob Beyers of the Stanford News Service reported that the march was "led by Leonard Siegel and 13 torch-bearers."[31] I don't remember leading the march. Perhaps Beyers named me because he recognized me.

This event was literally a breakthrough, for demonstrators broke windows along the way, primarily at financial institutions. When they returned to campus, they reportedly broke two or three oversized plate glass windows at the Lou Henry Hoover Building, part of the right-wing-led Hoover Institution. Beyers reported that each of those windows cost several hundred dollars. To my knowledge, this is the first time Stanford protestors engaged in window-breaking for its own sake, a practice that soon became known as "trashing."

There are a number of reasons why trashing emerged as an activist practice, not just at Stanford, but across the country. First, it reflected growing frustration with the continuing escalation of the Southeast Asian War and the failure of institutions such as Stanford to stop participating in the War. Second, it made the news, enhancing the perception that campuses and communities in much of the U.S. were in turmoil over the War and other issues.

Third, at a practical level, it was a hit-and-run tactic, with the rock-thrower facing little chance of prosecution. If one could be suspended from college or go to jail simply for trying to attend a meeting or sitting in a hallway, trashing was a safer alternative.

Though one marcher was temporarily detained during the Stanford TDA action, no formal arrests were made that night or after the fact. The third Radical Guide to Stanford, *Fire and Sandstone*, later reported, "The Movement learned that night

---

Bobby Seale had been separated from the other seven defendants, so they were no longer the Chicago 8.

31. "About 300 Persons...," Stanford University News Service, February 17, 1970. http://a3mreunion.org/archive/1969-1970/69-70/files_1969-1970/69-70_Press_5.pdf

**Fig. 7.6. Cover photo from *Chaparral* magazine,
February 16, 1970.**

that police or FCM [Free Campus Movement, the new name of the organized right-wing on campus] photography doesn't mean shit after dark."[32]

Finally, the student Movement was increasingly identifying with revolutionary movements throughout the world. No one expected the National Liberation Front or the African National Congress to lay down their arms, so why would American revolutionaries eschew property damage in which people were unlikely to be injured, let alone killed. Furthermore, many national leaders who counseled against property destruction or violence were responsible for carpet-bombing and mass murder in Southeast Asia.

Coincidentally, another Bank of America was the target of demonstrators in Isla Vista, near the University of California Santa Barbara, the following week. The burning of that retail bank building was soon memorialized in a poster in the form of a personalized check. When the Bank and its friends argued that the world's largest bank was still the people's bank formed by Italian immigrant A.P. Giannini at the beginning of the 20th Century, my friends at the Pacific Studies Center researched and published their own poster, listing the bad things the bank was doing around the world.

Low-key activities characterized the remainder of winter quarter. We organized tours of ROTC facilities. On February 18, on one of those tours, Colonel Ramey answered questions put forward by *Chaparral* Editor Mike Sweeney and me.[33] On March 2, we demonstrated outside an Academic Council (full faculty) meeting at Dinkelspiel where the professors voted to

---

32. "Stanford Movement," *Fire and Sandstone,* Stanford Radical Caucus and New Left Project, Fall, 1970, p. 19. http://www.a3mreunion.org/archive/1970-1971/70-71/files_70-71/70-71_Fire_and_Sandstone_1-4.pdf

33. Ralph Kostant, "Radicals Face Ramey," *Stanford Daily,* February 19, 1970, p. 1. I don't remember this event, but one of my functions in the Movement was to lead tours. archives.stanforddaily.com/1970/02/19?page=1&section=MODSMD_ARTICLE3#article

put the Academic Senate's reversal decision to a mail vote of the entire faculty. On March 3 I debated Mike Wolf, a ROTC cadet, before a small crowd of 35.[34]

With the help of a friendly cadet who passed along the ROTC schedule, Off ROTC activists harassed the trainees.

> The New Moratorium organized the infiltration of ROTC classes and a limited education program in the dorms. [On February 28] The "People's Army" took to the countryside, armed with water balloons, laying a guerilla ambush for a ROTC field maneuver.... ROTC forces never showed.[35]

On another day, protestors even traveled to an Army training area near the East Bay town of Dublin to challenge the ROTC trainees.

On March 30, as Spring quarter began, the results of the Academic Council mail vote were announced. By a narrow margin, 390 to 373, the faculty endorsed the Academic Senate plan, which had been proposed by Pitzer. That night, Chicago 7 celebrity Tom Hayden spoke to an overflow crowd at Dinkelspiel Auditorium. Taking advantage of the critical mass of activists attracted by Hayden, some three hundred anti-ROTC demonstrators marched on ROTC headquarters, hoping to board it up. After protestors threw rocks through the second-story windows, Santa Clara County Sheriff's Deputies charged the crowd. Demonstrators broke into small groups, breaking windows elsewhere on campus.

---

34. John Coonrod, "Siegel, Wolf Join In Debate Over Military's Presence Here," *Stanford Daily,* March 4, 1970. I don't remember this event, either. archives.stanforddaily.com/1970/03/04?page=1&section=MODSMD_ARTICLE4#article

35. "Stanford Movement," *Fire and Sandstone,* page 19. http://a3mreunion.org/archive/1970-1971/70-71/files_70-71/70-71_Fire_and_Sandstone_1-4.pdf      For      more details, see Marshall Kilduff, "People's Army Ambush Fails," *Stanford Daily,* March 2, 1970, p. 1 archives.stanforddaily.com/1970/03/02?page=1&section=MODSMD_ARTICLE2#article I did not take part in these maneuvers.

**Fig. 7.7. Siegel and other Off ROTC protesters confront Stanford "police" chief William Wullschleger.**

The following night, Friday, April 1 was pretty much a repeat of Thursday. Demonstrators, many of whom were organized into affinity groups, attempted to board up the ROTC building. Right-wing counterdemonstrators tried to get in their way. Sheriff's deputies charged the protestors, arresting four. Rock-throwers broke windows. Men who we believed to be plainclothes cops maced me, Bruce Franklin, and a *Daily* reporter in the face.[36]

At an April 2 mass meeting, the Off ROTC demonstrators voted again to ask KSZU, the campus radio station, not to broadcast the debate. We had a long history of meeting in the open, but those who were concerned turned out to be right. After later meetings were broadcast, some Stanford administrators actually testified in court that they had been listening to KZSU

36. "ROTC Protests Continue, Four Marchers Arrested," *Stanford Daily,* April 2, 1970. archives.stanforddaily. com/1970/04/02?page=1&section=MODSMD_ARTICLE5#article

to identify activists who were proposing to violate the law or campus disruption policy. That night the Movement snaked a peaceful march around campus, gathering people from the dorms as we moved. The *Daily* estimated 800 participants.[37]

Interwoven with our challenges to the Stanford war machine were continuing demands for more democracy on campus: student power. Most student votes didn't mean much because student government had no power. Our demands for open meetings of the Trustees and faculty grew out of the old SDS aphorism: People have a right to make the decisions that affect their lives.

In the wake of the mail ballot, there were no significant items on the April 3, 1970 Academic Council agenda. But the Off-ROTC Movement decided to attend the meeting, held that afternoon in the Physics "Tank" lecture hall where I had spent hours learning about optics, mechanics, and electricity and magnetism. About 150 of us, including one wearing a paper-maché pig's head, entered the building.

Our coordinating committee, made up of representatives of our affinity groups, had chosen me as spokesperson. Later I wondered whether representatives from other factions preferred that I take the heat for whatever action we took. For me the event stands out because I spent days on trial and five days in jail for speaking out that afternoon.

I "rudely and illegally" attempted to call the meeting to order, angering a number of professors.[38] Then President Pitzer asked us to leave. I politely shouted, "General Pitzer, we would

---

37. "800 March For Third Night In Peaceful ROTC Protest," *Stanford Daily,* April 3, 1970. archives.stanforddaily. com/1970/04/03?page=1&section=MODSMD_ARTICLE2#article

38. These were the adverbs used by the judge in the subsequent civil judgment against me. I think that many in the establishment were aghast that Stanford students could be so impolite. George H. Barnett, "Board of Trustees vs. Alhadeff *et al.*, Memorandum and Order," Santa Clara County Superior Court, July 7, 1970, page 5. http://a3mreunion. org/archive/1969-1970/69-70_off_rotc/repression/files_69-70_off_ repression/69-70_ROTCRepression_Court_Order.pdf

like to know why the meeting is closed… the issues which have to be discussed here today affect all of us." Pitzer said that there were other communications channels available. He had the campus Public Safety Director declare our attendance a disruption, and most of us left, singing "We Shall Overcome" and chanting "Off ROTC!"[39]

**Fig. 7.8. On April 3, 1970, I "rudely and illegally" tried to call to order a meeting of Stanford's faculty, the Academic Council. I spent five days in jail for the exercise. The scrawled number is part of Stanford's systematic use of photography to identify and punish protesters.**

39. Ed Kohn, "Demonstrators Invade Movie, Move on Academic Council," *Stanford Daily,* April 6, 1970. archives.stanforddaily. com/1970/04/06?page=1&section=MODSMD_ARTICLE5#article See also "Case of the Academic Council Meeting of April 3, 1970," Stanford Judicial Council Case No. 37, 1970. http://a3mreunion. org/archive/1969-1970/69-70_off_rotc/repression/files_69-70_off_ repression/69-70_ROTCRepression_SJC_37_1-2.pdf For the one-hour KZSU recording of the meeting, go to http://www.a3mreunion. org/archive/audio/audio_1970_april3.html

There were many nights of trashing, and they've blended together in my memory. After a while, the university gave up on replacing broken windows. Some were boarded up for years. To the best of my recollection, I never broke a window on campus. I was aware that students opposed to the Movement were watching me, hoping to catch me in the act.

But mostly I would go over to the *Stanford Daily* offices. I had friends, perhaps roommates by then, on the *Daily* staff.[40] This is when I learned the art of "spin." My friends would disperse around campus, throwing rocks. I would go to the *Daily* and explain why. I explained the "Cost-Benefit Analysis," a strategy in which the Movement tried to make the retention of ROTC too costly. While broken window repairs and police costs ran into the tens of thousands of dollars, the negative publicity was more significant. It threatened to undermine the university's constant pitches for tax-deductible contributions.

While our affinity groups were also discussion groups, they served a strategic purpose. For example, at the end of our April 6 meeting in the Old Union Courtyard, we broke up into affinity groups, which sent representatives to a Coordinating Council. According the *Daily,* the Coordinating Council chose two targets, Pitzer's office and the new Durand Space Science Building, and the representatives informed their groups.

> At least 55 windows were quickly smashed by more than 250 anti-ROTC demonstrators last night in the fifth evening of protest against officer training. Within 10 minutes the well-organized radicals broke 15 windows in President Kenneth Pitzer's office and 34 in the Aeronautics and Astronautics building, their two primary targets. Uniformed police were not in evidence, and no arrests or injuries were reported.[41]

40. One year I played as a "ringer" in the Ink Bowl, the traditional touch football contest between the staffs of the Berkeley and Stanford dailies, played on Big Game weekend. I scored a touchdown for Stanford.

41. "Protestors Smash Windows In Scattered Guerilla Attacks," *Stanford Daily*, April 7, 1970, p. 1.

I did chair one or more meetings in the Old Union Courtyard, in which hundreds of protestors would gather before taking action. When everyone was reluctant to make any motion, for fear of prosecution, I entertained a motion to not trash. That motion was defeated, and people felt authorized to continue attacking buildings. When one of the two Shoch brothers spoke, I identified him as a third, fictional Shoch brother, "Hymie." I had mixed feelings about breaking windows. I didn't believe that breaking windows was always the wrong thing to do. I enabled it to some degree. But I thought we needed to expend more energy organizing and educating the Stanford community. The *Daily* reported, "Leaders like Paul Rupert and Lenny Siegel question the effectiveness of the window-breaking in building a mass movement."[42]

I recall one point where I urged a specific limitation on window-breaking. One of the Movement's favorite targets was the new Space Science Building,[43] which was home to some of the campus's remaining military contracts. One end of the building, where Radar Astronomy was located, was repeatedly attacked because it was a convenient target. An activist graduate student there reminded me that Radar Astronomy did basic research, with little or no military money. So I suggested that people find better targets.

There were demonstrators who saw trashing as an end in itself. It served as a personal release. On the other side, there were people—equally committed to our goals—who equated it with violence, who saw passive resistance as the

---

https://archives.stanforddaily.com/1970/04/07?page=1&section=MODSMD_ARTICLE5#article

42. Bill Freivogel, "Radicals Go Revolutionary," *Stanford Daily,* April 8, 1970, p. 1. archives.stanforddaily.com/1970/04/08?page=1&section=MODSMD_ARTICLE3#article

43. *Fire and Sandstone* contains a photo of the Durand building with broken and taped windows. I wrote the caption: "People who work in glass buildings should not do war research." page 26.

http://a3mreunion.org/archive/1970-1971/70-71/files_70-71/70-71_Fire_and_Sandstone_1-4.pdf only way to challenge ROTC and end Stanford's participation in the war. This tension remained through the Stanford spring.

After the April 6 night-time trashing, window-breaking died down for several days, as militants challenged those who criticized them to come up with alternative forms of protest. The Off ROTC Movement tried blockading the ROTC building, boarding it up, and disrupting ROTC classes. The April 7 "mill-in" in the ROTC building stands out for me because I spent another five days in jail for that. It also prompted Pitzer to issue "an emergency regulation closing the Athletic Building and the ROTC Departments to all but employees or students having classes there."[44]

About 100 of us had entered the building and tried to join ROTC classes. One of the demonstrators was beating a drum in the hallway. It was my snare drum, which I had used at the Dillingham/Palo Alto Square demonstration in January. As we left the building, I retrieved the drum. That night, about 45 protestors "audited" an ROTC class in the Business School, throwing paper airplanes and squeaking their chairs.

The Movement considered a variety of creative day-time tactics. There was even talk of a "nude-in" at ROTC drills. Some students fasted in protest. On April 9 there was a "stuff-in" in the ROTC building doorway.

> After marching to the building at about 1:30 p.m., the protesters encouraged 53 of their group to cram into the seven by 12-foot doorway. A dog joined them. A few more of the crowd then moved around to block the back entrance of the building.

---

44. "Pitzer Closes Building After Mill-In At ROTC," *Stanford Daily,* April 8, 1970, p. 1. https://archives.stanforddaily.com/1970/04/08?page=1&section=MODSMD_ARTICLE4#article

Then they plastered cartoons of Pitzer on the building's entrances, and Sheriff's deputies were called to clip off a bicycle lock that had been clamped to the front door handles to prevent anyone from opening the doors.[45]

In addition to the handful of arrests made during nighttime demonstrations, the university attempted to punish demonstrators by bringing dozens before the Stanford Judicial Council, and on April 13 it filed civil contempt citations against five of us, using the Injunction granted after the Encina Hall sit-in the previous Spring.

It was indeed a busy time. Radicals organized a teach-in on the war. Chicago 7 Yippie Jerry Rubin spoke to 1400 students in Memorial Auditorium. Anti-violence centrists organized a 500-strong march to Memorial Church. On April 16, as part of the national Moratorium against the war, 8000 people attended a dawn rally in Frost Amphitheater, where elected officials spoke and the San Francisco cast of the musical *Hair* performed. As described above, April 22, the first Earth Day, drew thousands of people to White Plaza during the day and 1,200 to Memorial Church at night.

Meanwhile, the Associated Students included another ROTC referendum in its Spring elections. This time, some of the Movement affinity groups campaigned, and it was clear that the tide had turned since the previous year: "Students also voted 3616-1898 to bar credit from ROTC courses, but chose to keep the program on campus by a slim 138 vote margin (2919-2781)."[46]

Furthermore, it was beginning to look like the Navy and Air Force ROTC units were preparing to leave campus, because it appeared that they might not get the academic credit they

---

45. Bill Freivogel, "Police Summoned To Unlock ROTC," *Stanford Daily*, April 9, 1970, p. 1. archives.stanforddaily.com/1970/04/09?page=1&section=MODSMD_ARTICLE1#article
46. Margie Wolf, "Shea, Shoch Win; ROTC Credit Out," *Stanford Daily*, April 17, 1970. archives.stanforddaily.com/1970/04/17?page=1&section=MODSMD_ARTICLE7#article

sought and, in the case of the Air Force, enrollment had declined below the "normal minimum."[47] Still, the larger Army program was slated to remain.

Spurred by activists who didn't support rock-throwing, the Movement threatened a sit-in. Five hundred people pledged to sit in if their anti-ROTC and amnesty demands were not met. On April 23, following a noon rally, nearly 500 Off ROTC demonstrators moved to the Old Union, where right-wing FCM members unsuccessfully tried to keep them out of the open building. Though Pitzer declared the Old Union closed at 5:00 pm, demonstrators stayed, ate dinner, and enjoyed live rock music in the courtyard. Demonstrators voted to leave if the police showed up.

I did not enter the building, for fear of implicating others as violators of the anti-disruption injunction. But I think I still received a letter from the Judicial Council, charging me as a "usual suspect."

Around 1:00 am on the 24th, deputies swept through the building without warning, arresting 22 of the remaining 125 demonstrators. The *Daily* called it a blitzkrieg and reported, "Police admitted they were tired of being assaulted by rocks in recent weeks and never arresting their assailants."[48] Even Bob Beyers reported that there was no warning between 5:00 pm and the police action.[49] Immediately protesters roamed the campus, breaking a reported $30,000 to $40,000 worth of windows.

---

47. "It now 'seems likely'...," Stanford University News Service, April 16, 1970. http://a3mreunion.org/archive/1969-1970/69-70_off_rotc/off_rotc/files_69-70_off_rotc/AirForcewithdraws.pdf

48. Ed Kohn and Philip Taubman, "Police Arrest 23; Break Up Sit-In With Swift Early Morning Sweep," *Stanford Daily,* April 24, 1970, p.1. archives.stanforddaily.com/1970/04/24?page=1&section=MODSMD_ARTICLE1#article

49. "Moving with Great Speed," Stanford University News Service, April 24, 1970. http://a3mreunion.org/archive/1969-1970/69-70_off_rotc/april_23-24/files_69-70_off_apr23/69-70ROTC_April_23_Press_3.pdf The Western Civ instructor who had kicked me out of his class my freshman year was arrested after being pushed into the building by deputies.

True to form, liberals—faculty members, *Daily* editors, etc.—who had been upset when the Movement damaged property were upset by the Sheriff's deputies use of force. Some Movement members asserted that the non-violent sit-in was dead as a tactic at Stanford. The night after the sit-in, Movement leaders split over next steps. Some argued for "mobile, militant action," while those who proposed a class boycott and a "liberation college" the next week prevailed in a close vote. The boycott didn't attract much support, but hundreds attended the teach-in.

As many as 500 people, including Movement opponents from student government, attended a hot-tempered meeting in the Business School's Bishop Auditorium Tuesday night, April 28. In the end, swayed by the support of two-time Nobel Prize winner Professor Linus Pauling, the group voted to conduct a non-violent, non-destructive, but disruptive sit-in in President Pitzer's office.[50]

This might have been the meeting where I proposed that we sit in at the Business School because we were already there. Pitzer immediately declared his office closed to unauthorized persons for 30 days.

On April 29, demonstrators showed up at Pitzer's office at 8:00 am. Finding it locked, they moved to the Old Union. Once again, those of us named in the civil injunction stayed outside. The sit-in was largely non-disruptive, and as usual they held multiple meetings to decide whether or when to leave the

---

50. Larry Diamond and John Sloan, "Sit-in Set For Pitzer's Office, Building Closed For 30 Days," *Stanford Daily*, April 29, 1970. archives. stanforddaily.com/1970/04/29?page=1&section=MODSMD_ ARTICLE4#article Linus Pauling, who had won Nobel Prizes in both Chemistry and Peace, had been one of my heroes in high school. In fact, he was one of the reasons I chose physics as a major. The same day the *Daily* headlined that rock-throwing anti-ROTC demonstrators had caused the closure of U.C. Berkeley, Stanford's so-called rival. "Cal Campus Closed Following Violence," *Stanford Daily*, April 29, 1970, p. 1. archives.stanforddaily. com/1970/04/29?page=1&section=MODSMD_ARTICLE5#article

building. Mid-day, a large crowd watched a performance of "Alice in ROTC-Land" on the Old Union steps. At least 100 chose to stay past the 5:00 pm closing time. Some of those left when Professor Pauling suggested that they avoid confrontation. Assured by administrators that they would be able to leave when police arrived, most agreed to do so.

That evening, everything changed. In fact, everything changed for the rest of the school year, not only at Stanford, but at campuses across the United States. The news reported that the U.S. and its South Vietnamese allies had invaded Cambodia.

## Perfect Storm

As events unfolded far beyond their control, there was no way that Stanford administrators and the faculty leaders allied with them could keep a lid on the campus. The front page of the April 30, 1970 *Stanford Daily* illustrated the coincidence of dramatic events. One article described the National Guard's fatal shooting of four unarmed anti-war demonstrators at Kent State University in Ohio. Confrontations over the Vietnam War were sweeping American campuses. Violent suppression was inevitable. Meanwhile, U.S. forces and their South Vietnamese allies "thrust" into Cambodia, destroying any remaining illusion that President Nixon intended to de-escalate the War. President Pitzer issued a statement calling the Cambodia action a "mistake."

The banner headline read, "Violent Fights Erupt After Sit-in; Students Battle Police For 4 Hours." After police arrested non-violent demonstrators sitting in the Old Union, several hundred rock-throwing demonstrators confronted them in hit-and-run confrontations throughout the main campus. At one point, Black Student Union leader Leo Bazile egged protestors on by telling them to "go home" because they weren't going to do anything serious. At least that saved him from a charge of inciting to riot.

The following night four or five thousand people met in Frost Amphitheater at a rally that "shouted approval of a campus-wide strike ... to protest U.S. involvement in Cambodia."[51] The Frost convocation was "sponsored by students and faculty seeking a nonviolent response to President Nixon's Cambodian policy."[52] But it didn't turn out that way. This event unleashed the most violent political confrontation in Stanford history.

**Fig. 7.9. Police guard the Old Union after expelling and arresting "Off ROTC" protesters, April 29 or early morning of April 30, 1970.**

The tone changed with the performance of "Alice in ROTC-Land."[53] This clever street drama, written by Jeff Blum and Marc Weiss, was performed by an on-campus theater troupe,

51. "Campus Strike Called Today To Protest Cambodia Action," Stanford Daily, May 1, 1970, p. 1. https://archives.stanforddaily.com/1970/05/01?page=1&section=MODSMD_ARTICLE2#article
52. "Violent Street Fighting Continues, Windows Smashed In Night Rampage," *Stanford Daily*, May 1, 1970, p. 1. archives.stanforddaily.com/1970/05/01?page=1&section=MODSMD_ARTICLE1#article
53. Jeffrey M. Blum and Marc A. Weiss, "Alice in ROTC-Land," May 1, 1970. http://a3mreunion.org/archive/1969-1970/69-70_off_rotc/off_rotc/files_69-70_off_rotc/alice-in-rotc-land.pdf

complete with a director, with Sigourney Weaver playing the title role. It parodied Lewis Carroll's work, localizing key characters, and made the Off ROTC Movement's key arguments against ROTC. Mid-way the play included a rewritten version of the Beatles' popular "All Together Now."

> *1-2-3-4*
> *We are bringing home the war*
> *5-6-7-8-9*
> *REV—olution*
>
> *boom boom boom*
> *Throw the rocks*
> *Trash the pigs*
> *Seize the quad*
> *Shut it down*
> *All together now (4 times)*
>
> *1-2-3-4*
> *We are bringing home the war*
> *5-6-7-8-9*
> *REV—olution*
>
> *boom boom boom*
> *Stop the war*
> *Burn the banks*
> *Smash the state*
> *Coming soon*
> *All together now (4 times)*

The song was repeated, as the grand finale, and the crowd joined in.

The Off ROTC coordinating council asked me to make a call to action, so soon after the emotional "Alice" finale and a short speech by Fred Cohen, I took the stage. The *Daily* reported:

> Fred Cohen addressed his remarks to Nixon's speech. "Anyone who watched [Nixon's] speech tonight would realize that the only reasonable thing to do is riot." Lenny Siegel went on to

explain the purpose of violent tactics. "We aren't here to destroy your education; we're here to make it relevant. People who feel that education means action should go to the ROTC building now."[54]

**Fig. 7.10. April 29 or 30, 1970. Police attempt to clear protesting students from White Plaza.**

And they did.

In 2019, playwright Marc Weiss reminisced:

> Our most raucous and memorable performance was the closing act on stage at Frost Amphitheater in front of 5,000 wildly cheering protesters on the night that Nixon invaded Cambodia. After the play concluded, several thousand people immediately marched onto the campus singing in unison our song from the play, "All Together Now," and initiated what indeed became the largest disruptive demonstration

54. "Campus Strike…,"*Stanford Daily,* May 1, 1970, p. 1. https://archives.stanforddaily.com/1970/05/01?page=1&section=MODSMD_ARTICLE2#article

and police battle in Stanford history, such that Dick
Lyman even suggested that the actors who staged the
play should be arrested for "inciting to riot."[55]

That night over a thousand rock-throwing demonstrators
faced off against 225 off-campus police armed with tear gas and
billy clubs. This one night, at least, militancy transcended both
ideology and strategy. It appeared to me that many demonstrators
took part simply because they regarded the region's police forces
as an occupying army. The Stanford News Service reported, "The
rock-throwers hit buildings plus the campus homes of Provost
Richard W. Lyman and Emeritus Provost Frederick E. Terman
in the most extensive 'trashing' yet on campus."[56] The mobile
night-time action triggered the arrest of fewer people than at the
sit-ins, but in general the charges were more serious.

Over the two nights, there were a few dozen injuries
on both sides. Unlike Kent State and later Jackson State (in
Mississippi), police at Stanford were instructed not to use their
lethal weapons. They fired tear gas canisters and wielded billy
clubs, but officials must have been worried that they might shoot
a Rockefeller, a Bechtel, a McNamara, a Katzenbach, or a Laird.
After two nights of street battles, the San Jose police said they
would not return to campus.[57]

As many as three hundred non-violent protestors attempted
to interpose themselves between rock-throwers and police, but

---

55. Personal e-mail, November 11, 2019. Weiss made similar
comments in his Oral History interview. Weiss, Marc A., Movement
Oral History Project, Stanford Historical Society, June 22, 2018, (pp.
41-42). https://historicalsociety.stanford.edu/publications/weiss-marc
56. "For the second straight night...," Stanford University
News Service, May 1, 1970. http://www.a3mreunion.
org/archive/1969-1970/69-70_off_rotc/april_29-30/
files_69-70_off_apr29/69-70ROTC_April_29_Press_1.pdf
57. "Three Shotgun blasts...," and "The San Jose Police Department...,"
Stanford University News Service, May 2, 1970. http://a3mreunion.
org/archive/1969-1970/69-70_off_rotc/april_29-30/files_69-70_off_
apr29/69-70ROTC_April_29_Press_2.pdf

in the absence of an established battlefront their effort was only symbolic.

As protest energy shifted to daytime on Friday, May 1, confrontations that night were relatively subdued. Demonstrators near Encina Hall greeted a police helicopter by spelling out "FUCK YOU" in drill-team fashion.

Also that night, the Los Altos home of ROTC Colonel Ramey was sprayed with shotgun pellets, but most campus protestors didn't consider that a part of their mass, militant protests.

Outraged by the Cambodia invasion and hoping to calm the campus down, the university establishment—administration, faculty, and student government—condemned Nixon, organized a delegation to go to DC, and reconsidered their position on ROTC. President Pitzer proposed that the Advisory Committee on ROTC review its position on ROTC credit, and he convened a meeting of the Academic Council, made up of all full faculty members. The technically powerless Academic Council called upon the Academic Senate, the representative body with more power, to condemn the invasion as "unwise, immoral, and harmful." In another divided vote, it asked the Senate to terminate academic credit for ROTC at the end of the academic year.[58] On May 7, the Senate voted to terminate credit for ROTC classes.

Though there was at least one more night of rock-throwing on May 18, after the arrest of several well-known radical activists, by May 1 street-fighting had pretty much run its course at Stanford. With a substantial boost from Richard Nixon, we had driven Stanford to the forefront of the national student strike. The Cambodia strike, in retrospect, was the high tide of the Stanford anti-war movement. The entire campus was electrified. While most students and faculty were already tacitly anti-war, the Cambodia strike brought forward a new set of leaders, primarily graduate students who organized in their academic

---

58. Frank Miller, "ROTC Credit, Cambodia Draw Requests For Senate Review," *Stanford Daily,* May 4, 1970, p. 1. archives.stanforddaily. com/1970/05/04?page=1&section=MODSMD_ARTICLE3#article

departments. They were motivated both by a sincere desire to end the war and a hope that they could bring calm back to the campus. Rather than oppose the new leaders, radical activists embraced them, using our resources to help educate students and nearby communities about not only the war, but the key role of Stanford's Community of Technical Scholars in prosecuting that war.

**Fig. 7.11. Students blockade the main administration building, Encina Hall, during the Cambodia strike, May, 1970. Notice the plywood windows.**

As a class boycott, the Cambodia strike was enormously successful. Professors cancelled classes or devoted them to discussing the War. Students, particularly undergraduates, skipped classes and attended teach-ins, marched for peace, or reached out to people beyond the campus. The *Daily* reported 20% attendance at classes at the Graduate School of Business,[59]

59. Ed Kohn, "University At Near Standstill As Strike Action

184

traditionally a more conservative enclave on campus. Initially, demonstrators blockaded classes in departments, such as Engineering, where there was less voluntary support, but over time the most persistent blockades were at Encina Hall, where strikers attempted to selectively block operations, and the ROTC building.

Pitzer suspended classes on Friday, May 8, and the university devised ways for students to get class credit and even to graduate without completing their Spring quarter coursework.

Mass meetings became routine. On Sunday, May 3 a rally of 1,200 endorsed the national Yale Demands. On May 4 Nobel Laureate Linus Pauling led a march in Palo Alto. That night, there was a convocation of a reported 1,000 people at the Medical school. On May 7, 2,000 people met again and adopted more detailed demands. Joan Baez sang to 1000 people at a noon rally in White Plaza while at least 33 men turned in their draft cards. On May 12, 1,400 people gathered in Memorial Auditorium to demand the release of Burnell Mack, a black student beaten and charged with assault with a deadly weapon and resisting arrest in March 31 campus disorders."[60] I missed much of the on-campus action due to my time spent in court, described later in this chapter.

Building off the graphic skills that Leif Erickson demonstrated for Grass Roots, the Movement developed four posters and a popular T-shirt design. There was a dinosaur poster documenting the interlocking directorates of the Stanford Board of Trustees;[61] a flaming map showing many of the campuses taking part in the national strike;[62] a particularly pedagogic poster called "A Small Circle of Fiends," with a large red fist in

---

Continues," *Stanford Daily,* May 6, 1970, p. 1. archives.stanforddaily.com/1970/05/06?page=1&section=MODSMD_ARTICLE5#article

60. Larry Liebert, "Black Demands Supported," *Stanford Daily,* May 13, 1970, p. 1. archives.stanforddaily.com/1970/05/13?page=1&section=MODSMD_ARTICLE4#article

61. "Strike Against the Stanford Empire," May, 1970. http://www.a3mreunion.org/archive/posters/posters_1970_strike.html

62. "National Student Strike," May 6, 1970.
http://www.a3mreunion.org/archive/posters/posters_1970_nss.html

the center, attacking both ROTC and the Dillingham project;[63] and a crudely drawn (by me) map of the Stanford Industrial Park, identifying the companies there and what they did for the military.[64]

Perhaps the most visible emblems of the strike were silk-screened T-shirts emblazoned with red fists and the words "Strike" and "Do It!" Volunteers must have produced hundreds. Today this sounds unimpressive, because almost everyone wears shirts with printed words or graphics, but back in those days t-shirts were only plain white or a single color.

Throughout my years at Stanford, people who were skeptical of Movement actions repeatedly charged that no one would listen to us activists because we were too militant, and then they would ask why we had taken militant action. So each time we took direct action, from sit-ins to heckling to trashing, we would speak at teach-ins, convene dorm meetings, and produce new, well-researched publications.

I believe this is when I was invited to an earnest discussion of U.S. foreign policy, as well as Stanford's role, at a row house, Stanford's version of a sorority. The women who lived there were anxious to learn, but I remember that one asked why activists hadn't set up literature tables in White Plaza. I replied that groups that I worked with had set up tables almost every day of the academic year.

As the Cambodia strike got underway, we published more than educational posters. Through the Pacific Studies Center, on May 4, 1970 we mass-produced a four-page analysis of Nixon's escalation of the War, "Operation Total Victory."[65] We

---

63. "A Small Circle of Fiends," May, 1970. a3mreunion.org/archive/posters/posters_1970_small_circle.html

64. "Stanford Industrial Park," May, 1970. http://www.a3mreunion.org/archive/posters/posters_1970_sip.html

65. "Operation Total Victory," Pacific Studies Center, May 4, 1970. http://www.a3mreunion.org/archive/1969-1970/69-70_cambodia/files_1969-1970_cambodia/69-70Cambodia_Total_Victory_1-2.pdf On May 10 we started distributing a longer version: "Operation Total Victory: 2nd Edition," Pacific Studies Center, May 10, 1970.

also published an 8-page pamphlet, "Engineering at Stanford," updating our critique of the Community of Technical Scholars.[66] I believe I raised money for and produced both versions of "Operation Total Victory" as well as the Engineering pamphlet, but I'm pretty sure someone else wrote the former.

On May 5, some 500 students met with Professor William Zimbardo to form the Political Action Coordinating Committee, led by Psychology graduate students. PACC served as an umbrella organization for almost anyone who wanted to "carry out alternatives to 'business as usual.'"[67]

One of the many projects instigated by striking students and faculty was civil disobedience at Hewlett-Packard's headquarters in the Stanford Industrial Park. I think it was led by the Stanford History Department. H-P was a symbol of Stanford's military complex because of Hewlett's nerve gas denial on March 11, 1969 and Packard's selection by Richard Nixon as Deputy Defense Secretary. I encouraged protestors to focus on electronic warfare companies, whose products were directly enabling the air war in Vietnam, but the Group for Civil Disobedience wrote:

> While H-P is not nearly as heavily involved with De-
> fense contracts as are some of the other big companies
> in the Industrial Park, H-P produces, nevertheless, sev-
> eral types of defense-related electronic equipment…
> Some one-third of H-P contracts are defense-related.[68]

http://a3mreunion.org/archive/1969-1970/69-70_cambodia/files_1969-1970_cambodia/69-70Cambodia_Total_Victory_3.pdf

66. "Engineering at Stanford," Pacific Studies Center, May, 1970. http://a3mreunion.org/archive/1969-1970/69-70_cambodia/files_1969-1970_cambodia/69-70Cambodia_Stanford_Engineering.pdf

67. "Liberation College," May 5, 1970. This document lists the initial projects proposed at the May 5 meeting. http://a3mreunion.org/archive/1969-1970/69-70_cambodia/files_1969-1970_cambodia/69-70Cambodia_Liberation_College.pdf

68. "Hewlett-Packard and the War," Group for Civil Disobedience, May, 1970.

**Fig. 7.12. Durand "Aero and Astro" Building during Cambodia Strike, May, 1970. Notice the windows. Another photo of Durand appeared in fall, 1970 *Fire and Sandstone* with the caption, "People who work in glass buildings should not do war research."**

Several Biological Sciences graduate students, a post-doctoral fellow, and faculty members created the Stanford Biology Study Group. They published an 11-page pamphlet, "The Destruction of Indochina," focused on the ecological damage and health consequences of the U.S. military's spraying of highly toxic defoliants in South Vietnam.[69] At the time, few people, even in the anti-war movement, were aware of the

http://a3mreunion.org/archive/1969-1970/69-70_cambodia/files_1969-1970_cambodia/69-70Cambodia_HP_p_1_4.pdf and http://a3mreunion.org/archive/1969-1970/69-70_cambodia/files_1969-1970_cambodia/69-70Cambodia_HP_p_2_3.pdf

69. Bruce Bartholemew *et al.*, "The Destruction of Indochina," Stanford Biology Study Group," May, 1970. http://a3mreunion.org/archive/1969-1970/69-70_cambodia/files_1969-1970_cambodia/69-70Cambodia_Destruction_pp_1_11.pdf

ecological consequences of the war. This pamphlet combined the interests of the anti-war movement and the nascent ecology movement. Notably, the pamphlet's foreword was written by Biological Science Department chair Donald Kennedy, later to become Stanford University president.

The strike gave students the opportunity to reach out beyond the campus. Stanford students have long believed they have wisdom to share.

> The Medical School, which is helping to organize a nationwide labor strike, said it had received some support from the Teamsters and the Longshoremen's unions. It distributed 15,000 leaflets at local industrial plants yesterday morning.[70]

On May 17 and 24, students welcomed hundreds of people from off campus to Open Campus days, modeled after similar efforts in Paris, France in the Spring of 1968.

On June 4 the Academic Senate endorsed a proposal by the Advisory Committee on ROTC that any future ROTC training for Stanford students be off campus. Students in the existing programs would be allowed to finish their education at Stanford. Freshmen admitted with ROTC scholarships would be offered alternate final assistance.[71]

ROTC was forever transformed. In 1983, the Stanford News Service reported that 75 Stanford men and women were enrolled in off-campus ROTC programs, but they received no Stanford academic credit for their military training.[72]

---

70. "Strike Momentum Maintained," *Stanford Daily,* May 8, 1970, p. 1. https://archives.stanforddaily.com/1970/05/08?page=1&section=MODSMD_ ARTICLE6#article

71. "An eight-man faculty-student committee...," Stanford University News Service, June 3, 1970. http://a3mreunion.org/ archive/1969-1970/69-70_off_rotc/advisory/files_1969-1970_off_ advisory/ReportReleased.pdf

72. "ROTC Enlistment Rising among Stanford Students," Stanford University News Service, November 23, 1983. http://a3mreunion.org/ archive/1972-beyond/72-beyond_rotc/files_rotc/EnlistmentRising.pdf

**Fig. 7.13. Poster produced during the Cambodia Strike.**

As the Spring 1970 term ended, so did the strike. Hundreds of graduating seniors forewent their robes and mortarboards, raising money instead for a Peace Commencement Fund. Otherwise, the Stanford Corporation returned to near normal.[73]

73. "Caps And Gowns May Go For Peace," *Stanford Daily,* May 18, 1970, p. 1. https://archives.stanforddaily. com/1970/05/18?page=1&section=MODSMD_ARTICLE5#article

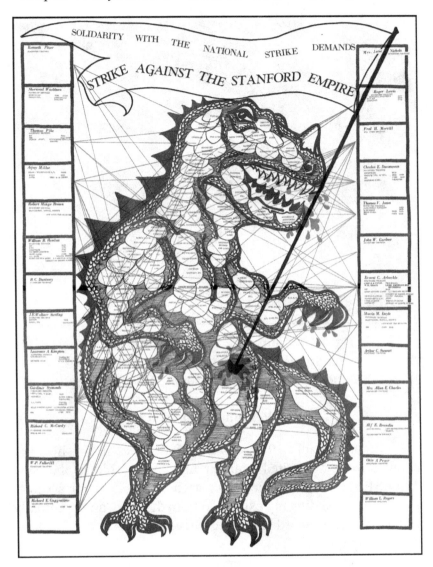

**Fig. 7.14. Perhaps the best of many representations of the corporate connections of the Stanford Board of Trustees, produced during the Cambodia Strike.**

**Fig. 7.15. Cambodia Strike at the Graduate School of Business, one of the campus's most conservative enclaves. May, 1970.**

## My Personal Crossroads

Looking back, 1970 was a decisive year in my life. For about a year, I awaited trial for my visible role in the May 1969 SRI Hanover Street demonstration. I settled for a year's probation, extending my exclusion from the draft, and eventually I had my arrest record expunged because I was under 21 at the time of my arrest.

At some point, my supervisor fired me from my bookstore job because I refused to punch the time clock 15 minutes early. This freed me to become more engaged in escalating Movement activities. As the Cambodia strike began, I went to work, for $200 per month, for the Pacific Studies Center to produce "Operation Total Victory" and "Engineering at Stanford." I am still there, fifty years later, though I've also taken income from sources such as San Francisco State University and Apple Computer.

My status as a student morphed from pay-a-fine-to-register to *suspended,* as I was hauled before the Judicial Council as a usual suspect in sit-ins and other questionable protests, whether or not I had participated. But I didn't care. I had become disillusioned with the Community of Technical Scholars that had attracted me to Stanford. I was happy not to become a cog in the military industrial complex. Little did I realize that some of my friends would play key roles in shifting the region's technical prowess from weaponry to civilian pursuits.

My parents, though supportive of my most militant activities, were disappointed that I did not graduate. Explaining that at one of our Movement reunions, I said "My parents always wanted me to *finish* Stanford." Thinking about it, I spontaneously quipped, "But it's still here." Eventually Stanford's alumni magazine recognized some of my successes and called me "Lenny Siegel, Class of 1970." It turns out that one is forever connected to one's undergraduate class, even if one does not earn a degree.

Wednesday night, May 13, 1970 there was an event that could have made a huge difference in my life. In fact, it was the only time in my activist career that I felt my life was in danger. Shortly before midnight, five San Mateo County Sheriff's Deputies showed up at the house I rented on Oakwood Drive in East Palo Alto with a warrant for the arrest of one of my roommates, Jimmy Johnson. Jimmy was one of the few African-American students who bridged the gap between the Black Student Union and SDS and its predominantly white successors. He also had a habit of antagonizing police, shouting things like "You better get eyes in the back of your head" at them. At the time Jimmy had left his Chemical Engineering studies and was working at the university telephone switchboard. I enjoyed imagining him politely answering random phone calls.

It's not clear why the Deputies arrived at our house at that date and hour, since the Santa Clara County Sheriff's office told the *Daily* they were serving an arrest warrant stemming "from an incident at the Old Union sit-in on April 29 at which Johnson allegedly kicked a police officer."[74] It would have been normal for the Sheriff's department to contact the lawyers who routinely represented activists to arrange for Johnson to turn himself in, but pounding on our front door and hiding at our back door late at night could have triggered violence. Johnson immediately grabbed his handgun, and it took all my persuasive powers to convince him to put it down.

The police had an arrest warrant, not a search warrant. As master tenant, I objected to the search, which may be why I was booked as well. One of our other roommates reported:

> The police entered the house without permission and searched the house without permission. "Legally, the police could only search for Johnson, but they were looking in trunks and bookcases; Johnson isn't that small," he said.[75]

We were jailed in a crowded cell in the County jail in Redwood City with what appeared to be average criminals, including some big, threatening guys. I tried to act tough, so no one bothered me. It may have helped that the TV news, shown inside the jail cell, referred to us as something like "dangerous radicals."

The Deputies walked several of us prisoners from the jail to the San Mateo County Courthouse for arraignment the following day. That's when I noticed that design tiles in the Courthouse, which had been built well before the rise of the German Nazi Party, displayed reverse swastikas.

My charges were dropped, and Johnson jumped bail. He was eventually caught in Trinidad and extradited back to California.

My favorite encounter with the "justice" system was the trial of five of us activists for Contempt of Court for violating the civil injunction the University obtained a year earlier against

---

74. "Siegel, Johnson Arrested At Home," *Stanford Daily,* May 15, 1970, p. 1. https://archives.stanforddaily.com/1970/05/15?page=1&section =MODSMD_ARTICLE7#article
75. *ibid.*

campus disruption. The trial began on May 7, at the height of the Cambodia Strike, at the Northern Santa Clara County Courthouse in Palo Alto. It must have taken a few days, because I believe it was over by the time I was arrested at my East Palo Alto house. Because it was a civil trial, not a criminal trial, we were not prosecuted by the District Attorney's office. Instead, we were "prosecuted" by Stanford's high-priced San Francisco law firm connected to the Stanford Board of Trustees. We were represented by Movement lawyer Jim Wolpman and a public defender, and I think some of us defended ourselves.

Our charges were almost laughable: Speaking out at the April 3 meeting of the Academic Council; beating a drum in the ROTC building; squeaking a chair in a ROTC class. We saw the trial as a political exercise, and I knew we were gaining ground when Stanford's attorney asked a witness, "And then what did General Pitzer do?" My *nom de guerre* for Pitzer tying Stanford to the military industrial complex had stuck.

Another time this attorney challenged one of our witnesses who said that Pitzer was angry. The lawyer asked how the witness concluded that. In response, Avram Goldstein, a medical school professor and world-renowned pharmacologist, gave a detailed description of Pitzer's anger symptoms, including the pulsating blood vessels in his neck.

We knew we had won the public relations battle when, during a break in the proceedings, the Court clerk or recorder approached me. Remember, this was at the height of the Cambodia strike, in the wake of the most violent confrontations in Stanford history. We five had been picked out as leaders of this militant movement. She queried, "My nephew is thinking of applying to Stanford. Do you think it's a good school?" Astounded that, after hearing all the evidence of disruption and presumably watching the news, she would ask me such a question, I replied, "It depends upon what he is looking for."

In early July, I was sentenced to ten days in jail, and three of my co-defendants were sentenced to five days each.[76] When we served our time that summer, the other two men and I were kept separate from criminal inmates because we were civil prisoners. In fact, the jailers thought we had hepatitis because we were incarcerated in an isolation cell. I spent overlapping time with both of them.

During my ten days, my only visitor was my brother, who lived in San Francisco, and his one-year-old son. When I was released very early in the morning, I spent time wandering the streets around the County Jail because I was unable to reach my roommates, one of whom was supposed to pick me up. One of them forgot about my impending release and was tying up the house's only phone line on a lengthy long-distance call. I was actually stopped by police. I had to show my release papers to avoid arrest for loitering.

Our trial and light sentences destroyed the deterrent effect of the civil injunction process. The process was much more costly for Stanford than it was for us. To my knowledge, no Stanford activists were ever again tried for civil contempt.

To close the circle on how 1970 shaped the rest of my life, I met my wife-to-be, Jan Rivers, later that year. But we didn't start seeing each other regularly until the Laos Invasion of 1971.

---

76. Barnett, "Board of Trustees vs. Alhadeff et al." http://www.a3mreunion.org/archive/1969-1970/69-70_off_rotc/repression/files_69-70_off_repression/69-70_ROTCRepression_Court_Order.pdf

# Chapter 8: How New Is My Left—The Laos Invasion and the 70-71 Academic Year

*A revolution is not a dinner party.* — *Chairman Mao Tse-Tung*

## A Movement Divided

I was never much of a political theoretician. In fact, for years I pinned a cartoon from Cuba above my desk, explaining, "The duty of the theoretician is to hope that someone else will make the revolution." As a physics major, I never took a class in political science, modern history, or economics. Compared to my comrades, I read relatively few books by radical historians, Left economists, and Marxist stars such as Marx, Engels, Lenin, and Rosa Luxemburg. I did participate in a short-lived study group reading Volume I of Marx's *Das Kapital.* Two books that shaped my views were French Leftist André Gorz's *Strategy for Labor* and George Orwell's personal recounting of the Spanish Civil War of the mid-1930s, *Homage to Catalonia.*[1]

Orwell's book reinforced my suspicion of Old Left politics. Though my family was a victim of the anti-Communist excesses of the early 1950s, I considered the world's Communist governments to be largely undemocratic. While autocracy might have been a rational response to counterrevolution in some places, I felt that American democratic traditions created new opportunities for participatory socialism.

Besides, the American Communist Party—though many of its members still did great labor and civil rights organizing—had been tamed by repression and spent much of its energy supporting slightly liberal Democratic Party politicians. Furthermore, my

---

1. In 2012 my wife and I visited Spain, and we had the opportunity to take a Spanish Civil War tour of the Ramblas district of Barcelona, based on Orwell's book.

progressive father—a lunch-bucket worker—never had much hope that a Movement for fundamental change would be led by the American white working class. The New Left, particularly SDS, had represented an attractive alternative.

In 1969 I was surprised by the transformation of national SDS into three factions, all of which had Old Left characteristics. At Stanford, Bruce Franklin's Peninsula Red Guard had joined with East Bay revolutionaries to form the Bay Area Revolutionary Union (RU), only, for the most part, to split from the RU in late 1970 to form Venceremos.[2] It was easy to see why many of the students I worked with, including activists I had personally brought into the Movement, were attracted to the RU and then Venceremos. Bruce was an articulate, charismatic leader, offering wondering youth the certainty of ideology. The group identified domestically with the Black Panther Party and like many others, the armed revolutionaries of Southeast Asia and southern Africa. They argued that white activists should follow African-American (later a broader "Third World") leadership.

While a few of the RU/Venceremos activists were well read, in the Marxist-Leninist tradition, most understandably loved the simplicity of Chinese Communist leader Mao Tse-Tung's *Little Red Book*. Who could argue with Mao's pithy slogans, such as "A single spark can set a prairie fire"; "A revolution is not a dinner party;" and "Where the broom does not reach, the dust will not vanish of itself"? By 1971, they seemed to represent the largest share of the most active campus progressives.

Like other Old Left groups, the RU and Venceremos practiced what they called "democratic centralism." Once they—or at least, their decision-making body—made a decision, all members were expected to support it. This posed a challenge to those of us who worked with them in coalitions, because in coalition meetings

---

2. Police agencies referred to Venceremos as the Venceremos Organization, to distinguish it from the Venceremos Brigade, cane-cutting and other volunteers who traveled to Cuba, and the slogan, "Venceremos!"

their organizational discipline made it difficult for us to propose alternative activities, or even compromise. In fact, it was easy to identify secret members—people who had joined but not disclosed it to others—by the energy with which they pursued the "party line."

Finally, they were intolerant of other groups claiming the Marxist-Leninist mantle. At one point in 1970 RU members beat up activists from the locally smaller Progressive Labor Party.

But there were others of us who still clung to the ideals of the New Left. Going back through my files, I realize how important these differences were, because I wrote about them often. My fundamental views have remained consistent over the years.

In July 1970, I circulated a two-page ditto (purple ink reproduction) proposing the formation of a new campus organization that would be an alternative to the RU. This new group, which became the New Left Project, would view "revolution" not primarily as the seizure of central state power, but rather the assertion of local control over institutions such as universities and workplaces. Our organization would be anti-authoritarian. We would not only tolerate, but encourage independent public expression by our members. Later, in one of its initial public documents, the New Left Project wrote:

> Because we believe that the organization of the revolutionary movement will structure the consciousness of the post-revolutionary society, the New Left Project operates on the basis of self-discipline, not on the basis of discipline from above by a central committee.[3]

In my writings, I promoted Gorz's concept of revolutionary or structural reforms. Recognizing that the American ruling class had repeatedly compromised with and coopted demands from labor and racial/ethnic interest groups, I argued that the Left should make

---

3. "The New Left Project," Fall, 1970, p. 3. The sophistication of this document suggests that I didn't write it. http://www.a3mreunion.org/archive/1970-1971/70-71/files_70-71/70-71_New_Left_Project.pdf

demands for control of our institutions. Challenging Stanford's participation in the Indochina War was an example of this approach.[4]

The New Left Project continued the critique of elite American universities that had been growing at least since the 1964 Free Speech Movement at the University of California at Berkeley. We wrote:

> Because the content of study is decided in large measure by the needs of the corporate elite, higher education is a process of absorbing pre-digested material and acceptable attitudes passively. The university prepares those whom the elite must recruit to replenish its numbers. A student who does not accept discipline and moral compromises of university life will not be fit for the elite.[5]

We embraced the concerns and struggles of fellow students, distinguishing ourselves from Marxist-Leninists who saw campuses as a source of human power to go out and fight the "real" struggles.

> What are the aims of the New Left Project and others who share our ideology? We seek human liberation. The impediments to realizing the possibility of a free society are what make us radicals. There was a New Left slogan in the 1960's: "A liberal wants to free others; a radical wants to free himself." This slogan pinpoints a major difference which divides New Left radicals from corporate liberal, social democratic, and Marxist-Leninist students. With the increased dogmatism of some elements of the student Left, one sees more and more "a kind of abstract devotion to alleviating the plight of arbitrarily defined others.

---

4. See, for example, Leonard Siegel, "Illusory Power," *Stanford Daily*, October 12, 1970, p. 2. https://archives.stanforddaily.com/1970/10/12?page=2&section=MODSMD_ARTICLE5#article

5. "New Left Project," p. 2. http://www.a3mreunion.org/archive/1970-1971/70-71/files_70-71/70-71_New_Left_Project.pdf

When you are for 'the working class' or 'third world'
you have annihilated the concrete existence of persons
and destroyed genuine contact with the reality of your
own situation." (Arnold Sachar)[6]

We also questioned Venceremos' appeal to follow black or Third World leadership. Undeniably, the Civil Rights and Black Power Movements gave birth to the predominantly white student movements outside the South. But it was clear that Venceremos had chosen which leaders of color to follow. The myth of following non-white leadership fell apart in July of 1971 when the Panthers changed their tune, and a majority of Venceremos decided to "follow" other militants of color.

Finally, we felt that our lifestyles and views should be compatible. In my original paper, I wrote:

Our style of organizing must reflect our ideals.
Clearly we cannot make a revolution merely by being
"beautiful people." But to attract and deserve support
we must demonstrate our humanity, humor, etc.[7]

I don't want to make it seem like there were only two active anti-war groups on campus. Non-violent students managed to create a theme house on campus, Columbae House, in the fall of 1970. Unlike the university administrators and faculty leaders who hypocritically preached non-violence to the Movement, Columbae students were serious activists. For example, they led a March blockade of the San Francisco draft board.[8]

---

6. *ibid.,* p. 3.
7. Leonard Siegel, "Over the past few months…," July 7, 1970, p. 1. http://a3mreunion.org/archive/1970-1971/70-71/files_70-71/70-71_ NewLeftProposal.pdf
8. "Thirteen Stanford students…," Stanford University News Service, March 11, 1971. http://a3mreunion.org/archive/1970-1971/70-71_columbae/ files_70-71_columbae/70-71Columbae_Press_3.pdf

The medical school was a bike ride away from the main campus, so students, staff, and faculty there formed their own Stanford Medical Community for Peace and published the *Axon* from a room they called the Nerve Center.[9]

After the February 1971 Laos Invasion, a group of campus women, led by faculty wives, formed Stanford Women for Peace. In late February they led a protest outside the university placement center against weapons contractor FMC,[10] the same company that Bill Hewlett had explained, on March 11, 1969, had sold its nerve gas factory to the government. This was the first of many Women for Peace actions at the Placement Center. In April of 1971 Women for Peace sent a letter to President Richard Nixon "calling for total withdrawal of American forces from Southeast Asia." It was signed by 1600 women: faculty, faculty wives, staff, and students, including University President Lyman's wife Jing.[11]

Faculty members with a history in the anti-war movement formed the Faculty Political Action Group (FPAG) after the Cambodia strike in the spring of 1970. Its program was broader, addressing educational issues as well as the Vietnam War.[12] As the university administration clamped down on activists, including Professor Franklin, FPAG focused more and more on opposing campus political repression.

---

9. "1970-71: *The Axon*," April Third Movement Historical Archive. http://www.a3mreunion.org/archive/1970-1971/70-71_axon/1970-1971_axon.html

10. "About half a dozen faculty wives...," Stanford University News Service, February 26, 1971. http://www.a3mreunion.org/archive/1970-1971/70-71_career/files_70-71_career/70-71Career_Press_2.pdf Remember, at this time, the Stanford faculty was overwhelmingly male.

11. "Nearly 1600 women students, faculty, staff, and wives...," Stanford University News Service, April 21, 1971. http://a3mreunion.org/archive/1970-1971/70-71/files_70-71/70-71_Press_12.pdf

12. See "1970–1971: Faculty Political Action Group," April Third Movement Historical Archive. http://www.a3mreunion.org/archive/1970-1971/70-71_faculty/1970-1971_faculty.html

Still, most campus activists were not members of any of the aforementioned groups. Many had been through the April Third Movement and/or Cambodia Strike with the people affiliated with the organized groups. They showed up at teach-ins, rallies, and marches. To some degree, the challenge for the organized groups was to attract the attention and participation of these unaffiliated activists, people who were already opposed to the War and in tune with the Movement on a wide range of issues.

The differences between the New Leftists and our more doctrinaire friends was more than a theoretical debate. It turned out to have significant implications for campus activism during this period. The New Left Project emphasized the continuation of the battle to extricate Stanford from the Indochina War, while the RU, its successor Venceremos, and the Radical Caucus that served as the instrument for much of their on-campus activity were more focused on workplace issues and support for the Panthers. This was a matter of degree, because the Marxist-Leninists continued to protest the war, while the New Leftists supported labor organizing and demonstrated in support of the Panthers.

**Fig. 8.1. Protesting FMC recruiting**

## A New Academic Year

In the wake of the Cambodia strike in the spring of 1970, the Stanford Left began the 1970-71 academic year with anticipation. We published, *Fire and Sandstone: The Last Radical Guide to Stanford.* Some people may have viewed the "Last Radical Guide" reference as bravado, a threat to put Stanford out of business. However, to me it meant that I would never work on a major publication again with some of the people on our writing team. Indeed, the title page explained:

> This booklet was prepared by members of the Stanford Radical Caucus and the New Left Project. In preparing the guide, numerous differences emerged over the nature of the articles to be included.... If you don't like the booklet blame the group that you don't like.[13]

The New Left Project kicked off the new academic year at the Freshman Convocation, where Richard Lyman, in his second day as university president, was speaking to 1400 new students. The *Daily* reported, "Demonstrators ... chanted 'Give 'em the Axe,' a chant normally reserved for Big Game," the annual football contest against Cal.[14]

Two weeks later I circulated a memo that advocated a "Road to Peace Lies in the Streets Campaign." The Movement would continue to question Stanford's role in the Vietnam War, but we would also challenge Stanford and SRI's programs elsewhere in the Third World. We would begin again with research and education. I wrote:

---

13. *Fire and Sandstone: The Last Radical Guide to Stanford,* Stanford Radical Caucus and the New Left Project, Fall, 1970, p. 2. http://a3mreunion.org/archive/1970-1971/70-71/files_70-71/70-71_Fire_and_Sandstone_1-4.pdf

14. Dan Bernstein, "Protest Greets President," *Stanford Daily,* September 28, 1970, p. 1. https://archives.stanforddaily.com/1970/09/28?page=1&section=MODSMD_ARTICLE4#article

Though our approach to the decision-makers [university trustees and administrators] would be antagonistic, we should attempt to convince people like ourselves that making war is not the best way to live.[15]

**Fig. 8.2. This photo appeared on the back cover of *Fire and Sandstone,* Fall 1970. It was probably taken during the Spring 1970 Cambodia Strike.**

To my knowledge, like other proposals I drafted, the strategy was never formally endorsed by any organization, but it helped to set the stage for a school-year that was punctuated by a series of guest speakers, rallies, and demonstrations. At no point, however, did the level of anti-war activity galvanize the entire

15. Leonard Siegel, "The Road to Peace Lies in the Streets," October 13, 1970, p. 1. http://a3mreunion.org/archive/1970-1971/70-71/ files_70-71/70-71_Looking_for_issue.pdf

campus the way it did during the spring, 1969 April Third Movement and the spring, 1970 Off-ROTC Movement and Cambodia Strike.

One of the first on-campus anti-war protests in the fall of 1970 was at the Placement Center, the central campus building that had hosted The Experiment my freshman year. The New Left Project and a group of former Lockheed engineers, a total of as many as 100 demonstrators, picketed a Lockheed recruiter and handed out leaflets. At the time, and for many years earlier, the Sunnyvale-based Lockheed Missiles and Space Company had been one of the nation's largest weapons contractors and the largest employer in what would soon be known as Silicon Valley.[16] The New Left Project and the Pacific Studies Center, which I now directed, had attracted a group of young engineers who specialized in research *about* the weapons industry. I was not the only tech student disillusioned by the military's dominance of new technologies.

During this period Stanford activists also took part in demonstrations in San Jose against the visiting Richard Nixon and in San Francisco protesting South Vietnam's "cowboy" president Nguyen Cao Ky.[17] On campus, on November 23, about 100 demonstrators reacted to a U.S. raid on Hanoi, North Vietnam by breaking windows at campus science and engineering buildings.

On November 6, New Left Project members, in cooperation with counterparts in Berkeley, initiated a local War Crimes Commission, to investigate local participation in the Vietnam

---

16. See "Peaceful Picketing and Leafleting against Lockheed...," Stanford University News Service, October 28, 1970; "Lockheed"; and Dick Stovel, "To the Stanford Engineering Student." a3mreunion.org/archive/1970-1971/70-71_career/files_70-71_career/70-71Career_Press_1.pdf
a3mreunion.org/archive/1970-1971/70-71_career/files_70-71_career/70-71Career_Lockheed.pdf and
http://a3mreunion.org/archive/1970-1971/70-71_career/files_70-71_career/70-71Career_to_Engineering_Student.pdf
17. Actually, he was all hat and no cattle.

War as well as other elements of U.S. foreign policy.[18] Though the U.S. undeniably committed war crimes in Southeast Asia, the characterization didn't seem to stick when applied to Stanford and SRI research.

I successfully argued that we rename the War Crimes Commission "The Inquisition," in an attempt to bring a little humor to a very serious subject. In January we explained in a campus leaflet "that the notion of 'war crimes,' as commonly understood, was too narrow to include all the areas which we are investigating." In addition, I felt our critics would look silly if they asserted, "The Inquisition is nothing but a witch hunt."[19]

In the late fall, I came up with a fun way to raise money for the New Left Project. Stanford's football team, led by "Heisman Trophy candidate" quarterback Jim Plunkett earned its way to a January 1, 1971 Rose Bowl showdown with Ohio State University. Stanford's sports publicity machine was so effective that Plunkett's name seldom appeared in print without the three words prepending. Plunkett not only won the Heisman trophy for his college football achievements, but he later led the Oakland Raiders to two Superbowl championships.

Meanwhile, prodded by Native American students and their supporters, Stanford was in the midst of a multi-year process phasing out its Indian mascot. We seized on the opportunity by identifying Stanford teams as "Reds." They eventually became known as Cardinal, for the color, not the bird.

We ordered and sold buttons—for 25 cents, I think—that stated simply, "Go Reds: Smash State." Many football fans bought and wore them, unaware of the political entendre, while many activists bought and wore them, not realizing they were for the Rose Bowl. The last time I talked to Richard and Jing Lyman, following Dick's 2009 lecture to the Stanford Historical Society, both of them recalled the button with a smile.

---

18. Larry Liebert, "'Purge War Criminals'—Scheer Says," *Stanford Daily,* November 10, 1970, p. 4. https://archives.stanforddaily. com/1970/11/10?page=4&section=MODSMD_ARTICLE12#article
19. "The Inquisition," January, 1971 http://a3mreunion.org/ archive/1970-1971/70-71/files_70-71/70-71_Inquisition.pdf

On January 1, 1971, Stanford did indeed smash Ohio State, 27-17. A group of us stayed at my boyhood home in Culver City so we could attend the game. But I missed it because I came down with the stomach flu. In February, as I prepared for a judicial hearing at Stanford, someone put out a light-hearted flier suggesting I had been a victim of germ warfare.[20]

## Lodge

Our first action under the new name—carried out with strong participation by Venceremos and the Radical Caucus— was to protest the presence on campus of Henry Cabot Lodge, Jr., who as U.S. Ambassador to the South Vietnam had been in charge of the U.S. war effort in its early years. In a January 11, 1971 column in the *Daily*, the "Grand Inquisitor" documented Lodge's bellicose service, writing, "It is time we started confronting the real war criminals, without who [sic] My Lai would never have been possible."[21] On January 12, 150 protestors shouted Lodge down.

The following day I wrote the following report:

> Monday, January 12, Henry Cabot Lodge was prevented from speaking at Stanford University by a crowd of anti-war demonstrators.
>
> Lodge had been scheduled to speak to a conference on the United Nations sponsored by Stanford's Hoover Institution on War, Revolution, and Peace, but Lodge—and his role in the Southeast Asian War— rather than the ultra-conservative Hoover Institution, was the primary target of the demonstrators.
>
> A half hour before the program was to begin, a bomb threat cleared Dinkelspiel Auditorium, the site of

20. "The Sky's the Limit Until Leonard Is Set Free," February, 1971. http://a3mreunion.org/archive/spoofs/files_spoofs/Sky's_the_limit. pdf
21. The Grand Inquisitor, "Henry Cabot Lodge: The Real War Criminal," *Stanford Daily*, January 11, 1971, p. 2. archives.stanforddaily. com/1971/01/11?page=2&section=MODSMD_ARTICLE6#article

the conference. Fire marshals searched the building, found nothing, and the conference opened at 2:00 pm, as scheduled.

Eight or nine hundred people filled the auditorium. Though a majority was hostile to Lodge, only 150 demonstrators participated in the heckling, chanting, and rhythmic applause.

Hoover Director Glenn Campbell (not the singer), also one of most reactionary members of the Board of Regents of the University of California, was heckled during this opening remarks, but was able, with difficulty, to finish his speech.

When Ambassador Lodge took the podium he was greeted with the chant, "N-L-F, Pathet Lao, U.S. out of Asia Now!" and continued rhythmic applause. One student, upon asking the hecklers if they were afraid to let him hear Lodge's views, drew loud applause. The heckling and handclapping continued.

Many of the anti-war demonstrators had expected to engage Lodge in a discussion on Southeast Asia, and did not take part in the heckling. They were unaware that Lodge had refused to discuss Vietnam at his press conference earlier, and planned to do the same in the question period following his address.

Finally, Lodge left the stage and Sheriff's deputies escorted him to another building, where he eventually spoke to a crowd of 150. Prophetically, as Lodge left the podium, he said: "I'm really not that dangerous, you know."[22]

Of course, not everyone on campus was pleased with this outcome. For one, we had been impolite. Secondly, it triggered

---

22. Lenny Siegel, "Monday, January 12, Henry Cabot Lodge was prevented from speaking...," January 12, 1971. http://a3mreunion. org/archive/1970-1971/70-71_lodge/files_70-71_lodge/70-71Lodge_ Report.pdf

yet another debate about free speech. Religion professor Robert McAfee Brown, an outspoken opponent of the War, wrote a *Daily* column emphasizing the importance of protecting free speech. He concluded, "If the purpose of Monday's disruption was to downgrade Mr. Lodge in the eyes of the nation, it certainly failed."[23]

I saw, and I continue to view, free speech from a different lens. I believe in the right to be heard. For the anti-war protestors, heckling may have been our only way to be heard beyond the campus. Like other federal officials, Henry Cabot Lodge had easy access to the global media. By shouting him down, we were not preventing an unpopular view from expression. Rather, we were holding him accountable for a genocidal war. I, for one, would not have shouted down someone simply because he or she thought the war was good thing.

In retrospect, the University's response to the Lodge demonstration was the first salvo in a successful two-year campaign by the university administration to expunge Bruce Franklin from the university. Berkeley Tomkins, the Hoover official moderating the event, singled out Bruce from the podium, even though Bruce was not chanting and clapping with the rest of us. I remember Bruce smiling and laughing as activists near him stood up and chanted, but he did not join them.[24] Nevertheless, just one week later President Lyman filed disciplinary charges against Franklin. In the end, the Advisory Board that recommended Franklin's firing acquitted Franklin on the charge that he disrupted Lodge's speech.

---

23. Robert McAfee Brown, "Lessons Learned from Lodge," *Stanford Daily,* January 18, 1971, p. 2. archives.stanforddaily. com/1971/01/18?page=2&section=MODSMD_ARTICLE5#article Usually identified as "noted theologian," Brown became increasingly progressive over the years. He and his wife, Sydney Thomson Brown, became personal friends, and Bob was happy to officiate at my wedding in 1976.

24. I wrote about this in April of that year. See Lenny Siegel, "Franklin Singled Out," *Stanford Daily,* April 1, 1971, p. 3. archives.stanforddaily. com/1971/04/01?page=3&section=MODSMD_ARTICLE8#article

It was another busy time. On the evening of January 20, the Inquisition and other activists organized a protest at the main SRI building in Menlo Park. The Association of Old Crows (see Chapter 6) was holding a secret briefing on the "Wild Weasel" weapon systems, air-to-ground weapons that homed in on anti-aircraft radar sites. This system was manufactured by Professor Rambo's company, the Applied Technology Division of Itek, in the Stanford Industrial Park. The Inquisition wrote, "It is timed to occur as the men who designed the electronic equipment used to bomb North Vietnam arrive to discuss the success of their work."[25]

About 150 demonstrators picketed the entrance, at times impeding the arrival of vehicles. As tensions mounted, the police dispersed the crowd, arresting nine. Some of the protestors returned to campus and broke windows in the engineering area.[26]

### Laos Invasion and the Computation Center[27]

On February 1 campus anti-war activists formed a new coalition against the war in Indochina, called appropriately the Coalition Against the War in Indochina. Though rumors were circulating that the U.S. would escalate the war again by invading Laos, the Coalition's fundamental position was more general: a call for immediate U.S. withdrawal from all of Indochina.[28]

---

25. "Stanford Inquisition Protests SRI's Electronic Warfare Briefing," January, 1971. a3mreunion.org/archive/1970-1971/70-71_sri/files_70-71_sri/70-71SRI_Demonstration_2.pdf
26. Dan Bernstein and Lang Atwood, "Nine Arrested As Police, Dissidents Clash at SRI," *Stanford Daily,* January 21, 1971, p. 1. archives.stanforddaily.com/1971/01/21?page=1&section=MODSMD_ARTICLE3#article
27. Much of this section is based upon a summary of events that I wrote up immediately. See Lenny Siegel, "Last week students at Stanford reacted angrily...," February 13, 1971. http://a3mreunion.org/archive/1970-1971/70-71_laos/files_70-71_laos/70-71Laos_Report.pdf
28. "Who We Are," Coalition Against the War in Indochina. http://a3mreunion.org/archive/1970-1971/70-71/files_70-71/70-71_Who_We_Are.pdf

At first, Stanford activists hoped for a national campus reaction to the Laos Invasion, similar to the strikes and militant demonstrations that followed the Cambodia Invasion the previous spring. We began with similar tactics to our Cambodia/ Off ROTC actions, and we sustained roughly two weeks of protest. Noon rallies drew from 500 to 2000 people, night-time trashings occurred, and several campus buildings were briefly occupied. But our actions did not command the participation of the majority of the student body—most felt powerless, especially since little else seemed to be happening nationwide. I remember that one of our activists contacted friends at Harvard, to hear how they were protesting Nixon's latest escalation. He reported, "It's snowing there."

Sunday night, February 7, 200 people marched through campus, trashing buildings popularly associated with the war or U.S. imperialism. Several thousand dollars worth of damage was reported.

Following a massive noon rally Monday, three hundred people surrounded a meeting of the Stanford Board of Trustees at the Stanford business school, demanding that the ruling-class trustees sign the People's Peace Treaty with the Vietnamese. The demonstrators were forced out by riot police. Students then briefly occupied the Old Union administration building, but they were again evicted by police.

Tuesday, following a rally called by the Black Students Union in which the black students made their own demands on the University administration, 300 students and friends walked out of campus judicial proceedings in which numerous students were on trial for disrupting Henry Cabot Lodge's speech as well as disruption of earlier judicial hearings.

Meanwhile, the New Left Project and its offshoot, the Inquisition, continued to research Stanford and SRI's participation in the War. We got a break when a graduate student who was using the campus Computation Center found a print-out left behind by an SRI researcher. It's hard to imagine, now that billions of people carry smart-phone computers around in their pockets, but in those days to run a computer program one had to key in instructions and data on punched "IBM cards," leave them to be input into a mainframe computer by computer operators, and then return hours later to see how well the program worked.

The SRI print-out was called Gamut-H, and our researchers quickly discovered that it was "a computer simulation of an amphibious assault, designed toward optimum speed and efficiency in the deployment of helicopters, troops, and artillery." In our initial Inquisition flier, we asserted, "This work is directly applicable in Indochina."[29]

On February 8, the Inquisition issued an open letter to the Stanford community, enumerating six demands focused on ending campus war research and connections with the military industrial complex. If I recall correctly, we issued them ourselves because we thought a broader set of demands, likely to be proposed by other factions,[30] would dilute their impact at a time when the Laos invasion had heightened the visibility of the War.[31]

Well over 1500 people showed up at a noon rally Wednesday in Stanford's White Plaza. Venceremos leaders, including Bruce Franklin, advocated for a strike, as they had at a Tuesday night meeting. But it was clear, in the light of the publicity about Gamut-H, that the crowd wanted to march to the Computation Center. Bruce ended up advocating for a strike that would begin at the Computation Center.

---

29. "SRI Does Indochina War Research at the Stanford Computation Center," The Inquisition, February, 1971. http://a3mreunion. org/archive/1970-1971/70-71_laos_computer/files_70-71_laos_ computer/70-71LaosComputer_SRI_at_Comp_1.pdf

30. See, for example, the demands adopted at a Tuesday night, February 9 meeting, listed in Chris Peck, "Meeting Calls for Strike, Plans Noon Rally Today," *Stanford Daily,* February 10, 1971, p. 1. https://archives.stanforddaily. com/1971/02/10?page=1&section=MODSMD_ARTICLE1#article

31. "Open Letter to the Stanford Community," The Inquisition, February 8, 1971. http://a3mreunion.org/archive/1970-1971/70-71_ laos_computer/files_70-71_laos_computer/70-71LaosComputer_ Open_Letter.pdf

Several hundred marched, and over a hundred broke into the $5,000,000 facility and shut it down. Late in the afternoon, police arrived to evict the demonstrators, arresting four in a scuffle outside. Slogans were scrawled on the inside of the building, but no permanent damage to the computers was reported.[32]

**Fig. 8.3. Audience at January 12, 1971 Lodge protest. "Where's Bruce?" How did Hoover's Berkeley Tomkins spot Bruce Franklin in this crowd?**

The discovery that SRI continued to do war research on campus following the severance of SRI from the university was embarrassing to the administration. SRI announced it would stop using the Computation Center, but we learned nine months later that Provost William F. Miller, for some unknown reason, deliberately delayed disclosing that SRI had discontinued Gamut-H processing. In October, 1971, participants in the

---

32. The *Daily* reported that protestors cut some wires and mishandled some magnetic storage tapes. Ed Kohn, "Unknown Assailant Shoots 2 Last Night; Radical, Police Clash at Comp Center," *Stanford Daily,* February 11, 1971, p. 1. https://archives.stanforddaily. com/1971/02/11?page=1&section=MODSMD_ARTICLE1#article

occupation testified at Bruce Franklin's disciplinary hearing that the occupation would not have occurred if SRI's decision had been made public.[33]

**Fig. 8.4. Protesting SRI's war gaming program, Gamut-H, at the university Computation Center, February 10, 1971.**

Still, the very day of the Computation Center occupation, just two days after the Inquisition circulated its six demands, Provost William F. Miller responded. Of course the university did not meet our demands, but Miller obliquely addressed the immediate issue:

> Information concerning utilization of the Computation Center by non-University organizations and individuals, which is relatively minor and controlled carefully, will be available.[34]

33. Jonathan Dedmon, "Witness Says Miller Withheld Data," *Stanford Daily,* October 27, 1971, p. 1. https://archives.stanforddaily. com/1971/10/27?page=1&section=MODSMD_ARTICLE3#article
34. "The Following Remarks were made by Provost William M. Miller....," Stanford University News Service, February 10, 1971.

215

Wednesday night, in response to the occupation of the campus by 150 riot police who checked I.D.'s and enforced a limited curfew, students marched across the campus. Scuffles

**Fig. 8.5. Police rout peaceful demonstrators from the area around the Computation Center after the occupation ended. Professor Bruce Franklin was fired, in part, for arguing with the police that the dispersal order was unjustified and illegal. February 10, 1971.**

and rock-throwing occurred between the demonstrators on the one side and the police and their right-wing student supporters on the other. Eleven demonstrators were arrested. A right-wing student who was photographing protesters was severely beaten. Two people were shot by an unknown assailant while standing near the headquarters of the right-wing Free Campus Movement. The next day I called the beating and shooting "unnecessary and counterproductive," but I remained uncertain as to who fired the gun. I also pointed out that "other demonstrators tried to prevent the beating."[35]

---

http://a3mreunion.org/archive/1970-1971/70-71_laos_computer/
files_70-71_laos_computer/70-71LaosComputer_Press_2.pdf
35. See Lenny Siegel, "People's War Critique," February 11, 1971.

Thursday evening several hundred students voted to strike, demanding that the U.S. get out of Indochina, that political prisoners be freed, and that the university cease participation in the war effort. However, the movement seemed to be waning, with many students reacting fearfully to the previous night's shooting. Three hundred students, including about 100 high school students, marched to Hewlett-Packard in the war-oriented Stanford Industrial Park and to Stanford's Hoover Institution. On Friday students voted to stage a class boycott and another march Tuesday, following the long week-end.

Meanwhile, high school, community college, and community groups in the Palo Alto area had been holding protest marches and rallies all week. On Tuesday, February 16, 1,000 people marched from Stanford's quad through downtown Palo Alto, finishing with a rally in El Camino Park. This march brought together campus and off-campus radicals as well as faculty leaders critical of the Movement's militant tactics.[36]

Also on Friday, the University obtained a superior court restraining order against disruptions and destruction, and it announced its intent to ban Venceremos leaders from the campus. President Lyman announced the suspension of Bruce Franklin. Once again, Franklin was singled out for something he did not do: inciting the occupation of the Computation Center. At the February 10 White Plaza rally he had argued for a strike, not an action at the Computation Center. When it became clear that the masses wanted to go to the Computation Center, he acquiesced and suggested that the strike begin there. Following his suspension, Bruce taught his class, Literature in the 1930's, on February 16. An overflow class of 250 students attended, even though the official enrollment was 150.[37]

---

http://a3mreunion.org/archive/1970-1971/70-71_laos/files_70-71_laos/70-71Laos_PeoplesWarCritique.pdf I don't remember if this was published.

36. Don Tollefson, "1000 March Against Asian War," *Stanford Daily,* February 17, 1971, p. 1. archives.stanforddaily.com/1971/02/17?page=1&section=MODSMD_ARTICLE3#article

37. Larry Liebert, "Prof. Franklin Ignores Suspension As Overflow

Though I played a key role in the Inquisition's Gamut-H research and education activities, I did not take part in the Computation Center occupation, for two reasons. First, the previous spring my presence at demonstrations deemed disruptive by the Stanford administration had made other protestors susceptible to civil prosecution, because I was subject to the spring 1969 injunction. Second, as Director of the Pacific Studies Center I was devoting time to raising money for, publishing, and distributing pamphlets such as the third edition of "Operation Total Victory."[38] Primarily written by Banning Garrett, this report provided context for the Laos Invasion and warned of further escalations. We not only circulated it locally. We shipped thousands to other campuses and communities.

Anti-war activity continued, less intense, on campus through the end of the academic year. Most large demonstrations took place off campus, but there were small demonstrations at judicial hearings and at the Placement Center.

More nationally known peace advocates visited Stanford in 1971. On February 18 Chicago Seven (Eight) defense attorney William Kunstler spoke on a panel at the Stanford Law Forum "to an overflow audience of 400 at the Bishop Auditorium."[39] On March 29 activist actor Jane Fonda spoke to an overflow crowd at Dinkelspiel, after a performance by the satiric San Francisco MimeTroupe.[40] David Harris spoke to an audience of 2,400 in Memorial Church on

---

Crowd Attends Class," *Stanford Daily,* February 17, 1971, p. 1. archives.stanforddaily.com/1971/02/17?page=1&section=MODSMD _ARTICLE4#article

38. Banning Garrett, "Operation Total Victory: February, 1971," Pacific Studies Center. http://a3mreunion.org/archive/1970-1971/70-71_laos/ files_70-71_laos/70-71Laos_Total_Victory.pdf

39. Bob Litterman, "Justice: 'A Monstrous Lie,'" *Stanford Daily*, February 19, 1971, p. 1. archives.stanforddaily. com/1971/02/19?page=1&section=MODSMD_ARTICLE1#article

40. Don Lindemann, "Fonda Favors People's Treaty," *Stanford Daily,* March 30, 1971, p. 1. archives.stanforddaily. com/1971/03/30?page=1&section=MODSMD_ARTICLE2#article

April 2. His wife at the time, folk diva Joan Baez, sang "Carry it On," the theme song for their joint documentary.[41]

## Packard

On that very day the Inquisition and the Palo Alto Committee to Defend the Right to Live, a women's organization, announced plans to arrest Deputy Secretary of Defense David Packard for war crimes when he spoke at a banquet of the Western Electronics Manufacturers Association (WEMA) at Rickey's Hyatt House (nicknamed Hickey's Riot House) in Palo Alto on April 8. An anti-war coalition adopted the slogan, "Packard before Calley."[42]

Packard wasn't just a convenient target for a protest. He was an important symbol of what the Stanford Movement was up against. He was a high-tech pioneer and at the time one of the wealthiest men in Silicon Valley, before it earned that nickname. He was a Director of Lockheed before Nixon tapped his management skills to essentially become the Pentagon's chief operating officer. He also had appeared to be a leader of the Stanford Board of Trustees' intransigence in response to Movement demands to demilitarize the university. Finally, there were so many Hewlett-Packard directors on the Stanford Board that I sometimes referred to Stanford/H-P as one corporation. I later learned that Valley leaders considered him a brilliant manager who brought many innovations to the high-tech workplace, but his support for the War was undeniable.

To avoid a confrontation, at the last moment WEMA moved the dinner to the Imperial Ballroom—an appropriate moniker— at the San Francisco Hilton, forty miles away. Because of the change, only 600 of the 700 with tickets to the speech and dinner were able to attend.

---

41. "Harris Plea: 'Revolutionary Love,'" *Stanford Daily,* April 5, 1971, p. 1. archives.stanforddaily.com/1971/04/05?page=1&section=MODSMD_ARTICLE1#article

42. Lt. William Calley was a U.S. Army officer convicted of mass murder for the March 1968 massacre of Vietnamese civilians at My Lai.

Confused by press announcements, only 200 protestors rallied in Palo Alto Square at 5:30 pm on April 8, where a march to Rickey's had been planned to start. Car pools were organized, and the demonstrators from Palo Alto were joined by a number of hastily-mobilized people from San Francisco. No real attempt was made to arrest Packard in San Francisco, as security at the Hilton was tight. Demonstrators simply picketed and chanted. Apparently using the excuse of "cursing," the San Francisco police Tactical Squad declared the demonstration an unlawful assembly, and they charged the crowd. Seven people were arrested. Several were beaten.

The People's Peace Treaty Collective in Palo Alto, one of the sponsoring organizations, called the move to S.F. a victory, stating that "David Packard is afraid to return to the city that he owns." Packard was on leave as Board Chairman of Hewlett-Packard, Palo Alto's largest private company. A member of *Venceremos* called the action a "People's Injunction," noting that while several area radicals had been banned from the Stanford academic campus by court injunction, Packard was banned from Palo Alto by the "People's Arrest Warrant." None of us could recall a similar relocation of an appearance by a major administration official.

Packard's speech was misleadingly entitled, "The Department of Defense in a Generation of Peace." He criticized WEMA for moving the speech:

> It is unfortunate that the leaders of this industry are unwilling to stand up to that bunch of radicals down on the Peninsula. The David Harrises, Jane Fondas, and all those what support them are your deadly enemies. They want to destroy you, me, and everything this nation stands for. Do not let them do it.[43]

---

43. This quote and much of this section are from a contemporaneous report that I wrote up on February 9. Lenny Siegel, "Packard Flees Arrest," April 9, 1971.
http://a3mreunion.org/archive/1970-1971/70-71_packard/files_70-71_packard/70-71Packard_Arrest_Packard_3.pdf

In his presentation, Packard accurately prophesized, "The nation will increasingly rely on machines rather than men to preserve its strength around the world." As the Nixon administration "Vietnamized" ground combat—that is, reducing the role of U.S. Army and Marine ground combat fighters—it was relying increasingly on what was known as the automated battlefield and the air war. This is what we were already researching at the Pacific Studies Center.

Nationally, on April 23, more than 800 anti-war Vietnam veterans turned in their medals on the steps of the U.S. Capitol, and the following day hundreds of thousands of protestors marched in the streets of D.C., while hundreds of us from Stanford joined the crowd of 150,000 that rallied against the war at the Polo Grounds in San Francisco's Golden Gate Park. A week later thousands were arrested trying to shut down the federal government by blocking commuter traffic in DC. Palo Alto-area activists threatened to shut down SRI's main campus in Menlo Park, but the small crowd of demonstrators was overwhelmed by a major, pre-emptive police presence.

## Labor and the Hospital Sit-In

People on the radical Left have always had an affinity for the labor movement. I grew up learning songs of the labor movement, and while at Stanford I read a great deal of labor history. Many of us romanticized the labor movement, supporting strikes and fighting for racial and gender equity within the labor movement. Some activists, such as Progressive Labor, the RU, and Venceremos for a while, saw workers as the heart of a radical or revolutionary movement. Others were more skeptical, viewing class struggle through a more complicated lens.

As a working class kid, I was influenced by my father's lack of confidence in the people he worked with. So while I supported labor organizing, particularly among lower-income workers such as the California farm workers, I did not think organized labor, even radical elements within organized labor, would spearhead fundamental change within the U.S. When I

221

worked at the Stanford Bookstore, I attended meetings of United Stanford Employees (USE), a new effort to represent non-faculty university employees. Though a number of the leaders were peace activists or members of radical groups, I was struck that the average employee was most concerned about issues that at the time I considered mundane, such as getting good health insurance!

As I spent more time studying the Silicon Valley electronics industry, I learned that this industry, which most people thought staffed primarily by technical professionals, was built on the backs of women factory workers, primarily non-white, in both Asia and in the U.S. For many years I worked informally with a network of researchers learning about this tech division of labor and providing information and analysis to organizers on both continents.

Though I remained focused on getting Stanford out of the war, many of my friends, particularly those aligned with Venceremos, emphasized labor organizing. After twelve employees were laid off at the Tresidder student union, they organized a boycott in an attempt to force re-hiring. After library worker John Keilch was suspended for his participation in the Lodge heckling event, United Stanford Employees led protests demanding his reinstatement.

But the biggest labor conflict in the spring of 1971 was the struggle to rehire Sam Bridges, a black maintenance worker at the Stanford Hospital, led by the Black United Front and supported by USE and Venceremos. Negotiations culminated in an initially peaceful sit-in at the hospital, on April 8, the same evening as the Packard confrontation in San Francisco. Since I was focused on the Packard protest, I only have second-hand knowledge of what happened at the hospital.

*Venceremos* reported:

> On Friday evening, April 9th, 175 members of the Palo Alto Police Force and the Santa Clara County Tactical Squad launched a brutal attack on a peaceful sit-in that was taking place in the administrative corridor of the Stanford Hospital. The sixty unarmed

protesters fought courageously for 45 minutes against battering rams, clubs and mace before being driven from the hallway.[44]

The *Daily,* in a special Sunday edition," reported that two dozen demonstrators and 13 police were injured.[45]

This was the most violent sit-in in Stanford history. I can only speculate why it turned out that way. First, many of the demonstrators were African-American, drawing the ire of racist police officers. Second, this was the only Stanford sit-in where demonstrators barricaded themselves inside a building. And third, the hospital is a good distance from the main campus, so there were no large crowds of students outside, observing.

That 30-hour sit-in ended up triggering a long legal battle testing the limits of the First Amendment to the U.S. Constitution:

> In an apparently unprecedented action, four Palo Alto and two Stanford policemen, using a search warrant to gain entry, thoroughly searched the offices of the *Daily* yesterday seeking evidence that might lead to new prosecutions for last Friday's violent hospital sit-in. The officers left empty-handed after spending nearly an hour searching the entire office including photo files, desks, personal correspondence, and several garbage cans.[46]

They found nothing, because a *Daily* photographer had placed an envelope containing the photographs in the mail.

---

44. "But Why the Hospital," *Venceremos,* April, 1971. http://a3mreunion.org/archive/1970-1971/70-71_hospital_sit-in/files_70-71_hospital_sit-in/70-71HospitalSit-In_Why_the_Hospital.pdf
45. Ed Kohn, "Police Break Up Hospital Sit-In," *Stanford Daily,* April 11, 1971, p. 1. archives.stanforddaily.com/1971/04/11?page=1&section=MODSMD_ARTICLE1#article
46. Bob Litterman, "Police Search *'Daily'* for Evidence," *Stanford Daily,* April 13, 1971, p.1. https://archives.stanforddaily.com/1971/04/13?page=1&section=MODSMD_ARTICLE1#article

The *Daily* went to court to challenge the search warrant, and it found support from the national news media and even Stanford President Richard Lyman. In October, 1972 District Judge Robert Peckham ruled in favor of the Daily, but it wasn't until early 1977 that a three-judge panel of the Ninth U.S. Circuit Court of Appeals upheld his finding that the search was unconstitutional.[47]

---

47. Bob Beyers, "Palo Alto Police use of a search warrant...," Stanford University News Service," February 4, 1977.
http://www.a3mreunion.org/archive/1970-1971/70-71_hospital_sit-in/files_70-71_hospital_sit-in/70-71HospitalSit-In_Press_5.pdf

# Chapter 9: The Struggles Continue—1971-72

I realize that the *Daily* does not have a comic page, but I am beginning to think that Lenny Siegel, "long time campus figure," and his Association of Young Crows is filling that vacuum.
*~Assistant Dean of Engineering Al Kirkland,*
*November, 1971*

By the fall of 1972, most of the students I knew from my early years at Stanford were gone, but a new generation of leaders stepped up to continue the struggles against war research, recruiting by the military and its contractors, and repression of the Movement. Those campaigns were interwoven throughout the academic year, escalating in spring quarter as President Nixon escalated the Indochina War. I was on campus less, spending most of my time at the Pacific Studies Center office in "Whiskey Gulch," the block of University Avenue in East Palo Alto but west of Highway 101.

However, my PSC colleagues and I continued to research and disseminate information about Stanford's role in an increasingly technological war that depended less and less on American ground combat troops. In 2009, when I last talked to Richard Lyman, I argued that Stanford's anti-war movement remained more vibrant than its counterparts on other campuses because of our unshrinking focus on the Community of Technical Scholars gone awry. Lyman seemed to understand my point because he saw Stanford as one of only a handful of America's "great research universities."

## Military-Sponsored Research

Back in 1969, in the wake of the April Third Movement, two physics graduate students and an undergraduate member of the Associated Students Council of Presidents formed the Stanford

225

Workshops on Political and Social Issues (SWOPSI). Under the sponsorship of faculty members, these were generally student-led teams that conducted original research.[1]

In the spring on 1971, a team of seven graduate students and two undergraduates, headed by Stanton Glantz, who was also a student member of the Committee on Research of the Academic Council, conducted a serious review of the remaining, hundred-plus Defense Department-sponsored contracts and grants at Stanford.[2] Eight of the nine were engineering or science majors. As background, Congress in 1969 had passed the first version of the Mansfield Amendment, which mandated:

> None of the funds authorized by this Act may be used to carry out any research project or study unless such project or study has a direct and apparent relationship to a specific military function.[3]

In Volume I, the SWOPSI researchers found that university documents, supplied primarily by faculty principal investigators, consistently described projects without mentioning their military

---

1. Joel Primack and Frank von Hippel, "Public Interest Science in the University: The Stanford Workshops on Political and Social Issues," *Advice and Dissent: Scientists in the Political Arena* (New York: Basic Books, 1974). https://dynamics.org/SWOPSI/ADVICE_AND_DISSENT/

2. Glantz *et al.*, *DOD Sponsored Research at Stanford,* Stanford Workshop on Political and Social Issues. *Volume I: Two Perceptions. The Investigator's and the Sponsor's.* June, 1971. *Volume II: The Impact on the University,* November, 1971.

3. This was first enacted as Section 203 of the Defense Authorization Act of 1970. An editorial in *Analytical Chemistry* warned at the time, "In university circles, the Mansfield Amendment is bound to play into the hands of campus radicals who will not acknowledge the possibility that basic research relevant to a military invasion can also be beneficial to the peaceful pursuits of society." Herbert Laitenen, Editor, "Reverberations from the Mansfield Amendment," *Analytical Chemistry,* June 1, 1970, p. 689. https://pubs.acs.org/doi/pdf/10.1021/ac60289a600

applications. The Department of Defense (DOD) listed the same projects with explicit reference to their potential military applications. In the second volume, the student researchers concluded:

> Although proposals for research contracts may reflect the wide range of interests of scientific and engineering scholars, the Defense Department, through a process of natural selection, can decide what is studied and what is not. This judgment does not deny the existence of non-military applications of much DOD sponsored research and development (DOD classifies about fifteen percent of Stanford's projects as exploratory, advanced, or engineering development), but when assessing DOD's impact on the University, this random civilian "spillover" must be contrasted with the systematically organized program to develop military technology that underlies every DOD decision to fund or not to fund a proposal.[4]

The SWOPSI team observed that Stanford "gently pressures many faculty towards DOD projects," because research funding helped to pay faculty salaries and graduate student stipends; funded equipment and computer time; and provided substantial amounts of money to the university as overhead (indirect costs), helping to pay for new buildings and infrastructure.[5] They warned:

> This policy has its costs: Stanford is severely dependent on the federal government, in particular the Department of Defense. Pressures tend to locate the decision on which technologies to develop in Washington, leaving the faculty free only to decide how to develop them. In seeking this funding, the University has perverted academic freedom

---

4. Glantz *et al.*, Volume II, page 4.
5. In 1989 Stanford's excessive indirect cost charges became a scandal, leading to the firing of Stanford News Service's Bob Beyers for his honest reporting. See Chapter 6.

over the last twenty-five years. Stanford's fiscal policies, combined with the DOD's well-managed program of supporting research and development with high military potential, have skewed the academic development of significant portions of the University, particularly Engineering, Applied Physics and Computer Science.[6]

This was music to my ears. A group of highly motivated engineering and science students had come to the same conclusion as I: Defense Department funding at Stanford was not only supporting the war effort. It was limiting our academic choices.

Meanwhile, my PSC colleagues and I continued to learn how Stanford-related technologies were becoming increasingly important in the war effort. I regularly read the Association of Old Crows' *Electronic Warfare* magazine, later known as *Defense Electronics.* Electronic intelligence, radar-jamming and spoofing technology, and Wild Weasel radar-destroying systems made the air war possible.[7]

We also researched the "automated battlefield," the applications of surveillance and detection equipment, navigation systems, and communications to combat. In October, 1971 PSC published my report, "Vietnam's Electronic Battlefield." I not only documented the advanced technologies that the U.S. was bringing to the war, I described their shortcomings, particularly as used to interdict men and materiel on the Ho Chi Minh Trail:

---

6. Glantz *et al.*, Volume II, pages 4-5.

7. I recall a story about how the North Vietnamese attempted to overcome America's superiority in electronic warfare. I don't remember where I heard it, and I don't know whether it's true. When a plane flew over a location, a "sentry" would phone twenty miles ahead, so defenders there could shoot their guns into the air in the hope of intercepting the planes. In the 1990s, I was on an environmental committee with a scientist who was a top Defense official during the war. I asked him about this strategy. He said the warning system was simpler: Vietnamese agents at U.S. airbases in South Vietnam would radio ahead to North Vietnam, warning about incoming planes and their missions.

> Tom Lehrer once wrote a song about the deer hunter
> that killed "Two Game Wardens, Seven Hunters, and
> a Cow" by shooting at anything that moved. Despite
> America's technological accomplishments, the
> electronic battlefield can do no better. Many sensors
> cannot distinguish between mice and men, to say
> nothing of tigers or water buffalo. Early reports of
> unattended sensor use mentioned that devices were
> often set off by rain and even the wind rustling the
> elephant grass....
>
> The most difficult problem, of course, is detecting
> which people are "enemy," "friendly," or "neutral."[8]

This challenge, determining what is in the hearts and minds of
local populations in war zones, remains a major obstacle to U.S.
war efforts nearly 50 years later.

At the start of fall quarter, a bunch of us started a new
organization to pick up where the New Left Project left off.
We called ourselves the Association of Young Crows so people
would ask who the Old Crows—the electronic warfare specialists
I described in Chapter 6—were. I believe the emphasis on
"young" was because many of the most active members were
undergraduates who had arrived at Stanford since the Cambodia
strike. We handed out copies of a Pacific Studies Center
publication, "From Our Past," that contained selected Stanford
Movement documents from 1967 through 1971.[9]

We inserted fliers describing the goals and methods of the
Young Crows. We explained:

---

8. Lenny Siegel, "Vietnam's Electronic Battlefield," *Pacific Research
& World Empire Telegram,* Volume II, Number 1, September-October,
1971, page 7.
http://a3mreunion.org/archive/1971-1972/71-72_war_research/
files_71-72_war_research/71-72Research_VEB.pdf
9. "From Our Past," Pacific Studies Center, October, 1971.
a3mreunion.org/archive/1971-1972/71-72/files_71-72/71-72_From_
Our_Past_1-3.pdf

We will continually point out the non-democratic dichotomy between the Stanford Corporation and the Stanford Community. That any community be controlled by a tiny minority of its members (and non-members) is unacceptable, especially when the decisions reached regarding the resources of that community have very real consequences for human beings all over the world.[10]

We also promised, "We will present information and arguments concerning these issues in a joyful and imaginative manner."[11]

It didn't take long for us to find an opportunity to question the undemocratic nature of Stanford in an imaginative way. On October 6, 1971, the *Daily* reported that Joseph Pettit, Dean of the Engineering School for the previous 12 years, was leaving Stanford to become President of the Georgia Institute of Technology, commonly known as Georgia Tech.[12]

I quickly announced that I was running for Dean, and I ordered "Lenny for Dean" buttons. People reacted by saying that one cannot run for Dean. I responded, "That's the point." In late November, Al Kirkland, Assistant Dean of Engineering, without mentioning his position, wrote a letter to the *Daily* ridiculing my campaign and other activities.[13] I immediately retorted with my own letter:

I just read Al Kirkland's letter in Monday's *Daily*. I think people should know that Kirkland is Assistant Dean of Engineering and has hopes for promotion to

---

10. "Who Are We? What Do We Believe?" Association of Young Crows, October, 1971. a3mreunion.org/archive/1971-1972/71-72/files_71-72/71-72_Young_Crows.pdf

11. *ibid.*

12. Daniel Brenner, "Dean Pettit To Head Georgia Tech," *Stanford Daily,* October 6, 1971, p. 1. archives.stanforddaily.com/1971/10/06?page=1&section=MODSMD_ARTICLE3#article

13. Al Kirkland, "Edit Page Monopoly," *Stanford Daily,* November 29, 1971, p. 3. archives.stanforddaily.com/1971/11/29?page=3&section=MODSMD_ARTICLE10#article

> Dean. I hope in the future that all candidates for Dean
> will wage principled campaigns on this issue, and
> refrain from personal attacks.[14]

Kirkland actually was not much more likely to become Dean than I was, but I was glad he took my bait and helped underscore that key decisions about Stanford's importance to the military-industrial complex were not made by the full Stanford community.

The Young Crows built support by holding popcorn parties in dorms, explaining to new undergraduates how Stanford contributed to the Indochina War. In mid-October, to make more accessible the wealth of information in Volume I of the SWOPSI report, we launched the Red Hot Professor contest, a take-off on a minor Stanford tradition. The conventional Red Hot Professor contest was a charity drive in which students voted, paying cash, for their favorite professors. I think I wanted to call ours the Reds' Hot Professor contest, but our flier says otherwise.

We listed 20 Defense contracts, and we asked people to pay a penny for a positive vote and a nickel for a subtracted vote. Voters could target their donation for the Young Crows, anti-war sailors of the *U.S.S. Coral Sea,* or Medical Aid to North Vietnam. Almost all of the contracts were engineering studies that were designed to serve as building blocks for the weapons of Vietnam and subsequent wars.[15] But there was a dark horse.

Number 20 on the alphabetical list was a project conducted by popular, anti-war Psychology professor Philip Zimbardo. The results of Zimbardo's famous summer, 1971 prison experiment, in which assigned student "guards" became abusive as they

---

14. Lenny Siegel, "Personal Attacks," *Stanford Daily,* December 1, 1971, p. 2. archives.stanforddaily.com/1971/12/01?page=2&section=MODSMD_ARTICLE6#article

15. "Official Ballot: Red Hot Professor Contest," Association of Young Crows, October 16, 1971. http://a3mreunion.org/archive/1971-1972/71-72_war_research/files_71-72_war_research/71-72Research_Red_Hot_1-3.pdf

assumed their roles, had just been made public.[16] People at Stanford were surprised to learn that Zimbardo had a Defense contract, and that the Defense Department's description of the contract seemed aimed at anti-war GIs. The *Daily* reported on the SWOPSI findings:

> Zimbardo's research proposal outlined the goal of the work as "the discovery of the causal variables underlying violence and other forms of anti-social behavior. Not only is this class of behavior of tremendous social and practical concern, but it has vast theoretical significance for understanding the interaction of group and individual variables."

> The DOD's stated purpose is more specific as to the applications of this research. "U.S. military forces have recently experienced an apparent upsurge of problems involving negative reactions to authority, insufficient loyalty to the organization, failure to maintain (and even sabotage of) valuable government property, and racial conflict. This research aims at the production of a set of behavioral principles which could reduce the incidence of such undesirable behavior in the Navy and Marine Corps."[17]

Zimbardo won the contest, but that didn't keep the Young Crows from conducting a November 17 tour of the engineering buildings associated with the military work. Some of the professors defended their work, emphasizing the non-military applications. We presented the top contenders with gag gifts, the

---

16. Andy Israel, "Prison Experiment Too Realistic," *Stanford Daily,* October 12, 1971, p.1. archives.stanforddaily. com/1971/10/12?page=1&section=MODSMD_ARTICLE1#article In 2015 the Prison Experiment was made into a feature film.
17. Phil Revzin, "SWOPSI Course Reveals 19 Defense Contracts," *Stanford Daily,* October 4, 1971, p. 1. archives.stanforddaily.com/1971/10/04?page=1&section=MODSMD_ARTICLE2#article See also Glantz *et al.,* Volume I, pp. 285 ff.

most expensive of which was a bottle of Old Crow bourbon, which we left at William Rambo's office.[18] The tour set the stage for multiple protests at these buildings in winter and spring quarters.

On that tour I explained radar and countermeasures to a crowd predominantly made up of humanities undergraduates, sitting and milling in the hallway of the McCullough engineering labs. I said if you were sightless and wanted to know how far away the wall was, you could throw a ball and note how long it took to bounce back. That's radar. Countermeasures is the science of deflecting, catching, or destroying the ball, or perhaps throwing back several balls. Afterwards, one of the engineering profs complimented me, saying that this was the kind of description they wanted to hear from their graduate students.

Throughout the rest of the academic year, I would speak at rallies, marches, and teach-ins about the military applications of Defense-sponsored research at Stanford. I even created a one-man guerilla theater skit to explain both the power and the folly of the electronic battlefield. I performed it, among other times, at a January 10, 1972 rally outside the Business School:

> In the most entertaining speech of the afternoon, Young Crow Lenny Siegel, dressed in Army fatigues and a helmet and identifying himself as Captain Seagull of the Air Force, displayed "the latest technological advance," a "gook detector." It was a heater mounted on a cardboard box wired to a piece of styrofoam and headsets.
>
> Siegel said, "All we need is a volunteer to go over to Vietnam and plug it in."[19]

---

18. Robert Bacon, "Young Crows Present 'Red Hot Professor' Awards," *Stanford Daily,* November 18, 1971, p. 6 archives.stanforddaily.com/1971/11/18?page=6&section=MODSMD_ARTICLE22#article
19. Jonathan Dedmon, "Protestors Invade Biz School, DoD Recruiters Already Gone," *Stanford Daily,* January 11, 1972, p. 1. https://archives.stanforddaily.com/1972/01/11?page=1&section=MODSMD_ARTICLE2#article See the *Daily* photo.

## Dis-Placement

In addition to research and development, Stanford contributed to the war effort by funneling skilled professionals into positions with military contractors as well as federal agencies that were directly engaged in Southeast Asia, so recruiting by war-related institutions was a recurring target of the Movement, beginning, as far as I know, with the October 1967 anti-CIA demonstration. In the fall of 1971, activists from the Young Crows, Venceremos, Columbae House, and Stanford Women for Peace came together to once again protest corporate and military recruiters at the campus Career Placement Center, conveniently located at the foot of White Plaza.

While at times protestors essentially chased recruiters off the Stanford campus, I don't think anyone indulged in the misconception that we could keep students who wanted war-related jobs from connecting with prospective employers. The demonstrations were symbolic, but in the long run I think we were largely successful in causing graduating and graduate students to think twice before taking such jobs.

The campaign drew additional support in the fall of 1971 when the moderate Associated Students Council of Presidents[20] stepped forward and opposed military-related recruiting. On October 27, they wrote the Director of the Placement Service:

> We are deeply distressed at the news that you have scheduled two United States Military services and eight major military contractors to recruit at the Placement Center next week. We are distressed not merely because of the intimate involvement of these organizations with the making of war, but also because

"Gook" was the most common racial pejorative used by American troops to refer to Vietnamese.

20. Starting the spring of 1969, many candidates for student body president formed slates of co-presidents. This promoted greater symbolic diversity, but I hesitate to call it power-sharing because student government was essentially powerless.

this type of recruiting was specifically prohibited in the student referendum passed in last Spring's student body elections.[21]

They added:

> The issue goes far beyond the problem of military recruiting. The issue, it seems to us, is whether students are able to determine in an official referendum how their own facilities, at the very least, may be used. The Placement Center is a student facility, administered as a service to students.

The Council also sent letters to the organizations scheduled to recruit.

Not everyone on campus agreed. For example, in January 1972, 271 faculty members released a statement stating, "Restricting campus recruitment 'is not only offensive, but also impractical and unworkable in a university...'" They made a free speech argument:

> Unless we protect the minority who hold the unpopular, or as some think, immoral views—yes, even those who would interview with General Motors or Honeywell—then no minority and no individual is safe here.[22]

But the argument was never about free speech. Protestors, the Council of Presidents, and their faculty supporters made it clear: The recruiters were welcome to visit Stanford to discuss their policies and contracts, but not to recruit.

21. Larry Diamond, Diane Fields, Anne Kimball, and Doug McHenry, Letter to Ralph Keller, October 27, 1971, p. 1. http://a3mreunion. org/archive/1971-1972/71-72_recruiting/files_71-72_recruiting/71-72Recruiting_to_Keller.pdf

22. "Restricting campus recruitment...," Stanford University News Service, January 6, 1972. http://a3mreunion.org/archive/1971-1972/71-72_recruiting/files_71-72_recruiting/Restricting_Recruitment.pdf

Someone in the Movement put together a flier listing which entities were scheduled to recruit at the Placement Center November 1-5, 1971, and describing their military contracts. The Air Force entry simply stated, "Only we can prevent forests," a reference to the U.S. chemical (Agent Orange) defoliation program in Indochina.[23]

There were rallies and Placement Center protests all week. Demonstrators sought to debate the war with recruiters. The high point was probably Thursday, May 4. After a rally addressed by Princeton Professor Richard Falk, a war crimes expert, as many as 150 protestors "milled in" at the Placement Center, preventing representatives from Honeywell from conducting recruiting interviews. Honeywell had become a target of anti-war protest because of its manufacture of anti-personnel cluster munitions.[24] For their actions that day, four undergraduates were later charged with violation of the university's policy against disruptions.

There were several other anti-recruiting demonstrations, targeting, among others, FMC Corporation, the Navy, and the Marines. In mid-February, President Lyman warned that barring military recruiters could cost the university $16.4 million in Defense and NASA contracts, claiming that such a policy would affect one thousand "faculty, students, research associates, and staff dependent on these funds."[25] While Lyman was trying to line up the thousand contract-dependent people in support of "open recruiting," activists were not at all worried. We saw contracts and recruiting as two sides of the same coin. We would have been happy if limits on recruitment had hampered military contracts on campus. On similar lines, one of the student body

23. "Career Placement Interviews—Nov. 1-5," October, 1971 http://a3mreunion.org/archive/1971-1972/71-72_recruiting/files_71-72_recruiting/71-72Recruiting_Interview_Schedule.pdf

24. "Caution: Honeywell May Be Hazardous to Your Health." http://a3mreunion.org/archive/1971-1972/71-72_recruiting/files_71-72_recruiting/71-72Recruiting_Honeywell.pdf

25. "Barring Military Recruiting," Stanford University News Service, February 16, 1972. http://a3mreunion.org/archive/1971-1972/71-72_recruiting/files_71-72_recruiting/Cost_of_Barring.pdf

co-presidents reported in November that Lyman had argued that the university shouldn't exclude recruiters from companies that donate to the university.[26]

After the spring 1971 student referendum President Lyman asked the Committee on Services to Students for advice on recruiting policy. Made up of five students and four faculty and administrators, the Committee published its report in the March 9, 1972 *Daily* after taking testimony from both proponents and opponents of restricted, or "selective" recruiting. The Committee unanimously recommended that students be provided with more information about the activities of recruiting organizations, and by an 8 to 1 vote it urged that recruiters from the armed services be excluded from campus. It split on the issue of recruiting by war-related industries, with five committee members rejecting such a restriction.[27]

Lyman responded immediately, accepting the recommendations that more information be provided. Otherwise, he argued against restrictions, but he said he would seek additional advice from faculty leadership. He made it clear, however, that he would be making the final decision.[28] To my knowledge, Stanford never officially restricted recruiting by the military or its contractors.

## The Pied Piper

In January, 1972 Stanford University took the unusual, perhaps unprecedented step of firing a tenured professor, H. Bruce Franklin for acts of speech. The firing unleashed criticism, militant on-campus protest, and litigation that

26. David Thiemann, "Coalition Pickets Placement Office," *Stanford Daily*, November 2, 1971, p. 1. archives.stanforddaily.com/1971/11/02?page=1&section=MODSMD_ARTICLE5#article
27. Committee on Services to Students Report on Recruitment Policies," *Stanford Daily*, March 9, 1972, pp. 4 ff. archives.stanforddaily.com/1972/03/09?page=4&section=MODSMD_ARTICLE13#article
28. "President Lyman's Response to Report," *Stanford Daily*, March 9, 1972, p. 5. archives.stanforddaily.com/1972/03/09?page=5&section=MODSMD_ARTICLE14#article

eventually failed. Franklin went on to teach at New Jersey's Rutgers University. The English professor was not fired for weak scholarship. He was widely recognized for his expertise on Herman Melville and science fiction.[29] He was not fired for his actions. His charges were essentially inciting others to do what everyone knew they were going to do anyhow. He was fired because the FBI, Stanford Trustees, right-wing alumni, and many faculty believed he was, like the mythical Pied Piper of Hamelin, leading upper-class and upper-middle-class youth down a revolutionary path.

Franklin first caught the FBI's attention in 1966, as he participated in anti-war demonstrations such at the Stanford Committee for Peace in Vietnam's anti-napalm protests in Redwood City. Undercover agents monitored his activities and spied on his family. After Franklin spent the 1966-67 academic year at Stanford in France, the FBI upped its surveillance:

> He became the object of an illegal campaign by the government known as COINTELPRO, an organized effort implemented by the FBI to "discredit" and "neutralize" Prof. Franklin and his political associations as part of a massive drive to subvert the so-called "New Left."[30]

29. In the early 1990s I had the pleasure of taking my two children through the "Star Trek" exhibit at the Smithsonian Air & Space Museum in DC. Thoughtfully curated by Franklin, it explained the relationship of the pathfinding TV series to the civil rights and peace movements.

30. Press Statement, Colorado American Civil Liberties Union (ACLU), October 14, 1976, p.3. http://a3mreunion.org/archive/1971-1972/71-72_franklin_fbi/files_71-72_fbi/71-72FranklinFBI_ACLU.pdf This rather thorough memo is based upon 194 pages of documents obtained through the Freedom of Information Act. Nearly all of the documents are available at http://a3mreunion.org/archive/1971-1972/71-72_franklin_fbi/1971-1972_fbi-cointelpro-docs.html For other summaries of the documents, see "1971-1972: Franklin Firing: FBI COINTELPRO," April Third Movement Historical Archive. a3mreunion.org/archive/1971-1972/71-72_franklin_fbi/1971-1972_fbi.html

The FBI fabricated correspondence to and from Franklin, and it created false rumors designed to damage his reputation. Most pertinent, the FBI's campaign included:

> Using "cooperative news media sources" to have false and misleading information published about Franklin and then anonymously distributing copies to selected individuals for the purpose of getting him fired from his teaching position at Stanford, keeping him from getting a job after he had been fired, and generally "discrediting" and "neutralizing" him.[31]

The FBI actually sent news articles and a "circular" to "parents of Stanford students, selected alumni and Board of Trustee members 'encouraging them to take positive action ... and insist that Franklin be removed from his position at Stanford.'"[32]

The ACLU wrote that the FBI and its collaborators distorted Franklin's revolutionary ideas, but they didn't need to. Franklin had returned from France as a dedicated Maoist. He formed the Peninsula Red Guard, joined with others to form the Revolutionary Union, and then led a split in that organization to form the Venceremos Organization. He wrote a column on guns under a pseudonym. Even the pure truth was enough to scare the people who ran the university as well as many who sent their children there.

In fact, the articulate, dedicated Franklin was winning over the children of America's elite, but if anything, the establishment attacks on him enhanced his influence. It's important to recognize that Franklin's detractors considered him a menace because he was winning over students and others to his ideas, not because of any specific actions he had taken. As such, the campaign to fire Franklin was a direct attack on tenure, the promise that faculty were free to espouse their ideas.

---

31. *ibid.*, p. 1
32. *ibid.*, p. 4

Franklin was not the only tenured faculty member who took part in "disruptive" student protests. In particular, I remember Charles Stein, called by the Stanford News Service the Einstein of the Statistics Department. Stein often took part in sit-ins and sent funds to support Movement publications, but he was older and less charismatic than Franklin. If the real reason to seek Franklin's firing had been to prevent faculty participation in disruptive activities, Lyman would have gone after Stein.[33]

The January 11, 1971 shouting down of Henry Cabot Lodge gave Lyman the pretext to discipline Franklin. Hoover moderator Berkeley Tomkins had picked Franklin out of the crowd.[34] At the time, it looked like a set-up.

On February 10, hundreds of students protesting the Laos Invasion had occupied the Computation Center after learning that an SRI researcher was gaming amphibious assaults there. Lyman charged Franklin with inciting the occupation, even though anyone familiar with intra-Movement debates knew that he went along reluctantly. Franklin used his White Plaza speech to try to convince protesters that a "strike" was a better strategy.

After about three hours the police showed up, and demonstrators left the building without incident. Then Sergeant Don Tamm of the Santa Clara County Sheriff's office ordered the crowd to disperse. I wasn't there, but reading the various accounts of what happened, Franklin argued with Tamm that there was no reason for such an order. The crowd at that point included people who had been part of the occupation and others, such as Franklin, who had not gone inside. Lyman charged Franklin with inciting demonstrators to resist the order to disperse. Notably, criminal charges against those arrested for refusing to disperse at that point were dropped.

---

33. "Charles M. Stein, Extraordinary Statistician and Anti-War Activist, Dies at 96," Stanford University News Service, December 1, 2016. news.stanford.edu/2016/12/01/charles-m-stein-extraordinary-statistician-anti-war-activist-dies-96/
34. See Chapter 8.

That evening, hundreds of protestors gathered in the Old Union Courtyard. Franklin, among others, gave two speeches urging action. Again, he was charged with inciting disruptive, potentially injurious conduct. However, anyone who followed such evening rallies knew that militant action was a foregone conclusion. Rather than incite disruption or destruction, Franklin was attempting to provide ideological context.

In late March, Lyman filed charges with the Advisory Board of the Academic Council, made up of seven senior faculty members. He asserted that Franklin had violated the Trustees' Statement of Policy on Appointment and Tenure at Stanford University.[35]

The trial began at the start of fall quarter, 1971. The open hearings lasted 33 days. The proceedings had many of the trappings of a criminal trial, but it lacked a clear statute against which to measure Franklin's activities. "Franklin's hearing involved 165 hours of testimony and over 100 witnesses." Among the prosecution witnesses was Bob Beyers of the so-called Stanford News Service. "The administration and Franklin placed in evidence 227 photographs and 136 other exhibits."[36] As the hearing closed, Franklin received support from the *Stanford Daily's* editors[37] and nearly four dozen other faculty members, including Linus Pauling.

I appeared on October 13, testifying that Franklin had not shouted down Lodge. Based on news articles reporting on my testimony and three others, the FBI actually initiated inquiries,

35. Richard W. Lyman, "Statement of Charges in the Matter of Associate Professor Howard Bruce Franklin," Before the Advisory Board of the Academic Council, Stanford University, March 26, 1971. http://a3mreunion.org/archive/1971-1972/71-72_franklin_advisory/files_71-72_advisory/71-72FranklinBoard_Charges.pdf

36. Larry Liebert, "Franklin Makes Final Arguments as 33-Day Hearing Concludes," *Stanford Daily,* November 8, 1971, p. 1. https://archives.stanforddaily.com/1971/11/08?page=1&section=MODSMD_ARTICLE1#article

37. Editorial, "Reinstate Franklin," *Stanford Daily,* November 8, 1971, p. 2. https://archives.stanforddaily.com/1971/11/08?page=2&section=MODSMD_ARTICLE5#article

because of our testimony, to determine whether we were affiliated with Venceremos or other "subversive" organizations. At least in my case, that memo illustrated how poorly informed the FBI was about the Movement that it was harassing.[38]

On January 5 the Advisory Board issued its report, recommending by a 5 to 2 vote that Franklin be dismissed. Board chair and future Stanford President Donald Kennedy and Robert McAfee Brown instead supported a suspension. Ironically, the board unanimously could not sustain the only charge in which Franklin was accused of directly engaging in disruption, the shouting down of Henry Cabot Lodge. Perhaps my testimony was persuasive. In ruling out lesser penalties, the Board majority wrote:

> We are highly dubious whether rehabilitation is a useful concept in this case. Professor Franklin's announced convictions about the guilt of the university appear deeply-held, and his opposition to the institution in its present form seems implacable.

Reading the Board's findings carefully, it is clear that the majority was indeed responding to Franklin's views. They declared:

> Professor Franklin engages in a pattern of conduct that constitutes a continual challenge to the institution... This pattern of conduct, however, is guided by a set of perceptions which differ markedly from those of most faculty members: Professor Franklin views the University as a central agent in domestic repression and in an imperialist foreign policy.[39]

---

38. FBI SAC San Francisco, "The '*San Francisco Chronicle*' edition....," November 17, 1971. http://a3mreunion.org/archive/1971-1972/71-72_franklin_fbi/files_cointelpro/FBI_711117.pdf

39. Advisory Board of the Academic Council, Stanford University, "Discussion of Sanctions," *Stanford Daily,* January 6, 1972, p. 6. https://archives.stanforddaily.com/1972/01/06?page=6&section=MODSMD_ARTICLE14#article and Donald Kennedy *et al.,* "Summary of Advisory Committee

On January 9, Lyman accepted the dismissal recommendation. On the 22nd, with 120 protesters chanting outside in the San Francisco rain, the Board of Trustees upheld Lyman's action by a 20 to 2 vote. Ignoring the obvious reality of political persecution, Board President Robert Minge Brown immediately wrote the entire faculty:

> We assure you that the principles of academic freedom will continue unimpaired at Stanford University with the wholehearted support of the Board of Trustees. We believe that the Stanford community should recognize that, as stated by the Advisory Board in its decision, "The real issue in these hearings is Professor Franklin's behavior on the offenses charged, not his political views."[40]

The Advisory Board recommendation and subsequent implementation were greeted with widespread surprise and opposition. English Department Chair Bliss Carnochan called it "retaliation."[41] Linus Pauling called the decision "a great blow not just to academic freedom but to freedom of speech."[42] The *Daily* editorialized that the decision was "outrageous." The student government Council of Presidents attacked it as "insidiously twisted."

Report," January 5, 1972, p. ix. http://www.a3mreunion.org/archive/1971-1972/71-72_franklin_advisory/files_71-72_advisory/71-72FranklinBoard_Summary_of_Report.pdf

40. Robert Minge Brown, "To the Stanford Faculty," Stanford University Board of Trustees, January 23, 1972. http://a3mreunion.org/archive/1971-1972/71-72_franklin/files_71-72_franklin_firing/71-72Franklin_from_Trustees.pdf

41. Larry Liebert, "Lyman Accepts Decision, Asks Franklin Dismissal," *Stanford Daily,* January 10, 1972, p. 1. https://archives.stanforddaily.com/1972/01/10?page=1&section=MODSMD_ARTICLE3#article

42. Chris Peck and Glenn Garvin, "Campus Reaction Varies, Group Marches to Lyman,"*StanfordDaily,* January 6, 1972, p. 1. https://archives.stanforddaily.com/1972/01/06?page=1&section=MODSMD_ARTICLE1#article

**Fig. 9.1. Professors protest the prosecution of Bruce Franklin. Two-time Nobel Laureate Linus Pauling is wearing a home-made sign, "Try Lodge, Not Franklin." September 29, 1971**

Later, students voted support for Franklin:

> One of the largest groups in ASSU [Associated Students of Stanford University] history turned out Wednesday and yesterday for the referendum on Bruce Franklin, and 55 per cent of the voters indicated they want the suspended Maoist professor back.[43]

Speaking on campus that Friday, Daniel Ellsberg of *Pentagon Papers* fame called the firing "fatuous," stating:

> To talk about sitting in as violence in a Computation Center that's carrying on computations for amphibious assaults is absolutely absurd as a basis for dismissing a professor.[44]

43. Glenn Garvin, "Heavy Votes Favors Franklin's Retention," *Stanford Daily,* January 21, 1972, p. 1. https://archives.stanforddaily.com/1972/01/21?page=1&section=MODSMD_ARTICLE5#article

44. Robert Vining, "Ellsberg Labels Franklin Decision 'Fatuous,'"

The *Daily* sought my reaction, too:

> Lenny Siegel, Director of the Pacific Studies Center
> and professed candidate for Dean of Engineering,
> was hardly coherent for about two minutes after he
> was told of the decision. He finally managed to say
> that the verdict was "obviously an unjust response to
> pressure. I'd have to see the reasons they list before
> I can fully comment." "I will continue my campaign
> for Dean. I will not be intimidated," he added.[45]

Despite our ideological and strategic differences with
Franklin, anti-war activists from other campus factions
immediately joined Venceremos in protesting Franklin's ouster.
Though some of the Advisory Board members who voted for
Franklin's dismissal were on record against the Vietnam War,
they were defending the university's role in waging that war, as
well as other elements of domestic repression and imperialist
foreign policy. We knew that the actions that Franklin supposedly
incited still would have happened had he not been present.

A broad coalition formed the Stanford Rehabilitation
Movement, arguing that Stanford, not Bruce, needed to
be rehabilitated. Protests of Franklin's firing were woven
into demonstrations against military recruiters and military
contracting. There were many rallies, marches, and building
occupations.

One of the most unusual actions was the 350-strong
January 24 "eat-in" at the exclusive Faculty Club:

> While some food, mostly bread and pastries, was
> taken from the club kitchen, more substantial

---

*Stanford Daily,* January 10, 1972, p. 1.
https://archives.stanforddaily.com/1972/01/10?page=1&section=MODSMD_
ARTICLE1#article

45. Peck and Garvin, "Campus Reaction Varies..." *Stanford Daily,* January 6, 1972, p. 7. https://archives.stanforddaily.
com/1972/01/06?page=1&section=MODSMD_ARTICLE1#article

amounts were provided by residents of Columbae. The protestors took over the large dining room and, using the expensive silver and china place-settings, helped themselves to the food available. When they left at 6:30 p.m. more than $1,000 worth of silverware was missing.... After the main crowd left, several people stayed to help clean up...[46]

Most of us who "ate in" were unaware of the theft until it made the news.

With the support of the American Civil Liberties Union, Franklin challenged his firing in the state courts. The case dragged on for at least 15 years, but in the end the courts upheld the university.[47]

## Shockley

While Franklin was under attack from the right, progressive students targeted Electrical Engineering professor William Shockley and his racist views on human intelligence. Outside students disrupted one of his classes on January 18, and on February 3 a small group dressed as members of the Ku Klux Klan interrupted his class to award him a large wooden cross in "recognition for his furthering of racism and genocide."[48] These events precipitated the suspension and arrest of some of the demonstrators.

46. Bob Litterman, "Protesters Occupy Old Union, 350 Hold Eat-In at Faculty Club," *Stanford Daily,* January 25, 1972, p. 1. https://archives.stanforddaily.com/1972/01/25?page=1&section=MODSMD_ARTICLE2#article

47. See "1971-1972: Franklin Firing: Courts," April Third Movement HistoricalArchive. http://www.a3mreunion.org/archive/1971-1972/71-72_franklin_courts/1971-1972_courts.html

48. Bob Vining, "Shockley's Class Halted, Six Arrested by Police," *Stanford Daily,* February 4, 1972, p. 1. https://archives.stanforddaily.com/1972/02/04?page=1&section=MODSMD_ARTICLE1#article and Enid Hunkeler and Barbara Hyland, "KKK's Statement on Shockley," *Stanford Daily,* February 4, 1972, p. 2. https://archives.stanforddaily.com/1972/02/04?page=2&section=MODSMD_ARTICLE7#article

On February 16, 350 people attended a rally calling for Shockley's dismissal from the faculty. Shockley actually attended the rally and spoke in defense of his positions. The *Daily* reported:

> He said that he felt his proposed program of voluntary sterilization was necessary because of "the poor unfortunate illegitimate slum babies who have no shake" and are "disenfranchised and cut off from the mainstream of American life."[49]

Many on campus, particularly non-white students, had trouble understanding a construct of "academic freedom" that could protect Shockley's eugenics ideology but oust Bruce Franklin for anti-war protests.

At the time, few people in the Movement were familiar with Shockley's pivotal role in the development of the silicon-based semiconductor industry that soon was to give "Silicon Valley" its globally recognized nickname. Shockley was one of three men awarded the Nobel Prize in Physics in 1956 for inventing transistor technology at Bell Labs in the late 1940s. He returned to Palo Alto to teach at Stanford and form the Shockley Semiconductor Laboratory in Mountain View. Shockley was not an effective leader, so eight of his top employees left to form Fairchild Semiconductor, the first successful semiconductor company in Santa Clara Valley. Nearly all semiconductor companies in the Valley, which became known as Silicon Valley in the 1970s, descend from Fairchild.

So the site of Shockley Semiconductor is known as the birthplace of Silicon Valley. In August, 2018, while serving as Mayor of Mountain View, I spoke at a ceremony, attended by hundreds of current and former electronics professionals, celebrating that history with the opening of a monument in the middle of a new, commercial development, where Facebook

---

49. Rich Jaroslovsky, "350 Turn Out at Rally, Asking Shockley Ouster," *Stanford Daily,* February 17, 1972, p. 1. https://archives.stanforddaily.com/1972/02/17?page=1&section=MODSMD_ARTICLE2#article

employs a couple of thousand workers. Fortunately, that monument is a sculpture of the silicon atom, not Shockley. In the press coverage of the event, I was the only one who reminded people of Shockley's racist theories. I don't recall taking part in the anti-Shockley protests in 1972, but I remembered them.

### Packard and Agnew

In 1972 the Stanford Movement built on its tradition of protesting campus visits by current and former federal officials associated with the War, confronting them in the nearby community. On February 29 four to five hundred protestors mobilized by the ad hoc Committee for Just Rewards attempted to give David Packard the "Mad Bomber of the Year" award at Rickey's Hyatt House, while on April 8 a crowd of 1800 hoped to award Vice-President Spiro T. Agnew the "Mouthpiece of Empire" award at the Cabaña Hyatt House, on the other side of El Camino Real in Palo Alto.

I wrote a report about the Packard demonstration the next day:[50]

> Electronics tycoon and former Deputy Defense Secretary David Packard received two awards last night in his home town, Palo Alto. At a $10-a-plate dinner in the plush Rickey's Hyatt House, the Palo Alto Chamber of Commerce presented him with its "Distinguished Citizen Award." Outside, 400 to 500 chanting anti-war demonstrators attempted to crown Packard "Mad Bomber of the Year."
>
> Demonstrators, who were mobilized by the Committee for Just Rewards, gathered at 6:00 pm at an empty lot a quarter mile from Rickey's. The crowd, four hundred strong, marched down one lane of El Camino Real—a main thoroughfare—with a police escort.

---

50. Lenny Siegel, "David Packard: Mad Bomber of the Year," March 1, 1972. http://a3mreunion.org/archive/1971-1972/71-72/files_71-72/71-72_Mad_Bomber.pdf

Marchers carried NLF flags, red flags, and banners condemning Packard, who supervised creation of the electronic battlefield, as a war criminal.

The police, including units from several local cities, were out in force, but maintained a lower profile. The Palo Alto Police Chief handed out a leaflet entitled, "'Oink'—Suggestions for a Peaceful Demonstration from Palo Alto's Super-Pig."[51]

The marchers, led by a death-figure pulling a little red wagon carrying the Mad Bomber Award—a three-foot high mini-missile—attempted to enter the courtyard at Rickey's but were blocked by police and county sheriffs. After a brief confrontation with police, the demonstrators returned to El Camino, forming a picket line which blocked two lanes of traffic. In the course of the evening two people were arrested.

Inside the banquet, which was attended by the San Francisco Peninsula's most distinguished citizens, two anti-war representatives attempted to make statements condemning Packard's role in the Pentagon and at his company, Hewlett-Packard. Both, paying guests at the dinner, were ejected.

Packard, in his acceptance speech, defended Nixon administration policies in Indochina, and attacked campus "anti-military campaigns." Without specifically naming recently fired English Professor Bruce Franklin, Packard congratulated Stanford University for ridding itself of "purveyors of evil."

51. James Zurcher, "Suggestions for a Peaceful Demonstration from Palo Alto's Super-Pig," February 29, 1972. a3mreunion.org/archive/1971-1972/71-72/files_71-72/71-72_from_Super_Pig.pdf

"If there are mad bombers in this country," said Packard—the man who explained the ABM [Anti-Ballistic Missile system] to Congress—"they are probably in front of Ricky's tonight."

Vice-President Spiro Agnew, who eventually was forced to resign from office, was scheduled to speak to the conservative California Republican Assembly Saturday evening, April 8. The Committee for Just Rewards made plans to recognize him with the Mouthpiece of the Empire Award.[52] We drew a reported 1800 people to our rally in front of the Cabaña Hyatt House. The organizers of the event moved Agnew's speech up to lunchtime, and our old friend David Packard joined then-Governor Ronald Reagan in the dinner-time slot. The *Daily* reported:

> Although Agnew's aides vigorously denied it, the Vice-President was evidently switched to the luncheon and former Deputy Defense Secretary David Packard to the dinner session because of anti-Agnew demonstrations planned for the evening.[53]

The *Daily* called the Red Star singers' rendition of "Pig Agnew" the "entertainment highlight of the evening."[54] But we also presented a guerrilla theater skit, "Beware of Greeks Dropping Gifts." In our script, King Agnewixon announced a secret peace plan, a "wooden horse with eight points."[55] I was

52. "Guess Who's Coming to Palo Alto on Saturday, April 8," Committee for Just Rewards, April, 1972. a3mreunion.org/archive/1971-1972/71-72/files_71-72/71-72_Spiro_1-2.pdf
53. Frank Miller, "Agnew Addresses Luncheon," *Stanford Daily,* April 10, 1972, p. 1. archives.stanforddaily.com/1972/04/10?page=1&section=MODSMD_ARTICLE2#article
54. Phil Revzin, "Nearly 1800 Demonstrate at Republican Dinner," *Stanford Daily,* April 10, 1972, p. 1. archives.stanforddaily.com/1972/04/10?page=1&section=MODSMD_ARTICLE3#article
55. "Beware of Greeks Dropping Gifts," April, 1972. a3mreunion.org/archive/1971-1972/71-72/files_71-72/71-72_Beware-of-Greeks.pdf

both an author and an actor. My most memorable part of the evening was forgetting my lines and mumbling, "Oh shit!" before a crowd of nearly two thousand.

## Escalation

Richard Nixon had been trying to reduce American opposition to the Indochina War by limiting the number of Americans in ground combat. He called it Vietnamization, because it required the South Vietnamese Army to assume that role. In reality, it also relied upon the electronic battlefield and more visibly, the air war. This became particularly clear in April of 1972 when Nixon ordered the heavy bombardment of the North Vietnamese capital, Hanoi, and its harbor city, Haiphong. At Stanford and across the country, the peace movement met Nixon's escalation with escalation of its own.

The night of April 17, hundreds of protesters roamed the campus, throwing rocks at police and buildings. The next days, hundreds of students met to plan a campus strike. Since it was spring, not winter, campuses in the Northeast and Midwest were able to mobilize as well. President Lyman sent a strongly worded protest letter to President Nixon, condemned the window-breaking, and opposed the proposed strike. Still, activist groups from all perspectives supported the strike. At scores of campuses across the country, strikes were planned.

Thursday night, April 20, the Movement organized a torchlight parade.[56] Five hundred marchers who had gathered at Lytton Plaza in downtown Palo Alto met another two hundred, streaming from the Wilbur Hall parking lot, at the intersection of Palm Drive and Campus Drive. They were headed toward the Hansen electronics labs, site of war-related Defense research.

Police had confiscated torches at Lytton Plaza, declaring them a violation of the California Uniform Fire Code. "Despite these precautions, about 50 torches were produced and lighted as

---

56. Some people must have gone to a lot of trouble manufacturing the dozens of torches produced that night. See "How to Make a Torch," April, 1972. http://www.a3mreunion.org/archive/1971-1972/71-72_april_21/files_71-72_april_21/71-72April21_torch.pdf

the two groups joined."[57] The County Sheriff's office declared the protest an unlawful assembly and charged the crowd, dispersing them and forcing demonstrators to drop their torches. Protestors regrouped on campus, so there were continuing confrontations with police and sheriff's deputies. The law enforcement strategy was to rely primarily on billy clubs, not arrests, to quell the demonstration. I did not meet up with other protestors until they arrived in the area around the labs, so I never saw the torches. I did however, feel the unpleasant smack of a billy club on my jaw.

Stanford's version of the nationwide campus strike was the next day. We considered it successful. I wrote, at the time:

> "God tells us to love, not hate," said the Jesus-movement freshman to a "rally" at Stanford University on April 24. "It made me sad last Friday to see so many of my friends hating the pigs—oops...."

> Events at Stanford during that campus's one-day anti-war Strike on Friday, April 21 forced a lot of people to accept new realities. Over one thousand people, including initially over 200 high school students, had snaked around the Stanford campus for two hours or so, engaging in minor, hit-and-run confrontations with the police. The crowd poured off campus around three o'clock and blocked El Camino Real, a major thoroughfare bordering the forest which insulates Stanford from Palo Alto. Without warning, the Santa Clara County Sheriffs charged the crowd, beating several demonstrators and arresting over 200 demonstrators, including a few Jesus-movement freshmen from Stanford. The participation of these "Christian Brothers" and one or two hundred Stanford freshmen reflects a real victory for the Movement at Stanford. All year long people warned that this

---

57. Jim Wascher, "Police, Crowd Clash in Anti-War March," *Stanford Daily*, April 21, 1972, p. 1. https://archives.stanforddaily. com/1972/04/21?page=1&section=MODSMD_ARTICLE1#article

year's freshman class was much more conservative than previous years' classes. Stanford had admitted a large number of Jesus-freaks and gung-ho pre-meds. Campus organizers were not discouraged, however, and consistently organized discussions, popcorn parties, and study groups in the Stanford dormitories. Without Nixon's escalation of the War, Friday's activities would not have been possible. Without the organizing, however, the demonstrations would have been restricted primarily to a hard core of old-timers.

The one-day strike at Stanford was successful. Most people did not attend class. While the marchers confronted police, three to four hundred students attended a teach-in on the war and one to two hundred students leafleted for [Democratic presidential candidate] George McGovern or collected signatures to get the anti-Air War referendum on the California November election ballot. Demonstrators attempted, throughout the day, to halt work in administrative offices and laboratories housing War Research, but the Stanford police called in police immediately and in force.

Anti-war organizing and educational activities are continuing throughout the campus, in local high schools, and in local communities, but the Movement was unable to continue the strike or sustain the high level of mobilization. Groups are beginning to organize against different Vietnam War corporations in the local communities, but no one knows exactly what will have immediate impact and not get more people arrested or hurt. [58]

58. Lenny Siegel, "'God tells us to love...,'" April, 1972, p. 1. http://www.a3mreunion.org/archive/1971-1972/71-72_april_21/ files_71-72_april_21/71-72April21_reflection.pdf. I've made a few copy edits. The minor errors and extensive cross-outs remind me what

I missed the action at El Camino Real. If I recall correctly, I was speaking about Stanford war research and the electronic war at the teach-in at Cubberley Auditorium. For a detailed play-by-play of the El Camino confrontation, see the *Daily's* account, published in a special Saturday edition.[59] There were large noon rallies and numerous on-campus confrontations focused on Encina Hall, the electronics labs, and large lecture classes. In the continuing tradition of Stanford protests:

**Fig. 9.2. Students marching from White Plaza to El Camino Real in protest of Nixon's escalation of the War, April 21, 1972.**

The crowd arrived at the [Hansen] Labs at 8:05 to find eight Tac Squad members waiting for them. Suspended student [and Young Crow] Pete Knutson

---

a godsend word processing, which I had access to less than a decade later, was for my writing.

59. Rich Jaroslovsky, "Police Clear El Camino, Arrest 205," *Stanford Daily,* April 22, 1972, p. 1. https://archives.stanforddaily. com/1972/04/22?page=1&section=MODSMD_ARTICLE1#article The *Daily* also reported on on-campus confrontations that day.

led a dash past the main Labs to the annex in the rear, which he opened with a key.[60]

Anti-war rallies and protests continued. I recall an event at the Stanford Linear Accelerator Center (SLAC).[61] Following a rally, there were informal discussions on the lawn. I was in a group with Wolfgang Panofsky, SLAC's director. Initially, "Pief"—as he was affectionately known—was a hero to me. His Jewish German family emigrated to the U.S. in the mid-1930s. Under his leadership, SLAC refused classified research and welcomed collaboration with Iron Curtain (Communist) country physicists. It became a haven for left-leaning physicists. SLAC's reputation was a major reason I applied to Stanford in the first place, and I had a summer job there in 1969, doing unskilled work in the lab/office of Martin Perl, an activist professor who later went on to win the Nobel Prize in Physics.

Panofsky was known for his technical work in support of nuclear arms control. It was important, admirable work. But he also served as a consultant at the Jason Division of the Institute for Defense Analysis. As I wrote in "Vietnam's Electronic Battlefield," the Jason Division had in 1966 recommended:

> the construction of an anti-infiltration barrier across
> the De-Militarized Zone [between North and South
> Vietnam]. This barrier, known as the "McNamara

---

60. Glenn Garvin and Jim Wascher, "15 Arrested for Door Blocking, Large Crowd Roams Labs, Encina," *Stanford Daily,* April 22, 1972, p. 1. https://archives.stanforddaily. com/1972/04/22?page=1&section=MODSMD_ARTICLE3#article See also Scott Thacher, "Strikers Interrupt Morning Classes, Some Business Continues Normally," *Stanford Daily,* April 22, 1972, p. 1. https://archives.stanforddaily. com/1972/04/22?page=1&section=MODSMD_ARTICLE2#article 61. George Dobbins, "S. Viets Forced Back; Moratorium Plans Set," *Stanford Daily,* May 3, 1972, p. 1. The *Daily* mentioned plans for a rally at SLAC on May 3, but I'm not sure that the event that I remember was that day. archives.stanforddaily. com/1972/05/03?page=1&section=MODSMD_ARTICLE3#article

Wall" or the "Edsel Line," proved costly and ineffective. In 1969 it was abandoned, barely begun, but the technology developed for it led to the electronic battlefield.[62]

On the warm, comfortable SLAC lawn, I questioned Pief about the Jason recommendations. He justified it as an alternative to the carpet bombing of North Vietnam, deadly to the population and disastrous for its economic life. If I recall correctly, I said that he had been used. The Defense Department received technical guidance on automating the war, and it still chose to heavily bomb North Vietnam.

Despite the protests, Nixon again escalated the war. On May 9, Navy planes dropped anti-ship mines into Haiphong Harbor, North Vietnam's only major port. The U.S. had previously avoided such action, concerned that a Soviet or Chinese ship would be damaged or sunk, provoking direct intervention. Nixon told the nation that the only way to end the war was to cut off the inflow of supplies to North Vietnam.

At Stanford and other campuses the response was immediate. That night 450 protestors marched up to Lyman's house. The *Daily* reported, "Lenny Siegel urged using a variety of tactics to 'throw a tantrum' to show President Nixon 'there will be no peace in the US until there is peace in Vietnam.'"[63]

Lyman actually responded:

---

62. "Vietnam's Electronic Battlefield," page 2. http://a3mreunion. org/archive/1971-1972/71-72_war_research/files_71-72_war_ research/71-72Research_VEB.pdf Ford Motor company produced the unsuccessful Edsel model while McNamara was company president. Reportedly he opposed the Edsel.

63. Larry Liebert, "450 Walk to Lyman Home," *Stanford Daily,* May 9, 1972, p. 1. https://archives.stanforddaily. com/1972/05/09?page=1&section=MODSMD_ARTICLE2#article That doesn't sound like something I would say, but no doubt that is how I felt.

He added that he had heard that Lenny Siegel of the Pacific Studies Center had advocated "throwing a tantrum" on campus. "President Nixon is throwing a tantrum," said Lyman, "and I don't think we should imitate him. We don't need any more tantrums anywhere in the world."[64]

I get it that Lyman wanted peace on campus, but I still am shocked that he equated a few dozen broken windows with the death and destruction Nixon unleashed upon Vietnam.

For a few nights demonstrators roamed the campus, trashing windows on buildings where war research was conducted and skirmishing with police. On Friday, May 12 there was a fairly effective class boycott. Law professors and students led a march of about 700 people into downtown Palo Alto. I spoke at a Concerned Asian Scholars teach-in at Memorial Church, attended by more than 900 people. I struck a familiar chord: "Siegel told the audience that the war has become more and more dependent on electronic development and he said that much of this technology is being designed here."[65]

For the first time I can remember, on May 12 130 students picketed and leafleted Moffett Naval Air Station, on the northern edge of Mountain View.[66] Reportedly, Moffett-based P-3 prop-jets had taken part in the mining of Haiphong Harbor. Two weeks later several students, faculty, and staff were arrested blocking incoming traffic at Moffett Field.

---

64. "Outrage, Fear Mark Reaction to Speech," *Stanford Daily,* May 9, 1972, p. 6. archives.stanforddaily.com/1972/05/09?page=1&section=MODSMD_ARTICLE3#article

65. George Dobbins, "Peaceful Demonstrations, Picketing Here Friday," *Stanford Daily,* May 15, 1972, p. 6.archives.stanforddaily.com/1972/05/15?page=6&section=MODSMD_ARTICLE1#article

66. Ironically, I've spent the last three decades of my life promoting the environmental cleanup and non-military reuse of Moffett Field while organizing to preserve its massive, historic dirigible hangar, Hangar One.

Marine recruiters canceled a visit to Stanford scheduled for May 17-18 when faculty members threatened to block the entrance to the Placement Center. The head of the Placement Center said they canceled because there was a lack of interest.[67] Either explanation represented a small but clear victory for the Movement.

Despite the anger and widespread activity, the strikes and protests in the spring of 1972 did not "electrify" the entire campus. Unlike the spring of 1970, when Nixon invaded Cambodia, Stanford finished its school year. What was different? I think many students, faculty, and staff had become cynical. In 1970, campuses throughout the U.S. shut down, but the war had continued and in some ways grew. Campus revolutionaries continued to turn their backs on the student population, from which they had emerged, while liberals united behind the anti-war presidential campaign of Sen. George McGovern. Propelled by a June, 1972 primary victory in California, McGovern won the Democratic nomination, only to be smashed by Nixon in November.

In retrospect, one cannot have a high point every year. The spring 1972 protests were significant, but the role of universities in the national anti-war movement declined as other sectors, particularly the GI peace movement, grew. In fact, a number of former Stanford activists, such as Jeanne Friedman, played important roles supporting that movement. On many campuses, activism slowed, but Stanford's Movement remained potent through the end of the war, because even without the draft and American ground combat troops, emerging technologies tied Stanford to the war.

---

67. "Oakland War Protest Today," *Stanford Daily,* May 17, 1972, p. 6. archives.stanforddaily.com/1972/05/17?page=6&section=MODSMD_ARTICLE20#article

# Chapter 10: A Lasting Legacy

My parents always wanted me to finish Stanford, but it's still here.
*~Lenny Siegel at the 2009 A3M Reunion*

Anti-war organizing continued at Stanford after the spring of 1972, but with the exception of one brief period, it diminished in intensity. Peace negotiations, the January 27, 1973 Paris Peace Accords, and gradual moves by Congress to limit war funding reduced the immediacy of protest, and the growing Watergate scandal gave progressives hope that Nixon's reign would not last. The Stanford anti-war movement played a role in hastening the war's 1975 conclusion, and it left a lasting impression on the activists who took part as well as the university itself. It helped spawn a redirection in advanced technology, stimulated the growth of the women's movement, gay rights, civil rights, and the environmental movement, but it did not lead to the revolution that so many of us had concluded was necessary.

## The Light at the End of the Tunnel

The exception was the December 1972 "Christmas bombing" of North Vietnam. B-52 bombers, the U.S. Air Force planes with the largest payloads, repeatedly struck targets in the Hanoi/Haiphong area in the war's heaviest bombing campaign. A group of us summarized in a mini-pamphlet published in early January:

> Between December 18 and December 29 American warplanes carried out over 5,000 air strikes against northern Vietnam. They dropped between 3,000 and 6,000 tons of bombs per day on Hanoi and Haiphong, home of over a million people.

> Although the Pentagon says that U.S. planes are not attacking civilian targets, anti-war activists, newsmen, and international observers in North Vietnam have testified that hospitals and residential areas have been destroyed by repeated saturation bombing.[1]

Nixon claimed that the bombing forced the North Vietnamese leadership back to the negotiating table, but they were already negotiating when the onslaught began. Our pamphlet argued, "The Nixon Administration was telling the North Vietnamese: Give up your vision of a re-united Vietnam or we'll destroy you."[2] We also suggested that the enormous devastation was designed to warn other small countries not to stand up to the United States. In retrospect, it was supposed to be proof of U.S. strength before Nixon agreed to a peace deal—just one month later—that implied weakness. Some have also theorized that the bombing was also a ploy by Nixon and his National Security Advisor, Henry Kissinger, to convince South Vietnamese president Nguyen Van Thieu that the U.S. would not abandon him.

The bombing campaign unleashed protest throughout the U.S. and around the globe. We argued at the time that the protests, along with heavy losses of irreplaceable B-52 bombers, forced Nixon to halt the attacks:

> Around the world people and government declared their opposition. Thousands of people demonstrated in France, Sweden, and other countries. Dockers in Italy and Australia boycotted American cargoes. China and Russia threatened an end to their rapprochements with the U.S.

1. "Is Peace at Hand?," Committee of Concerned Asian Scholars at Stanford and Pacific Studies Center, January 3, 1973, p. 3. http://a3mreunion.org/archive/1972-beyond/72-1977/files_1972-present/72Beyond_is-peace-at-hand.pdf
2. *ibid.*, p. 3..

while the Swedish response was so strong that the U.S. asked Sweden not to send an ambassador to Washington. In the U.S., the "dead" anti-war movement woke up. Locally, 2,000 people marched in protest Christmas Eve. U.S. Congressmen and Senators—even Republican supporters of Nixon like Ohio's Senator William Saxbe— threatened to cut off war funds.[3]

I wrote a January 4 *Daily* column urging action. I began, "Astrology may not be in, but you can tell Nixon's going to escalate the War whenever the U.S. has a manned space-shot, if not more often."[4] That day 500 people gathered in White Plaza for a peace rally, and on January 12, folk-music diva and non-violence advocate Joan Baez led a noon march into Palo Alto. That evening she spoke to an overflow audience of over 2000 at Memorial Church on the Stanford Quad. Baez and other war critics had been in North Vietnam during the bombing, surviving in underground bomb shelters. She had visited the ruins of Bac Mai hospital. "She said she saw dead and wounded patients strewn everywhere and that her guide on the trip lost his entire family in the bombing."[5]

The Movement was not able to sustain a heightened level of activity, however, because Nixon had halted the bombing of Hanoi and Haiphong, and perhaps because it was winter. There was a universal, but fragile sigh of relief when, on January 27, the cease-fire between the U.S. and North Vietnam, embodied in the Paris Peace Accords, was announced.

---

3. *ibid.,* p. 4.
4. Lenny Siegel, "Peace Is Not At Hand," *Stanford Daily*, January 4, 1973, p. 2. https://archives.stanforddaily.com/1973/01/04?page=2&section=MODSMD_ARTICLE8#article
5. Bill Weinstein "Baez Relates Vietnam Experiences; Lambastes 'Outrageous Bombing,'" *Stanford Daily,* January 15, 1973, p. 1. archives.stanforddaily.com/1973/01/15?page=1&section=MODSMD_ARTICLE4#article

On February 6 the *Stanford Daily* wondered what the agreement meant for the local anti-war movement. It published an article, "Vietnam Truce Leaves Anti-War Movement In Limbo." Robert McAfee Brown, who had progressed from "noted theologian" to a "liberation theologian," reminded the reader of unresolved issues. Without using the word imperialism, Brown said that Vietnam was not an isolated problem. In the same article, I was quoted, "It's a mistake... to think that radicalism will disappear. But there will be less sensation in it."[6]

By then the Watergate scandal was growing in the public consciousness, reaching a high point with the opening of the bi-partisan Senate hearings in May. I remember a particular Saturday night in October (the 20th), when my wife and I were watching *Night of the Living Dead,* perhaps the first noteworthy zombie movie, with out-of-own guests at our Mountain View apartment. We were watching live TV, because that's all we had back then.

Still experiencing the intensity of the movie, we crashed back to reality when we heard that Nixon had fired his three top Justice Department appointees. We hurriedly scheduled a noon rally for Monday, and 400 people showed up. But Watergate never inspired the continuing organizing and street activism of the anti-war movement because Congress and the media were actually doing their jobs, culminating in Nixon's resignation on August 8, 1974.

Nixon did not have to preside over America's first clear-cut war defeat. His appointed successor, Gerald Ford, earned that honor less than a year later, on April 30, 1975, when North Vietnamese and National Liberation Front forces seized control of Saigon as Americans and their South Vietnamese supporters fled the country. The massive, growing opposition to the War

---

6. Dan Brenner, "Vietnam Truce Leaves Anti-War Movement in Limbo," *Stanford Daily,* February 6, 1973, p. 1. https://archives. stanforddaily.com/1973/02/06?page=1&section=MODSMD_ ARTICLE5#article

had fed the establishment's drive to hold Nixon accountable for the Watergate break-in and cover-up, and in turn his departure hastened the end of the war.

I believed then and I continue to believe that the national movement against the Vietnam War and the other wars in Indochina was a proud point in U.S. history. It was unprecedented, and it was effective. I wrote, in my January 4, 1973 column:

> Most people are tired of the same old tactics: marches, sit-ins, writing congressmen, supporting resisters in the military. But the old tactics have been effective.
>
> Had the anti-war movement not done these things, then hundreds of thousands of gung-ho American troops would now occupy Indochina. The war is not over, but the Vietnamese and other Indochinese have a fighting chance at independence.[7]

Like Robert McAfee Brown, many of us had learned that Vietnam was not simply a mistake. It was part of a global pattern, indeed a strategy, by America's rulers to maintain military, diplomatic, and economic hegemony. Did we curtail U.S. imperialism? As 20th Century Chinese Communist leader Chou En-Lai reportedly responded when asked about the continuing influence of the late 18th Century French Revolution, "It's too soon to tell." That is, in the 1970s and subsequent decades, U.S. influence in the world diminished, but it still remained a superpower exercising immense might. It's too soon to know how long that power will last.

Until the 1990-1991 Persian Gulf War, American leaders felt constrained by what they called the "Vietnam Syndrome," the American public's unwillingness to weather another military

---

7. Lenny Siegel, "Peace Is Not At Hand," *Stanford Daily*, January 4, 1973, p. 2. archives.stanforddaily.com/1973/01/04?page=2&section=MODSMD_ARTICLE8#article

quagmire. Upon the defeat of Saddam Hussein's Iraq, President George H.W. Bush declared, "by God, we've kicked the Vietnam syndrome once and for all."[8]

However, later wars have demonstrated that American military power remains constrained by our collective, though sometimes distorted, memory of the Vietnam War. Americans today accept military conflict only when casualties are limited, costs seem minimal, and victory is anticipated. The Gulf War met those criteria, but subsequent conflicts within Afghanistan, Libya, and Iraq have shown the U.S. can topple hostile leaders with bombing campaigns, automated or remote-controlled weapons, and even local allies. However, without committing huge numbers of American ground combat troops for a period of years it cannot impose governments friendly to American interests, and the American people will not tolerate such a total military commitment. This is not just because of Vietnam, but the crescendo of opposition to the Vietnam War continues to serve as a reminder that Americans will not support military action that does not achieve military and political objectives quickly.

The Movement also had a lasting, but uneven impact on Stanford University. In direct response to our activities, the Board of Trustees became more diverse and less conservative, students were offered more opportunities to influence university decisions, but Stanford remains a corporation run, in the final analysis, by a self-perpetuating body of corporate leaders.

Despite recurring efforts to reestablish ROTC on the Stanford campus, Stanford students must co-enroll with other Bay Area universities to participate in those programs.

Stanford to this day does not allow classified research on campus, and while Defense-sponsored research and development remains significant, over $72 million in 2018, it has fallen to 4.4% of the university's reported sponsored projects total. In the same year, Stanford received nearly $512 million from the

---

8. Online at "Public Papers of the Presidents of the United States: George H. W. Bush (1991, Book I)," p. 197. Government Publishing Office. https://www.govinfo.gov/content/pkg/PPP-1991-book1/html/PPP-1991-book1-doc-pg195-2.htm

federal Department of Health and Human Services. Since one of the functions of military sponsored was to channel students into continuing work for the military industrial complex, the change in funding mix offers today's students diverse opportunities that were not necessarily open to students in my generation. Of course, there are also issues with medical research, but it is better, as we declared in the spring of 1969, to "research life, not death."

Meanwhile, SRI—known since 1977 as SRI International —continues to depend heavily on the Defense Department. As with Doug Engelbart's pioneering work in the 1960s, some of that research has had significant civilian value. In the early 2000s, SRI researchers created the Speech Interpretation and Recognition Interface, commonly known as SIRI. In 2007 it spun off a company, SIRI, Inc., and in 2010 Apple acquired SIRI for incorporation into its iPhone.

Though the Defense Department played an essential role in the development of the Internet and commercial computing systems, it lost control of those technologies in the 1970s. Engineers, scientists, and programmers who in the 1960s and early 1970s felt trapped with only military-related job opportunities could finally find jobs with little or no application to warfare. One of the reasons the Defense Department lost its leadership was that it was constrained by an inflexible "Mil-Spec" acquisition system. The Pentagon took as much time to qualify a design for use in weapons systems as it took civilian industry to create a new generation (or two) of devices. In 1986 I explained:

> If any single invention marked the eclipse of the Pentagon's hegemony over high-tech electronics, it was the microprocessor. While the military purchased 70 percent of all integrated circuit production as late as 1965, it was an order from a Japanese calculator manufacturer that inspired engineers at Intel (a small Silicon Valley firm spun off from Fairchild) to design the first microprocessor. The device combined the circuits of a programmable computer on a single

265

silicon chip that could be mass produced for a few
dollars. As Regis McKenna, the public relations whiz
for Intel (and later Apple), pointed out, the "second
generation" microprocessor (the 8080, which was the
"brain" of many early microcomputers) was marketed
by Intel in 1974, second-sourced by Japan in 1975,
copied by the Soviets by 1977, and finally purchased
by the Pentagon in 1979.[9]

Furthermore, unbeknownst to me at the time, people from
the Movement and the counterculture were also contributing
to the evolution of computing technology. Fred Moore, a draft
resister, was one of the founders of the Homebrew Computer
Club in 1975. Meeting at locations such as the SLAC auditorium,
young hobbyists designed the computers that spawned the
personal computing industry. Lee Felsenstein, with whom I
worked on Stop the Draft Week in 1967, chaired many of those
meetings. Jim Warren of the Free University organized the West
Coast Computer Faires.

While many of the participants were anti-war activists,
the common theme was a desire to have a computing device
that one could own and control independent of corporations and
government agencies. Many factors contributed to the ubiquity
of computer telecommunications and the availability of smaller
and smaller personal computing devices. Furthermore, many
civilian, as well as military, applications of these technologies
are undesirable. But it's clear that the Defense Department
irreversibly lost control of the technologies that it pioneered.
Though I've spent much of my career criticizing the civilian tech
industry, I consider the shift in emphasis away from warfare an
epochal victory. My friends from the Movement, and others like
them, helped pave that path.[10]

---

9. Lenny Siegel, "Microcomputers: From Movement to Industry,"
*Monthly Review,* July-August 1986, p. 112.
10. For a comprehensive look at the relationship between the 60s
counterculture and the growth of personal computing, see John
Markoff, *What the Dormouse Said* (Penguin Books, 2006).

## The Reunion Cohort

In fact, I believe that the "veterans" of the Stanford Movement continued to have a positive impact long after our last rally, pamphlet, march, sit-in, or trashing episode. I only have anecdotal evidence, but it's my impression that a large share of Stanford activists continued to pursue actively their progressive ideals long after they left the campus. I credit that to the research and educational work that we did. People were not simply radicalized "at the end of a billy club." We learned as we absorbed research about the university and the war, and we engaged in seemingly interminable dialogue among ourselves.

We created a network of former Stanford activists, and we've held reunions in 1979, 1989, 1999, 2009, 2014, and 2019. Though we call it them "A3M Reunions," we have welcomed anyone who was active at Stanford and adjacent communities any time during the 1960s and 1970s. We have also invited current students, faculty, and staff, as well as family members of our original cohort. One of our largest was in 1989, attended by 300 people including my two young children. The Pacific Studies Center has sponsored each event.

Each reunion has included speeches, panel presentations, and open discussions. We revived old political arguments and instigated new ones. Some of our number even rekindled old flames. We re-enacted "Alice in ROTC-Land" without Sigourney Weaver. At one dinner Ed McClanahan read his essay, "Another Great Moment in Sports." We have honored the growing number of dead from our time at Stanford. We have shown, to disapproving sneers, the PBL documentary *Fathers and Sons.*

In 2009 we nailed a petition to the door of the university president's office asking that Condoleezza Rice, back at Stanford then, be held accountable for the Iraq War that she promoted. That year we also scheduled a dance, but the overwhelming majority of those at the Saturday night dinner insisted that we instead continue an enlightening discussion with History Professor Bart Bernstein.

Culminating each reunion, I have led tours of campus, re-telling some of the stories in this book but providing ample opportunity for others in our cohort to confess to violations of Stanford's disruption policy, or worse. On May 7, 1989, some 50 or 60 veterans of the Stanford anti-war movement wound our way into the basement of the Applied Electronics Laboratory building, where we had staged the 9-day sit-in in 1969.

We gathered again outside the building to hear Paul Rupert tell how a fictional call to his mother in April, 1969 quelled university president Kenneth Pitzer's from-the-floor-microphone attempt to sidetrack the sit-in. When my seven-year-old daughter and two-and-a-half-year-old son kept insisting on going back into AEL, Paul commented, "It's in their genes."

Ten years later, we placed a temporary commemorative plaque at the site of the Applied Electronics Laboratory. The building, as well as the Physics tank, had been razed for the construction of new, larger engineering buildings.

After people left Stanford, some became community, environmental, and labor organizers or leaders. Many more became lawyers, college professors, and journalists. As the AIDS crisis unfolded in the 1980s, several from our cohort engaged in related medical research. At least one, Dan Hamburg, served in Congress from California's far north. The preponderance of the people we've been able to contact, and I'm still discovering more, remain politically progressive, whether or not they are professional activists.

Veterans of our Movement fondly look back at what was, for most of us, the most formative period in our lives. However, that doesn't mean that no one has changed. At one reunion—I think it was 1989—many participants told me that they were glad to see that many old comrades had remained progressive but had retreated from the "gun fetishism" that had characterized a portion of our Movement.

I don't know if we'll have any more reunions. In 2019 many folks said they were not healthy enough to travel. But we still have an e-mail list of over 230 people where we continue

**Fig. 10.1. We never even threatened to tear down the Applied Electronics Laboratory, but at some time between 1989 and 1999 the university administration wiped it off the map.**

to debate ideology, policy, and politics. And 36 of us have been interviewed by the Movement Oral History Project, recording over 3,400 minutes of audio and video in cooperation with the Stanford Historical Society and the Stanford Library Archives.[11]

The Pacific Studies Center, which I still maintain as a library and non-profit organization, is the last remaining offshoot of the April Third Movement. It began as a subsistence-pay "halfway house" for Movement researchers on their way back to school or on to new careers. We initially saw ourselves as a small counterweight to the Stanford Research Institute, almost calling ourselves the Stanford Radical Institute. Noting SRI's focus on the Pacific Rim, we wrote about Asia. I personally wrote numerous articles about Indonesia, though I never traveled there.

---

11. See "Movement Oral History Project." https://historicalsociety. stanford.edu/discover-history/oral-history/projects/movement-oral-history-project-antiwar-protest-and-allied

When the Vietnam War ended in 1975, we consciously re-assessed what we were doing. Looking down from the stratosphere, we were in the heart of Silicon Valley, the new name of Frederick Terman's Community of Technical Scholars. By then our area was recognized globally as modern equivalent of the British Midlands in the First Industrial Revolution. We had already studied local military contracting, local land use, and the Asian production plants of Valley semiconductor companies. But there were also labor, environmental, equity (what became known as the digital divide), and privacy issues too.

We moved to a second-floor office that we carved out of a former manufacturing facility in downtown Mountain View, a few blocks from my apartment. We shared space with the Mid-Peninsula Conversion Project, which also researched and worked to transform the Valley's dependence on and support of the Department of Defense. Briarpatch Cooperative market was downstairs. In those days, rent was cheap. Now office rents in downtown Mountain View are among the most expensive, anywhere.

In 1977 we organized a conference, "Silicon Valley: Paradise or Paradox," nearby at the old Mountain View High School. Over 300 people attended. We published a pamphlet with the same name, addressing many of the problems we associated with high-tech. The pamphlet foreshadowed *The High Cost of High Tech,* a book that John Markoff and I wrote in 1985. Most of the issues we raised in 1977 and again in 1985 remain hot topics today, despite the Valley's evolution from military and then semiconductor production to primarily smart phones, software, and Internet services today. Ironically, though I never graduated, Stanford's alumni magazine called me the "Diogenes of the Diode" in 1985, noting that I was "class of '70."[12]

We worked with people organizing workers in Silicon Valley's tech industry and its offshoots in Asia and in the American southwest and west. I even took a few trips up to British Columbia to speak about the shortcomings of

------

12. "Diogenes of the Diode," *Stanford Magazine,* Fall, 1985, p. 106.

our supposed futuristic paradise. The PSC library, with its extensive files on Silicon Valley, became a destination for journalists and academic researchers from throughout the world.

In the early 1980s, I helped Ted Smith—who had arrived at Stanford during the AEL sit-in—form the Silicon Valley Toxics Coalition. It turned out that the semiconductor and other electronics manufacturers had poisoned the region's groundwater, including areas just a short bike ride from my house. As my work focused more and more on environmental contamination, PSC's library collected reports and files on military, Superfund, and brownfield contamination. In 2017 we donated most of our Silicon Valley files—from PSC's first 25 years—to the Stanford libraries, but we still hold the environmental files I collected over the Center's second quarter-century.

We also have retained the Movement historical files from the 1960s and 1970s. Those documents, scanned and presented on the A3M Reunion website, form the basis of much of this book, supplementing my memory.

## My Continuing Journey

As for me, I recall that Stanford Education Professor and one-time Congressional peace candidate Martin Carnoy commented at one of our early reunions that I had "never left." It seemed a strange comment from someone who has been a Stanford professor, living adjacent to campus, for five decades now. But in a way it rings true. While other Stanford activists dispersed around the world, PSC and I had moved from East Palo Alto, about five miles from campus, to downtown Mountain View, about eight miles away. More important, in the 52 years since I was first not allowed to register for classes, I have been doing pretty much the same thing.

When I moved to Mountain View, I recognized that even though rental households formed a majority of the housing stock, renters were seriously underrepresented in city government. I ran for City Council in 1976, placing 13th in a field of 13. I ran and lost two more times. In the wake of Proposition 13, the 1978 statewide limitation on property taxes—which benefited landlords but not tenants—I led two unsuccessful initiative campaigns for rent control and one successful campaign to control condominium conversions. I served as an appointed Planning Commissioner from 1978 to 1980. I tried to address the area's growing jobs-housing imbalance, proposing a moratorium on industrial growth in the city's rural North Bayshore area. I was unsuccessful. Now home to Google, Intuit, and Microsoft's regional headquarters, before the 2020 COVID-19 outbreak North Bayshore had more than 25,000 employees.

Though I occasionally returned to Stanford, my life focused on Mountain View. In 1979 my wife and I, with the help of our parents, bought a house on a quaint street in Old Mountain View. It seemed expensive at the time, but with the growing popularity of downtown Mountain View restaurants and the city's growing affluence, it became a very desirable place to live. The value of our house has appreciated by a factor of at least 25 over the last 40 years.

While researching Silicon Valley, I was active in diverse groups such as Briarpatch Market and Men Against Rape. In the 1980s, when my kids were born, I moonlighted as a contract technical writer for Apple Computer and a couple of start-ups formed by people I met at Apple. I was struck by how much more money I could make in tech than writing about it. As my publisher, Cornelia Bessie predicted, my co-authored book, *The High Cost of High Tech,* had the marketing shelf-life of a carton of milk. Still, the substance of the book remains as true today as it was in 1985. The *San Jose Mercury-News* called me, with an appropriate caricature, a gadfly.

All along I remained active in the peace movement. I took part, for example, in the movement for a Nuclear Freeze and opposed U.S. intervention in Central America. In 1990 I formed Mountain View Voices for Peace to oppose the Persian Gulf War. I was heartened by the fact that by creating a Mountain View group, as opposed to urging people to travel to Stanford or Palo Alto to protest, that some of my neighbors joined anti-war demonstrations. We re-activated the group in 2003 to oppose the Iraq War.

The early 90s marked a turning point for me professionally. I was working on three major projects. For Computer Professionals for Social Responsibility, I edited a critique of the FBI's proposed National Crime Information Center.[13] For the Service Employees International Union, I was providing research for an abortive multi-union, Silicon Valley-wide drive to organize the employees of electronics and computer firms. And for the National Toxics Campaign Fund, I prepared a report on military contamination, *The U.S. Military's Toxic Legacy.*[14]

The environmental thrust won out. Because of my research and my local involvement at the Moffett Naval Air Station Superfund site, I was appointed to what became the Federal Facilities Environmental Restoration Dialogue Committee (FFERDC), an official federal advisory committee. Because Moffett's base commander, Captain Tim Quigley, had invited activists, such as Ted Smith and me, to the official Technical Review Committee, Moffett Field became the national model for community engagement at federal hazardous waste sites. To me, the creation of site-specific advisory boards, what the Defense Department calls Restoration Advisory Boards, combined with technical assistance for public participants, was a pioneering approach to participatory democracy that provided constructive community oversight, even on highly technical issues.

Even though I opposed the overseas deployment of the U.S. military and argued for cuts in the military budget, I decided to cooperate with the military. Perhaps I overstated the case when I called my work "bringing environmental responsibility to

---

13. See "CPSR Reports on the FBI's National Crime Information Center," *CPSR Newsletter,* Spring, 1989. http://cpsr.org/prevsite/publications/newsletters/old/1980s/Spring1989.txt/ I can't tell if this is the full report that I edited, but it's related. A version was also included in *FBI Oversight and Authorization Request for Fiscal Year 1990,* Hearings before the Subcommittee on Civil and Constitutional Rights, Committee on the Judiciary, House of Representatives, 101st Congress First Session, 1989, Serial No. 48, pp. 513 ff.

14. Lenny Siegel, Gary Cohen, and Ben Goldman, *The U.S. Military's Toxic Legacy,* National Toxics Campaign Fund, released March, 1991.

the design and productions of weapons of mass destruction." The Pentagon environmental bureaucracy, as well as U.S. EPA and state environmental regulatory agencies, soon began to regard me as a constructive critic. They invited me, paying for travel, to Defense Department trainings and conferences. I became a frequent visitor at the Pentagon. During the Obama administration, a Deputy Undersecretary of Defense hosted me twice for lunch at the white-tablecloth Navy Executive Mess in the heart of the five-sided building. I never imagined such collusion when I was at Stanford, but I believe my new approach helped bring more, faster cleanup to contaminated military facilities and gave communities a say in how local military installations addressed environmental problems.[15]

Moffett Field was proposed for closure by the Navy in 1990 and again by a federal commission in 1991. In 1993 the Base Realignment and Closure (BRAC) Commission proposed that dozens of military bases across the country be shuttered, including most of the remaining Bay Area installations. In response, members of Congress proposed earmarks—dedicated appropriations—to fund programs designed to help impacted communities recover. San Francisco State University (SFSU) created a program, CAREER/PRO (a mis-acronym for California Economic Recovery and Environmental Restoration Project) to train base workers, who would lose their jobs due to closure, to do the environmental cleanup necessary to make the contaminated bases ready for reuse. San Francisco's Congressional representative, Nancy Pelosi, submitted an earmark to fund the project.

One of the people at SFSU leading the program was Mike Nolan, whom I first met when he was part of the team filming *Fathers and Sons* in 1968 and 1969. He hired me as a consultant because by then I was an expert in military base contamination. It turned out, however, that Congress had only appropriated

---

15. For a more detailed account of this progression, see Lenny Siegel, "Adaptive Cleanup of the 'Regional Plume' in Mountain View, California," Center for Public Environmental Oversight, May, 2011. cpeo.org/pubs/RegionalPlume.pdf

half the money needed to cover all the BRAC earmarks, so the SFSU grant was not a sure thing. As I heard it, a university Vice-President traveled to DC to lobby for the money. When he met with the Pentagon official responsible for allocating BRAC training money, the official said something like, "Oh, that's Lenny's project. Don't worry." That is, he made it clear that much of the funding would be forthcoming. He was one of the Defense managers I had been working with on the Dialogue Committee. Not too long after, SFSU hired me to serve as a CAREER/PRO Director.

The irony was not lost on me. After years of opposing any military funding at Stanford, I got a good job at San Francisco State by bringing in a Defense Department grant. Of course, I still think it's much different to support the cleanup of military bases in a way that promotes civilian reuse and retrains military civilian employees than to conduct electronics research and development in support of air combat and the electronic battlefield.

At CAREER/PRO, I initiated an award-winning environmental job training program for disadvantaged youth of color in cooperation with the Laborers International Union and four community-based organizations in San Francisco. But under my leadership CAREER/PRO shifted emphasis to promoting *community oversight* of remediation at military bases, Superfund sites, and brownfields, the civilian counterpart of base closure—that is, the redevelopment of former factories and other contaminated sites. Eventually we changed the name to the Center for Public Environmental Oversight after people on our staff rejected my proposed acronym of C3PO (the cute *Star Wars* robot).

Over time, our funding came primarily from U.S. EPA. We established Internet newsgroups, convened conferences, and served on national, regional, statewide committees. I served on about a dozen National Academies of Sciences (National Research Council) committees dealing with military cleanup and chemical weapons demilitarization. I traveled to almost every state, providing organizing and technical assistance to community groups and tribes, and I testified before Congress and met repeatedly with Congressional aides. Beginning 2003 I devoted much of my time to helping communities address the vapor intrusion pathway, the migration of subsurface chemicals into overlying buildings, because that issue had risen to the surface in Mountain View.

Though CPEO had offices in San Francisco and then DC, I normally worked from home in Mountain View, creating a library of files and reports on military environmental issues and brownfields at the Pacific Studies Center, which remained in downtown Mountain View until 2017 before downsizing and moving to a lower-rent district within Mountain View. The project left SFSU in 2001 for the Tides Center, a San Francisco-based non-profit, and in 2006 it became a project of PSC. Our federal funding ran out when the Trump Administration cut the EPA budget. I still try to help toxics-impacted communities and serve on a couple of committees, but the future of my environmental work and the PSC library are both uncertain.

Locally, much of my activism centered around Moffett Field and the nearby Superfund sites. When in 1990 the Navy first proposed to close the Naval Air Station, I organized unsuccessfully for the development of residential neighborhoods there. After NASA and other armed services took over the facility, in 1996 I led a successful campaign to prevent air package express companies from flying noisy planes in and out of the airfield in the middle of the night. Starting 2001, my allies and I fought successfully for a cleanup of the Moffett Field wetlands that would allow eventual tidal restoration. And in 2005 I spearheaded the formation of the Save Hangar One Committee, which prevented the Navy from demolishing Moffett's gigantic, historic dirigible hangar.

From time to time I would write the Mountain View City Council in support of housing development, but I didn't pay close attention until 2012, when the Council, including some of my personal friends, voted for a General Plan update that would allow 13,000 to 17,000 new jobs in North Bayshore, but no new housing there. As the city developed a North Bayshore plan that excluded housing, I asked various groups to organize to change it. When no one else took up the challenge, I formed the Campaign for a Balanced Mountain View. Our new group quickly gained traction, and in the November 2014 election pro-housing candidates came in first, second, third, and fifth for three seats. I came in third. My radical history was no secret, because there are still journalists and politicians around who remember the Movement. In fact, one of my constituents was a leader of the Stanford's right-wing blue-button crowd.

While serving on Council, I worked on many issues. We raised the minimum wage to $15/hour on January 1, 2018. We passed a progressive "head" tax on employers. We strengthened the city's commitment to sustainability. We provided city employees, at all levels, reasonable pay raises. Our police refused to become agents of deportation. I was the only Council member to support Measure V in 2016, a successful voter initiative which enacted apartment rent control and required just cause for residential eviction. Mountain View rotates the mayorship annually among elected Council Members, so I became mayor in 2018.

Mountain View became a regional leader in housing development, funding and approving a series of affordable (subsidized) housing projects and making plans that could lead to a 75% increase in our housing stock. Developers have been proposing large market-rate projects in Mountain View because they know the city wants to build housing, unlike some of our neighbors. At the end of 2017 our Council unanimously passed a new North Bayshore plan calling for the construction of nearly 10,000 housing units, with a goal of 20% below market (subsidized), in medium-density, mixed-use, car-light neighborhoods, complete with parks, a school, and retail, on previously commercial property.

In creating this plan, I cooperated closely with Google, by far Mountain View's largest employer, property owner, and taxpayer. Though I continue to be concerned that tech businesses are taking away our personal privacy, I felt comfortable working with one of the world's largest corporations, with a trading

**Fig. 10.2. I was elected to the nearby Mountain View City Council in 2014 on some of the housing and land use issues I worked on at Stanford in 1969-70. It was my turn to become mayor in 2018.**

value of over $1 trillion. Google should improve the treatment of its lower wage employees, many of whom are hired through contractors, but it deserves credit for being a regular, substantial donor to most good local causes. More relevant, Google's corporate planners share my "new urbanist" vision.

I lost my first re-election campaign in November 2018, even as voters overwhelmingly approved Measure P, the employer tax that I first proposed in 2015. There are many possible reasons for my loss, but I don't have polling data to back up any of the theories. After leaving the Council, I led the formation of the Housing Justice Coalition, committed to preserving and expanding rent control, protecting our homeless and vehicle residents, and opposing plans to tear down naturally affordable (and rent-controlled) apartments to build luxury, owner-occupied housing. In the fall of 2019 we successfully collected signatures on a referendum petition to keep Mountain View from outlawing vehicle residency on most Mountain View streets, and in March 2020 we defeated, 70% to 30%, a measure to weaken our rent control law.

My housing advocacy returned full circle to Stanford in 2018 and 2019. Land use planning for most of Stanford's academic campus is subject to the approval of the Santa Clara County Board of Supervisors through a General Use Permit. In early 2018 Stanford proposed significant employment expansion without planning for enough housing to match, and most of the cities in the area, as well as student activists, objected. In October 2018 I testified before the Board of Supervisors:

> When I entered Stanford University as a freshman physics major in 1966, I quickly learned that Stanford isn't just a great university. It is a major corporation with landholdings greater than the area of the city of Mountain View. It pioneered the practice of linking campus brainpower, federal funding, and university real estate, creating what we then called the Stanford Industrial Park. Stanford's "community of technical scholars" is largely responsible for the emergence of Silicon Valley as the global Mecca of high technology. Universities around the globe have mimicked, but not equaled Stanford's innovation.

> But Stanford's experiment has proven not to be sustainable. While it created what is essentially the area's only community land trust for senior faculty, it ignored the need to house the rest of its substantial workforce, as well as the much larger workforce in its Industrial/Research Park, Shopping Center, and Hospitals. In 1969, a group of us—students, faculty, and staff—formed an organization, Grass Roots, to challenge Stanford's land use decisions. In a pamphlet called "The Promised Land," we wrote:

> *Is the housing shortage a small oversight which*
> *can be solved easily, or is it grave and persistent,*
> *the local outcome of the way in which this area*
> *has been developed? Is the ecological crisis simply*
> *an abundance of beer cans and auto exhausts, or*
> *is it a larger problem, caused by the self-seeking*
> *decisions of local land developers and industrialists?*
> *Do the people in the area really control local land*
> *development through their elected officials, or do*
> *the City Councils and Planning Commissions serve*
> *the Trustees of Stanford, the directors of major*
> *corporations and the real estate kings of downtown*
> *Palo Alto?*

> I'm a lot older now, and I've learned how to partner
> constructively with major corporations and real estate
> "kings," but I'm still waiting for Stanford to address
> fully the housing impact of its growth. Today the Santa
> Clara County Board of Supervisors has the leverage
> to insist that Stanford accept responsibility for its
> significant share of our regional housing crisis, and
> to make sure that local elected officials and the public
> at large play their proper role influencing continuing
> decisions on housing development and other land use
> plans. Please exercise your authority.[16]

The Board listened to the cities, demanding full mitigation of employment growth. About a year later, Stanford withdrew its proposal, but no doubt it will be back.

In December 2018, after I had lost my re-election campaign, Stanford University President Marc Tessier-Lavigne invited four local mayors and their city managers to lunch at the Stanford faculty club, presumably to curry favor for its land use proposal. During our round of introductions, I explained that my

---

16. Lenny Siegel, "Stanford Housing Accountability," Testimony before Santa Clara County Board of Supervisors, October 15, 2018.

attempt to enter a luncheon there 50 years earlier (January 14, 1969) had ended my academic career. Tessier-Lavigne offered that I was no longer in trouble due to the "statute of limitations."

In November 2020, I lost my campaign to return to the Mountain View Council, and voters affirmed the motorhome ban that we petitioned against in 2019. However, two of my allies won. The new Mountain View Council will be more progressive than the current one. For the first time in Mountain View history, we will have a Council that supports rent control and other housing justice policies.

Why did I lose? The results seem to show a voter preference for women and people of color. This was particularly relevant when it came to the endorsements by organized labor and Democratic Party organizations.

In its endorsement of me and my three Housing Justice allies, the *Mountain View Voice*—now just an online newspaper, due to COVID-19—wrote:

> Former Councilman Lenny Siegel has long been a force for good in Mountain View, from his decades of environmental work on cleaning up the city's multiple Superfund sites to his efforts to increase housing and protect renters. Unfairly painted as a radical in some circles, he may have the background of a classic '60s activist but his nearly 50 years as a city resident reveal a far more nuanced portrait. Siegel combines a strong moral compass with a collaborative approach to problem-solving and a pragmatism born of years of working with federal agencies and local governments. He's not shy about taking up unpopular causes, but more often than not, he's been on the right side of history. We think he deserves another term on the City Council.[17]

17. Editorial: "Elect Lieber, Showalter, Nunez and Siegel to the Mountain View City Council," *Mountain View Voice,* September 9, 2020. https://mv-voice.com/news/2020/10/09/editorial-elect-lieber-showalter-nunez-and-siegel-to-the-mountain-view-city-council

It's quite possible that my history worked against me.

At the 2009 A3M Reunion, David Harris gave what some in attendance considered an inspirational speech, but he suggested that at our ages we were less able to organize. A couple of days later I responded:

> "I don't agree with those guys who said 'Look at us, we're over the hill,'" Siegel said, minutes before delivering a lighthearted speech and briskly leading the pack of several dozen people to Building 10. "I'm at the top of my game."[18]

Twelve years later, I still believe that I'm at the top of my game, though my career as an elected official is over. While many comrades have fallen,[19] many from our cohort remain professionally and politically effective in our seventies. Numerous old friends reported taking to the streets again, in the late Spring of 2020, participating in Black Lives Matter protests in the wake of George Floyd's murder. We learned a lot at Stanford University, and not just in our classes. While we and people like us have brought a great deal of progress to both the university and the country, the need for research, education, organizing, and protest remains as great as ever.

---

18. Gerry Shih, "'60s Anti-War Movement Reunited," *Stanford Daily*, May 4, 2009, p. 2. archives.stanforddaily. com/2009/05/04?page=1&section=MODSMD_ARTICLE4#article
19. See "In Remembrance," April Third Movement, a3mreunion.org/remembrance/remembrance.html for a partial list of remembrances.

# About the Author

Lenny Siegel grew up in southern California, organizing fellow high school students to work for peace and civil rights. He entered Stanford University in the fall of 1966, majoring in physics and hoping to eventually get a job in the area's growing computer and electronics industry.

He soon discovered that Stanford's pioneering "Community of Technical Scholars" had a powerful, seldom mentioned partner, the U.S. military. Along with other students, he spent much of his time at Stanford documenting the university's participation in the Vietnam War and organizing other members of the Stanford community to "halt all military and economic projects concerned with Southeast Asia." Siegel's participation in that Movement ended his academic career, sent him to jail for a dozen days, and ironically, kept him out of the military draft.

Siegel became head of the Movement-inspired Pacific Studies Center in 1970, researching and writing about Southeast Asia and the emergence of Silicon Valley as the planet's preeminent center of high technology. In 1985 he co-authored *The High Cost of High Tech: The Dark Side of the Chip*.

He moved to nearby Mountain View in 1972, buying a home in 1979. In the 1980s he and his wife, Jan Rivers, had two children, and he moonlighted as a contract technical writer at Apple Computer.

In the 1990s he became one of the environmental movement's leading experts on toxic cleanup, military environmental issues, and public engagement. 1994 he was hired as Executive Director of what became known as the Center for Public Environmental Oversight at San Francisco State University. CPEO affiliated with the Pacific Studies Center in 2006.

In 2014, Siegel formed the Campaign for a Balanced Mountain View, to address the jobs-housing imbalance that Siegel challenged during his days at Stanford. That led to his election to the Mountain

View City Council, on which he served from 2015 to early 2019. He served as mayor in 2018, becoming one of the San Francisco Bay Area's leading advocates of new housing development.

# Graphics Credits
(listed by page)

Links in this printed edition may be found online at a3mreunion.org/DisturbingTheWar.html.

Cover: *Lenny Siegel leads a march to SRI's Counterinsurgency Offices, April 21, 1969.* SDS March through Industrial Center Park. Stanford University, Stanford News Service records (SC0122). Dept. of Special Collections & University Archives, Stanford University, Stanford, California. Copyright © The Board of Trustees of the Leland Stanford Junior University. All rights reserved. (purl.stanford.edu/qh190rj0918)

19. Fig. 2.1. *1965 Peace March to Palo Alto.* Photo by Jeff Kane.

22. Fig. 2.2. *Stanford's first sit-in, May 19-21, 1966, in President Sterling's office.* Student sit-in protesting Selective Service Testing. J. E. Wallace Sterling, President of Stanford University, Papers (SC0216). Dept. of Special Collections & University Archives, Stanford University, Stanford, California. Copyright © The Board of Trustees of the Leland Stanford Junior University. All rights reserved. Photo by Leo Holub. (purl.stanford.edu/qx280rm9942).

23. Fig. 2.3. *Stanford students' effort to provide medical aid to Vietnam.* Rally—Blood Pledging for Vietnam, Stanford News Service records (SC0122). News Service #3404-11. November 2, 1965. Dept. of Special Collections & University Archives, Stanford

University, Stanford, California. Copyright © The Board of Trustees of the Leland Stanford Junior University. All rights reserved. (purl.stanford.edu/kv725vt8730)

31. Fig. 2.4. *"We Accuse" poster*

39. Fig. 3.1. *Resistance leaders David Harris and Paul Rupert burn draft documents in White Plaza, November 14, 1968.* Student Demonstrations, Stanford Historical Photograph Collection. Dept. of Special Collections & University Archives, Stanford University, Stanford, California. Photo by Chuck Painter. SC0122. Photo ID 8983. November 14, 1968. (purl.stanford.edu/ds432yr7260)

42. Fig. 3.2. *First poster promoting October, 1967 demonstrations at the Oakland Induction Center: People Get Ready!*

43. Fig. 3.3. *Second poster promoting October, 1967 demonstrations at the Oakland Induction Center: Stop the Draft Week Rally*

64. Fig. 4.1. *May 6, 1968 Mass meeting in the Old Union courtyard during the sit-in protesting the suspension of anti-CIA demonstrators, May 6, 1968.* Stanford News Service, Stanford University, Stanford, California. Photo by Chuck Painter.

77. Fig 5.1. *With a gold-painted spike, SDS nailed its demand to the Trustees' office door. Speaking Truth to Power.* http://www.a3mreunion.org/archive/photos/1968-1969_photos/1968-1969_speaking_truth/files_68-69_speaking/Page_02_w1160.jpg, p. 2

80. Fig. 5.2. *SDS marches to the Applied Electronics Laboratory.* Student demonstrations—April Third Movement—Applied Electronics Lab, Stanford Historical Photograph Collection. Dept. of Special Collections & University Archives, Stanford University, Stanford, California. Photo by Chuck Painter. SHPC Photo ID 9438. November 5, 1968. (purl.stanford.edu/rn803sv7246)

86. Fig. 5.3. *Lenny read the SDS demands to the Trustees.* Student Demonstrations, Stanford News Service records (SC0122). Dept. of Special Collections & University Archives, Stanford University, Stanford, California. Photographer, Stanford News Service. January 14, 1969. (purl.stanford.edu/tv256vk7681)

87. Fig. 5.4. *Demonstrators forced their way into the Trustees' lunchroom.* Student Demonstrations, Stanford News Service records (SC0122). Dept. of Special Collections & University Archives, Stanford University, Stanford, California. (purl.stanford. edu/dc539kc7478)

88. Fig. 5.5. *Inside the Trustees' lunchroom at the Faculty Club.* Student Demonstrations, Stanford News Service records (SC0122). Dept. of Special Collections & University Archives, Stanford University, Stanford, California. (purl.stanford.edu/gh741bp6463)

89. Fig. 5.6. *SDS entered President Pitzer's office.* Students for Democratic Society, Stanford Historical Photograph Collection Dept. of Special Collections & University Archives, Stanford University, Stanford, California. SHPC Photo ID 11238 (purl. stanford.edu/gh273fg6546)

92. Fig. 5.7. *March 11, 1969 Student-Trustee Forum in Memorial Auditorium.* Student Demonstrations—Trustees Meet Students, Stanford Historical Photograph Collection (SC1071). Dept. of Special Collections & University Archives, Stanford University, Stanford, California. (https://purl.stanford.edu/kr764zn6049)

102. Fig. 6.1. *The AEL Hallway.* Sit-In at Applied Electronics Laboratory. Dept. of Special Collections & University Archives, Stanford University, Stanford, California. News Service #7008-6. April 10, 1969. Stanford University, News Service, Records (SC0122). Copyright © The Board of Trustees of the Leland Stanford Junior University. All rights reserved. (purl.stanford.edu/xm684wd0552)

103. Fig. 6.2. *At AEL, decisions were made in public.* Student demonstrations, April Third Movement, Applied Electronics lab. Stanford Historical Photograph Collection. Dept. of Special Collections & University Archives, Stanford University, Stanford, California. SHPC Photo ID 9441. (purl.stanford.edu/rm436yx3237)

106. Fig. 6.3. *Small-group discussion in the AEL Courtyard.* Copyright (c) 2016 by Steve Rees. https://www.sixties-photos.com

111. Fig. 6.4. *Round-the-clock operation of the AEL print shop.* Copyright (c) 2016 by Steve Rees. https://www.sixties-photos.com

114. Fig. 6.5. *Mass meeting of student body.* Student Body Meeting—Frost Amphitheater, Campus protest against war in Vietnam. Stanford News Service records (SC0122). Dept. of Special Collections & University Archives, Stanford University, Stanford, California. Photographer, Stanford News Service. News Service #7075-2. April 18, 1969. Copyright © The Board of Trustees of the Leland Stanford Junior University. All rights reserved. (purl.stanford.edu/qg173bz5721)

133. Fig. 6.6. *Affinity group talking, listening, and thinking.*

135. Fig. 6.7. *Geodesic Dome on "Agitators' Grass."*

137. Fig. 6.8. *An A3M Affinity Group marches up Hanover Street.*

138. Fig. 6.9. *Motorists avoid the A3M blockade at Hanover and Page Mill.* April 3rd Movement demonstration at SRI, Stanford News Service records (SC0122). Dept. of Special Collections & University Archives, Stanford University, Stanford, California. May 16, 1969. Photographer, Stanford News Service. News Service #7194-2 . Copyright © The Board of Trustees of the Leland Stanford Junior University. All rights reserved. (purl.stanford.edu/nc911gw9623).

140. Fig. 6.10. *Demonstrators let concrete truck pass.* Student Demonstrations—April Third Movement—1969—SRI, Stanford Historical Photograph Collection (SC1071), Dept. of Special Collections & University Archives, Stanford University, Stanford, California. http://a3mreunion.org/archive/photos/sri-hanover/concrete_w1000.png

141. Fig. 6.11. *May 16, 1969 demonstration outside SRI.*

142. Fig. 6.12. *Preparing for the police sweep on Hanover Street.* Student Demonstrations—April Third Movement—1969—SRI, Stanford Historical Photograph Collection. Dept. of Special Collections & University Archives, Stanford University, Stanford, California. May 16, 1969. SHPC Photo ID 9435. (purl.stanford.edu/vb425fk2925)

143. Fig. 6.13. *Expended tear-gas canister under a desk at SRI.*

150. Fig. 7.1. *Linus Pauling speaks at Vietnam Moratorium mass meeting.* Stanford Historical Photograph Collection. Dept. of Special Collections & University Archives, Stanford University, Stanford, California. October 15, 1969. SHPC Photo ID 11514. (purl.stanford.edu/kp173hp7729)

151. Fig. 7.2. *Leafleting in the Industrial Park for the Vietnam Moratorium.* Photo by Jeff Kane.

152. Fig. 7.3. *November 14, 1969 Vietnam Moratorium Rally at Hanover and Page Mill.* Photo by Jeff Kane.

153. Fig. 7.4. *Poster illustrating the military contracting and other work done in the Stanford Industrial Park.* Produced by Lenny Siegel.

158. Fig. 7.5. *Grass Roots protests Palo Alto Square development.* Student Demonstrations, Stanford Historical Photograph Collection. Dept. of Special Collections & University Archives, Stanford University, Stanford, California. 1970. SHPC Photo ID 8980. (purl.stanford.edu/wr914dy8313)

166. Fig. 7.6. *Cover photo from Chaparral magazine.* February 16, 1970.

169. 7.7. *Siegel and other Off ROTC protesters confront Stanford 'police' chief William Wullschleger.* Student Demonstrations, Stanford Student Demonstrations Collection (SC0376). Dept. of Special Collections & University Archives, Stanford University, Stanford, California. Copyright © The Board of Trustees of the Leland Stanford Junior University. All rights reserved. (https://purl.stanford.edu/xt068gj5533)

171. Fig. 7.8. *Lenny tries to call to order a meeting of Stanford's faculty, the Academic Council.* Student Demonstrations. Stanford Student Demonstrations Collection (SC0376). Dept. of Special Collections & University Archives, Stanford University, Stanford, California. 1970. Copyright © The Board of Trustees of the Leland Stanford Junior University. All rights reserved. (purl.stanford.edu/pq662rj8118)

179. Fig. 7.9. *Police guard the Old Union.* Student Demonstrations—Strike—1970. Stanford Historical Photograph Collection (SC1071). Dept. of Special Collections & University Archives, Stanford University, Stanford, California. Donor is Donald T. Carlson. April, 1970. SHPC Photo ID 6782. (purl.stanford.edu/wh762vx0239).

181. Fig. 7.10. *Police attempt to clear protesting students from White Plaza.* Student Demonstrations—Strike—1970. Stanford Historical Photograph Collection (SC1071). Dept. of Special Collections & University Archives, Stanford University, Stanford, California. April, 1970. SHPC Photo ID 6799. Donor is Donald T. Carlson. (purl.stanford.edu/cn487hv1159).

184. Fig. 7.11 *Students blockade the main administration building, Encina Hall.* Student Demonstrations—Strike—1970, Stanford Historical Photograph Collection (SC1071). Dept. of

Special Collections & University Archives, Stanford University, Stanford, California. 1970. SHPC Photo ID 6809. (purl.stanford. edu/gq208dd6597)

188. Fig. 7.12. *Durand 'Aero and Astro' Building during Cambodia Strike.* Student Demonstrations—Strike—1970, Stanford Historical Photograph Collection (SC1071). Dept. of Special Collections & University Archives, Stanford University, Stanford, California. 1970. SHPC Photo ID 6817. (purl.stanford. edu/dw713kf8877)

190. Fig. 7.13. *Poster produced during the Cambodia Strike.* Design by Leif Erickson.

191. Fig. 7.14. *Representation of the corporate connections of the Stanford Board of Trustees.* Design by Leif Erickson.

192. Fig. 7.15. *Cambodia Strike at the Graduate School of Business.* Student Demonstrations—Strike—1970, Stanford Historical Photograph Collection (SC1071). Dept. of Special Collections & University Archives, Stanford University, Stanford, California. Photo by Chuck Painter. May 05, 1970. SHPC Photo ID 6814. (purl.stanford.edu/wm221tk1272).

203. Fig. 8.1. *Protesting recruiting at FMC placement center.* Stanford News Service records (SC0122). Dept. of Special Collections & University Archives, Stanford University, Stanford, California. February 26, 1971. News Service #8529-5. Photographer, Stanford News Service. Copyright © The Board of Trustees of the Leland Stanford Junior University. All rights reserved. (purl.stanford.edu/dq113fw5275)

205. Fig. 8.2. *Back cover of Fire and Sandstone, Fall 1970.* http://a3mreunion.org/archive/photos/1970/building10_h1000. png

214. Fig. 8.3. *Audience at January 12, 1971 Lodge protest.* Demonstration against Ambassador Lodge, Stanford News Service records (SC0122). Dept. of Special Collections & University Archives, Stanford University, Stanford, California. January 11, 1971. Photographer, Stanford News Service. News Service #8431-15. Copyright © The Board of Trustees of the Leland Stanford Junior University. All rights reserved. (purl. stanford.edu/sp739rg6071)

215. Fig. 8.4. *Protesting SRI's war gaming program at the university Computation Center.* Student Demonstrations— Computation Center, Stanford Historical Photograph Collection (SC1071) Dept. of Special Collections & University Archives, Stanford University, Stanford, California. Photo by Jose Mercado. February 10, 1971. SHPC Photo ID 9456. (purl. stanford.edu/fc158sg4582)

216. Fig. 8.5. *Police rout peaceful demonstrators from the area around the Computation Center.* Student Demonstrations— Computation Center, Stanford Historical Photograph Collection (SC1071) Dept. of Special Collections & University Archives, Stanford University, Stanford, California. Photo by Chuck Painter. February 10, 1971. SHPC Photo ID 9458.2. (purl. stanford.edu/xb449jt7628).

244. Fig. 9.1. *Professors protest the prosecution of Bruce Franklin.* Student Demonstrations—Franklin, H. Bruce—Dismissal. Stanford Historical Photograph Collection (SC3276). Dept. of Special Collections & University Archives, Stanford University, Stanford, California. Photo by Chuck Painter. September 29, 1971. (purl.stanford.edu/km419ng0302).

254. Fig. 9.2. *Students marching from White Plaza to El Camino Real in protest of Nixon's escalation of the War.* Campus Protest against War in Vietnam, Stanford News Service records (SC0122). Dept. of Special Collections & University Archives, Stanford University, Stanford, California. April 21, 1972.

269. Fig. 10.1. *Framed document commemorating AEL.*

278. Fig. 10.2 *Photo of Lenny Siegel as Mayor of Mountain View.*